Corpus-Assisted Ecolinguistics

Bloomsbury Advances in Ecolinguistics

Series Editors:
Arran Stibbe and Mariana Roccia

Advisory Board:
Nadine Andrews (Lancaster University, UK)
Maria Bortoluzzi (University of Udine, Italy)
Martin Döring (University of Hamburg, Germany)
Sue Edney (University of Bristol, UK)
Alwin Fill (University of Graz, Austria)
Diego Forte (University of Buenos Aires, Argentina)
Amir Ghorbanpour (Tarbiat Modares University, Iran)
Nataliia Goshylyk (Vasyl Stefanyk Precarpathian National University, Ukraine)
Huang Guowen (South China Agricultural University, China)
George Jacobs (Independent Scholar)
Kyoohoon Kim (Daegu University, South Korea)
Katerina Kosta (Oxford Brookes University, UK)
Mira Lieberman-Boyd (University of Sheffield, UK)
Keith Moser (Mississippi State University, USA)
Douglas Ponton (University of Catania, Italy)
Robert Poole (University of Alabama, USA)
Alison Sealey (University of Lancaster, UK)
Nina Venkataraman (National University of Singapore, Singapore)
Daniela Francesca Virdis (University of Cagliari, Italy)
Sune Vork Steffensen (University of Southern Denmark, Denmark)

Bloomsbury Advances in Ecolinguistics emerges at a time when businesses, universities, national governments and many other organisations are declaring an ecological emergency. With climate change and biodiversity loss diminishing the ability of the Earth to support life, business leaders, politicians and academics are asking how their work can contribute to efforts to preserve the ecosystems that life depends on.

This book series explores the role that linguistics can play in addressing the great challenges faced by humanity and countless other species. Although significant advances have been made in addressing social issues such as racism, sexism and social justice, linguistics has typically focused on oppression in human communities and overlooked other species and the wider ecosystems that support life. This is despite the disproportionate impact of ecological destruction on oppressed groups. In contrast, this book series treats language as an intrinsic part of both human societies and wider ecosystems. It explores the role that different areas of linguistic enquiry, such as discourse analysis, corpus linguistics, language diversity and cognitive linguistics can play at a time of ecological emergency.

The titles explore themes such as the stories that underpin unequal and unsustainable industrial societies; language contact and how linguistic imperialism threatens the ecological wisdom embedded in endangered languages; the use of linguistic analysis in ecocriticism, ecopsychology and other ecological humanities and social sciences; and emerging theoretical frameworks such as Harmonious Discourse Analysis. The titles also look to cultures around the world for inspirational forms of language that can lead to new stories to live by. In this way, the series contributes to linguistic theory by placing language fully in its social and ecological context, and to practical action by describing the role that linguistics can play in addressing ecological issues.

Corpus-Assisted Ecolinguistics

Robert Poole

BLOOMSBURY ACADEMIC
LONDON • NEW YORK • OXFORD • NEW DELHI • SYDNEY

BLOOMSBURY ACADEMIC
Bloomsbury Publishing Plc
50 Bedford Square, London, WC1B 3DP, UK
1385 Broadway, New York, NY 10018, USA
29 Earlsfort Terrace, Dublin 2, Ireland

BLOOMSBURY, BLOOMSBURY ACADEMIC and the Diana logo are trademarks of
Bloomsbury Publishing Plc

First published in Great Britain 2022
Paperback edition published 2023

Copyright © Robert Poole, 2022

Robert Poole has asserted his right under the Copyright, Designs and
Patents Act, 1988, to be identified as Author of this work.

For legal purposes the Acknowledgments on p. xv constitute an
extension of this copyright page.

All rights reserved. No part of this publication may be reproduced or
transmitted in any form or by any means, electronic or mechanical, including
photocopying, recording, or any information storage or retrieval system,
without prior permission in writing from the publishers.

Bloomsbury Publishing Plc does not have any control over, or responsibility for,
any third-party websites referred to or in this book. All internet addresses
given in this book were correct at the time of going to press. The author
and publisher regret any inconvenience caused if addresses have changed or
sites have ceased to exist, but can accept no responsibility for any such changes.

A catalogue record for this book is available from the British Library.

A catalog record for this book is available from the Library of Congress.

ISBN: HB: 978-1-3501-3855-1
PB: 978-1-3503-2042-0
ePDF: 978-1-3501-3856-8
eBook: 978-1-3501-3857-5

Series: Bloomsbury Advances in Ecolinguistics

Typeset by Integra Software Services Pvt. Ltd.

To find out more about our authors and books visit www.bloomsbury.com
and sign up for our newsletters.

Contents

List of Plates	viii
List of Tables	ix
Preface	x
Acknowledgments	xv
List of Abbreviations	xvi

1	An Introduction to Ecolinguistics and Corpus-Assisted Discourse Study	1
2	Corpus-Assisted Ecolinguistics	27
3	A Corpus-Assisted Diachronic Analysis of Representations of *Wilderness*	53
4	Corpus-Assisted Ecolinguistics for Literary Texts: A Keyness Analysis of Richard Powers' *The Overstory*	83
5	Roving Beasts and Bolting Bovines: Wordplay in the Reporting of Animal Escapes	109
6	Geographical Text Analysis for Corpus-Assisted Ecolinguistics	131
7	Conclusion	155

Notes	165
Bibliography	166
Index	182

List of Plates

Plate 1	Adjective + wilderness in the Google Books Corpus 1800–2010
Plate 2	Place name mentions globally across all corpora
Plate 3	Place name mentions in the United States
Plate 4	Place name mentions in the Rosemont Mine Truth Corpus
Plate 5	Rosemont Mine cartoon
Plate 6	Place and money
Plate 7	Place and money (United States)
Plate 8	Place and life

List of Tables

1	Top 50 4L-4R adjective collocates of wilderness 1810–2010	72
2	Evaluative adjectives increasing in use 1810–2010	74
3	Evaluative adjectives increasing in use 1950–2010	74
4	Adjectives decreasing 1810–2010	77
5	Adjectives decreasing 1950–2010	79
6	Keywords in *The Overstory* (sorted by BIC)	98
7	Verbal patterns with trees	104
8	Concordance lines of tree	105
9	Corpus of nonhuman animal escape articles	121
10	Framings	126
11	The Environmental Organizations Corpus	140
12	Semantic tag frequencies with place names	142

Preface

The exploitation and destruction of the environment continues essentially unheeded despite compelling and overwhelming evidence of the climate crisis and its varied consequences for peoples, nonhuman animals, and ecosystems around the world. In recent years, wildfires in Australia and across the American West start more frequently, burn more widely, and seem to even devour landscapes and communities with greater ferocity (Lindenmayer & Taylor, 2020; Patel, 2018). Over the same period, the Amazon region continues to burn at an alarming rate as loggers, ranchers, and others push the forest to a dangerous tipping point from which recovery may not be possible (Goodman & Giles, 2020). Additionally, severe coastal and inland flooding with climate crisis links grows more frequent (Seneviratne et al., 2012) while devastating hurricanes and typhoons with similar climate change connections occur with worrisome and growing regularity (Geophysical Fluid Dynamics Laboratory, 2021). This is hardly new information as numerous reports, studies, documentaries, and books from Bill McKibben's *The End of Nature* (1989) in the late 1980s to David Wallace-Wells' more recent *The Uninhabitable Earth: Life after Warming* (2020) describe in tragic detail the extent of the ecological crisis which the world now faces. It is undeniably clear that human action, and our inaction as well, continues to have significant and potentially irreversible impacts on ecosystems worldwide. As Jack E. Davis writes in his history of the Gulf of Mexico: "We still insist on harnessing it [the environment] to our will, as we perpetuate waste and blight in the natural world" (Davis, 2017, p. 9). Concerned citizens inspired by activists such as Greta Thunberg are increasingly unifying and demanding action, yet the reality is that the global community has done little to produce the transformational change necessary to ensure long-term ecological sustainability and well-being for human and nonhuman species on the planet.

Though applied linguists and ecolinguists may not be seen as key contributors to solving the ecological crisis, one of the most esteemed linguists of the past fifty years, M.A.K. Halliday, argued otherwise. For Halliday (1990/2001), addressing the ecological crisis is not solely a task for the chemists, biologists, and scientists—rather, it is a great challenge that all within the academy and beyond must urgently face, for it is too severe to be engaged by only a few. The crisis calls for increased trans-disciplinary, trans-agency, and trans-governmental action that expands and extends existing research and action capacities in order to enable "new forms of activity" (Halliday, 1990/2001, p. 176). The climate crisis is truly an "All hands on deck!" scenario in far greater orders of magnitude than other endeavors to circumnavigate the world, put a human on the moon, or solve the ozone crisis, to name only a few. And clearly, the consequences of continued inaction in the face of climate collapse for all of Earth's inhabitants are catastrophic.

Ecolinguists and scholars across the environmental humanities have contributed greatly to our understanding of language and its role in mediating our perceptions and understanding of the environment and environmental issues. However, ecolinguistics, in my view, has been limited by its somewhat narrow concentration on environmental communication alone. Drawing from Naess' distinction of shallow and deep ecology (1995), we may analogize this historical focus on language specifically about the environment as a sort of shallow ecolinguistics for the language under observation is immediately and explicitly recognizable as concerning the environment. Though the connotation of *shallow* may feel pejorative in this case, that is neither my desire nor intent. This book is greatly indebted to the extensive and valuable research on *greenspeak,* a term coined by Harre, Brockmeir, and Mühlhäusler to refer to language use specifically about the environment and environmental issues (1998). Indeed, analyses of *greenspeak* have yielded numerous insights into the patterns of language that reflect and perpetuate troubling conceptualizations of and problematic actions toward the environment, yet it is the language of popular and prevailing discourse that must be investigated for it is in these spaces where our ways of existing in and perceiving the world are profoundly and covertly enmeshed. There, in the language of the everyday, our attitudes and beliefs are manipulated and manufactured, and the systems and ideologies which perpetuate ecological degradation are normalized and reproduced. Thus, this book aims to forward a broader vision of ecolinguistics, a vision that goes beyond the study of *greenspeak* to the interrogation of language and discourses not actually *about* the environment in an immediate sense but which nonetheless function to reproduce, normalize, and perpetuate a range of ideologies, practices, beliefs, and attitudes that are harmful to sustainability and ecological well-being.

Such a call for ecolinguistic-informed analysis of discourses more broadly is not novel, and this book will not be the first to propose such an expanded vision for ecolinguistics. Notably, Alexander and Stibbe (2014) forwarded a similar call to move beyond ecological discourse analysis (i.e., the analysis of *greenspeak*) to the ecological analysis of discourses—this book is informed by and indebted to their work. However, this book is innovative in its application of techniques from corpus-assisted discourse studies to this broader ecolinguistic mission and framework. It is the aim of this text to illustrate the affordances of corpus-assisted discourse studies for the advancement of this wider vision for ecolinguistics. It is my belief that ecological interrogations of discourses beyond *greenspeak* will reveal the ways in which everyday language and communication reflect and reproduce the conditions and relationships underlying the present ecological crisis.

As evident in the title, this book aims to foster greater connection between ecolinguistics and corpus-assisted discourse study. It may be true that some ecolinguists conduct research in ecological discourse analysis but are somewhat unfamiliar with using corpora and implementing corpus techniques. It is also possible that these ecolinguists have concerns for what may seem the quantitative or technical aspects of corpus linguistics. This book attempts to address these concerns and relieve these worries. Similarly, there are perhaps readers conducting corpus-assisted analyses of academic writing, business communication, political discourse, and many other texts, genres, or discourses of interest. These applied linguists, though quite familiar with the principles and techniques of corpus-assisted discourse study, may be yet unacquainted with the domain of ecolinguistics. To these readers, I hope the book will inspire you to take your own ecological turn and pursue research which contributes positively to ecological well-being and sustainability for your communities. And finally, for readers from other disciplinary orientations and backgrounds, I hope this text will pique your interests and meet your expectations and that it will inspire you to critique the role of language in the ecological crisis and contribute new ways of thinking, new forms of acting, and new modes of being for an ecologically sustainable civilization.

Ecosophy

Before proceeding, it is necessary for me to make known my own positionality within this research enterprise in the form of an ecosophy. I am neither a distant nor wholly impartial observer for I too live on this planet, and I too feel the great burden of our present ecological crisis. As Bang and Døør assert, "We have no access to a point of view from nowhere" (1993, p. 10). This assertion reflects our positionality as citizens and scholars and how our own backgrounds, experiences, and values inform and influence how we perceive and interpret the world about us.

An ecosophy is an ethical framework which reflects and expresses the values of the researcher (see Stibbe 2015, 2021 for a more detailed discussion), and in ecolinguistics, forming and stating one's own ecosophy has become common practice. Importantly, an ecosophy is greater than a commentary on one's own ecological identity, beliefs, and values, for it also serves as the ethical and moral framework by which one may subsequently evaluate discourses as positive and beneficial or negative and destructive. In essence, when language use transgresses the values of my ecosophy, it shall be critiqued and challenged. For example, the reporting of nonhuman animal escapes in Chapter 5 demonstrates such a negative discourse deserving of critique. In contrast, when language use promotes ways of thinking and being that align with the framework, as in the illustration of Chapter 4, it will be praised and promoted. Though your ecosophy may diverge from my own, it is important that we all formulate an ecosophy to inform and guide our practice.

The following are the pillars of my ecosophy:

- Well-being: I am an advocate for the well-being of all human and nonhuman animals as well as of forests, lakes, rivers, oceans, and all ecosystems large and small. As Stibbe (2021) writes, "The goal is not just living in the sense of survival but living well" (p. 15). I similarly advocate for such a standard of life that makes life worth living for all species, and thus, I oppose practices that normalize and perpetuate inequality, oppression, and suffering and that do not contribute to the well-being of all species.
- Justice: For there to be well-being, there must also be justice. As the effects of the climate crisis increasingly materialize, it will be marginalized peoples and communities that will most significantly feel the effects of climate change. It is unjust that the excessive consumption and waste by the few should cause the suffering of the many. My calls for justice extend also to nonhuman animals and their right to life and well-being.
- Awakening and Transformation: Aspirational and optimistic, I believe an awakening is possible and that through revealing and challenging the practices, attitudes, and beliefs that contribute to the ecological crisis, transformational change is still achievable. This hope in the potential for transformation is not meant to deny the severity of the crisis nor project a flawed belief that life as we know it can carry on largely unchanged. It cannot. Radical change and comprehensive transformation will only be

possible if we rethink and restructure how we perceive, exist, and engage with and in the natural world. Such transformation will not be the result of shallow behavioral modifications that many global citizens have already adopted and integrated into their daily routines. In other words, while banning plastic straws and installing energy-efficient light bulbs are ecologically positive actions, the impact such actions produce is minimal in the face of ongoing political indifference and continued environmental crime and injustice. The COVID-19 pandemic has caused many to pause and bear witness to the changes in the global environment and the pervasiveness of inequality and injustice around the world. In a meta-analysis of research assessing the environmental impact of COVID-19, data indicated that air quality improved in many of the world's cities, greenhouse gas emissions declined, and water pollution decreased during the first year of the pandemic (Rume & Islam, 2020). This is evidence that behavior change is possible and that such transformation can indeed produce demonstrable environmental benefits. Transformation is achievable, and thus, I seek to challenge language practices that forestall such development and promote an awakening to discourses which contribute to sustainability and well-being.
- Compassion: Compassion and empathy for the lived conditions of humans and nonhuman species are required for transformational change.
- Sustainability: Sustainability now makes possible the achievement of alternative futures for generations that follow.

Notes on terminology:

1. **Climate crisis and ecological crisis:** These terms are used interchangeably to indicate not just the direct issue of climate change but all ecological issues that influence well-being.
2. **Nonhuman animal and animal:** In the text, I generally use the term "nonhuman animal" in order to challenge constructs that separate humans from other species. However, at times, I do use both terms out of concern for concision and to avoid excessive repetition that may become bothersome for the reader.

Acknowledgments

There are several individuals to whom I would like to express my gratitude. First, I am thankful for the careful reading and many forwarding comments provided by Dr. Shannon Fitzsimmons-Doolan. Any contribution to the field of ecolinguistics which this text may produce is surely greater as a result of her insightful comments throughout the writing process. I also wish to thank Yanisa Haley Scherber, Amelia Gaither, and Nair Tolomeo for assisting with the often-tedious task of corpus construction. I am also grateful to Zachary Brooks, Ivy Gilbert, and Nataliia Goshylyk for commenting on various sections of the manuscript. I would like to thank Arran Stibbe and Mariana Roccia for their efforts as co-editors of this series. I am grateful to them both for their support of this project from its inception to completion.

List of Abbreviations

BNC: British National Corpus
CADS: Corpus-Assisted Discourse Studies
CDS: Critical Discourse Studies
CL: Corpus Linguistics
COCA: Corpus of Contemporary American English
COHA: Corpus of Historical American English
NOW: News on the Web Corpus

An Introduction to Ecolinguistics and Corpus-Assisted Discourse Study

1.0 Introduction

This chapter briefly introduces ecolinguistics, corpus linguistics, corpus-assisted discourse studies (CADS), and critical discourse studies (CDS) to provide the historical, theoretical, and methodological foundations for corpus-assisted ecolinguistics as pursued in the balance of this text. Though many of the concepts of this opening chapter are revisited more deeply in later chapters, the discussions here provide a necessary foundation to the multiple research traditions and approaches informing this text's approach to corpus-assisted ecolinguistics. In closing, the chapter outlines the organization of the book and provides brief summaries of each chapter.

1.1 Defining Ecolinguistics

The word formation process which blends ecology and linguistics seems rather clear and transparent, yet defining and delimiting the resulting term has not been so easily achieved historically. An early definition of ecolinguistics established the field as one focused upon "the study of interactions between any given language and its environment" (Haugen, 1972/2001, p. 325). One may imagine a research enterprise reflective of this term, but it is quite likely the imagined research agenda would not capture the diversity of methods, approaches, and domains of application this definition has stimulated. Ecolinguistics, as pursued by this text, emerges from this early definition from Einar Haugen but more closely aligns with a research tradition which explores how language mediates and shapes how people think about and engage with physical spaces, nonhuman animals, and the environment generally. Ecolinguistics, in this tradition, thus, takes the position that "perceptions of nature are mediated through language and that in turn such perceptions and lifestyles feed back into the structure of discourse" (Mühlhäusler, 2003, p. 12). While Haugen's aforementioned conceptualization motivates "deeper reflections on the theories of language inspired by a holistic paradigm of ecology," this second discourse-focused strand of ecolinguistics applies a range of discourse analytic methods to the analysis of language use of ecological relevance and importance (Bang & Trampe, 2014). Most frequently in this discourse analytic tradition, at times referred to as ecological discourse analysis (EDA), researchers analyze features of the language system which produce an "unecological fragmentation" between humans and the environment (Fill & Mühlhäusler, 2001, p. 6). Essentially, ecolinguistics interrogates the "role of language in the life-sustaining interactions of humans, other species, and the physical environment" (International Ecolinguistics Association, 2019).

The underlying theoretical rationale informing research in the field aligns with a post-structuralist, constructivist notion that views language as mediating how we think and perceive, and therefore how we act and engage with/in the world. Though this rationale is shared with much critical discourse analytic work across the social sciences, ecolinguistics is unique for its particular focus on and critique of "forms of language that contribute to ecological destruction" (Stibbe, 2015, p. 1). While this may seem rather deterministic to some, ecolinguists believe language indeed has a contributing role to our ecological crisis. Such a theoretical orientation conflicts with structuralist beliefs of language that see the language system as simply encoding and reflecting an objective, preexisting reality. Ecolinguists view such an orientation to language and its use as flawed and insufficient, instead seeing language from a Hallidayan perspective as a complex semiotic system for construing reality and worldviews, not a system for capturing an external, objective truth. For ecolinguistics, language is constitutive for it both reflects and builds reality.

To exemplify this constitutive view of language use with samples from modern prevailing discourse is not particularly challenging as many such instances are present in mainstream communication. Though the previous discussion may feel esoteric, its essential thesis is reflected in evolving language use throughout society. For example, a sort of language engineering has occurred that has de-gendered such titles as *chairman* and *policeman* for the more inclusive *chairperson* and *police officer*. That change both reflects reality as more women occupy such positions, but it also builds such a reality by producing a cognitive space that views gender equality as preferable and such positions as achievable occupational goals for all genders. Similarly, the historically dominant use of masculine pronouns in science and academic writing has essentially disappeared in these respective discourse communities over the past few decades. There is also the campaign forwarded by Facebook executive Cheryl Sandberg to stop people from describing women and girls as *bossy* for actions their male counterparts are deemed *assertive* and praised for leadership. A view that language is an arbitrary system for encoding a preexisting reality would seemingly not object to the ascription of *bossy*, the gendering of titles, etc. In contrast, the critical discourse analyst argues that the ascription of the label reflects attitudes and beliefs about gender roles shared in a community or culture, but, and most profoundly, it normalizes and perpetuates such systems, thus reconstituting the system for years to come. In addition to critiquing the linguistic practice under inquiry, much critical discourse analysis seeks to motivate awareness of and ultimately change linguistic practices that normalize and perpetuate marginalization, exploitation, and inequality, a mission that is shared by ecolinguistics but extended to the physical environment and nonhuman species as well.

Though the aforementioned examples are not of immediate ecological relevance, this book explores similar linguistic practices that influence our conceptualization of and actions toward the environment. Ecolinguistics extends the scope of inquiry to discourses of nonhuman animals, depictions of physical spaces, representations of the climate crisis, and beyond. Through such work, ecolinguistics aims to challenge language patterns and practices that (re)produce attitudes, beliefs, identities, and ideologies which contribute to ecological destruction or identify and promote those practices that contribute to well-being and sustainability (Stibbe, 2015).

1.2 A Brief History of Ecolinguistics

It is worthwhile to look back at the field's origins in the nineteenth century through its development to the present. In a field so intimately focused on emergence and interconnection, a general orientation to the field's philosophical, scientific, and theoretical genesis seems quite necessary. Undoubtedly, some may tell a different history with different key figures and alternative points along their timeline, and readers are encouraged to review other histories of the field written previously (e.g., do Couto, 2014; LeVasseur, 2015; Mühlhäusler, 2003; Steffensen & Fill, 2014). This brief review begins with the brothers Alexander von Humboldt and

Wilhelm von Humboldt before moving to Charles Darwin and Ernst Haeckel. In the nineteenth century, few people were likely as well known around the world as Alexander von Humboldt, Charles Darwin, and Ernst Haeckel (Wulf, 2015). While we know them for their immense scientific contributions, their work underpins the theoretical and philosophical foundation of language ecology and ecolinguistics. From these figures of the nineteenth century, this history moves more rapidly through a series of key figures of the twentieth century before exploring more recent work central to the field today.

In 1807, the German naturalist, geographer, and explorer Alexander von Humboldt published *Essays on the Geography of Plants* in which he depicted in the sketch *Ein Naturgemälde der Anden* the interconnectivity and interrelatedness of all elements of the physical world. His transformational work is generally unknown in the modern world, but his radical rethinking of nature continues to exert immense influence on science and modern thought (Wulf, 2015). Though he did not coin the term *ecology*—the coinage is attributed to Ernst Haeckel—Alexander von Humboldt's views on the unity and interconnectedness of nature are the theoretical and philosophical genesis of *ecology*. Some may point to the inspirational image of *The Blue Marble* captured from the window of Apollo 17 for awakening modern ecological consciousness, but Humbolt's *Naturgemälde* from well over 100 years before the iconic *Blue Marble* image was the first to assert and inspire the conceptualization of an interconnected ecological system. In his work, he asserted a comprehensive, dynamic, and holistic view of nature as a complex and interactive system, a view which would later influence renowned naturalists such as John Muir, Henry David Thoreau, and George Perkins Marsh (Wulf, 2015).

Amazingly, Alexander von Humboldt was only one member of his family whose intellectual work would contribute to ecology. While Alexander expanded our conceptualization of the interconnectedness of the physical world, it was his brother, Wilhelm von Humboldt, who began to bridge ecological thinking with linguistic theory and analysis. Serving as an important precursor to the more well-known work of Edward Sapir and Benjamin Whorf, Wilhelm von Humboldt asserted that language must be more carefully studied in relation to context and culture for he argued variations in grammar reflects different views of reality (Swan, 2011; Wulf, 2015). Quite radical at the time, Wilhelm claimed that every language encodes a particular worldview and that language is not simply a tool for communication but that it actually functions to shape thought (Wulf, 2015). As captured in Andrea Wulf's biography of Alexander, the terminology used by the two brothers for describing nature and language were often the same, and they undoubtedly influenced each other's thinking.

Though Alexander von Humboldt's work was undeniably influential and would shape and inform the thinking of many of the great environmental writers of the next hundred years, the term *oecology,* which evolved to *ecology,* was first used by the German zoologist Ernst Haeckel in the 1866 monograph *Generelle Morphologie der Organismen (General Morphology of Organisms)* (Kingsland, 1991, p. 1) in an attempt to capture and explain the complex relationships Charles Darwin elaborated in his 1859 *On the Origin of Species* (from Macintosh, 1985, cited by Kingsland, 1991, p. 1). This coinage and his work helped launch Ecology as a science made distinct through its "application of experimental and mathematical methods to the analysis of organism-environment relations, community structure and succession, and population dynamics" (Kingsland, 1991, p. 2). In the decades following Darwin's classic text and Haeckel's elaboration, naturalists, botanists, and zoologists took a more "rigorous approach to natural history" (p. 2) and at the turn of the twentieth century, the domain of Ecology was described as a "dynamic, experimental approach to the study of adaptation, community succession, and population interactions" (Kingsland, 1991, p. 2). Increasingly, an ecology-driven approach was adopted by prominent naturalists in the United States who rejected more traditional, descriptive methods for the more quantitative and theoretical principles offered by the emerging science. In this time, Stephen Forbes published "The Lake as Microcosm" (1887), a seminal article that remains a frequently cited piece in ecology. In this piece, Forbes developed the conceptualization of the complex, interrelated interactions present within an ecosystem.

While scholars often apply metaphors, approaches, and theories from other fields and shape and transform them in a manner useful and insightful for their own pursuits, few seem to be so apt to borrow as language studies and linguistics. Ecology is one such example. Linguists in the early 1900s were beginning to extrapolate principles of ecology for language theory as the complexity of language and its interrelationship with people, places, culture, and thought was increasingly observed. The first applications of ecology to language through works of Franz Boaz, Edward Sapir, Benjamin Lee Whorf, and Charles and Florence Voegelin would emerge in the southwest of the United States.

While the roots of Ecology are undoubtedly European in origin, Sapir's work in the American southwest is often regarded as foundational in the area of language ecology. In Sapir's well-known and ultimately quite controversial essay "Language and Environment" (1912/2001), he cautioned against producing a view of human culture and human life in which all differentiation may be allocated to environmental influences. Indeed, he stated that deterministic arguments that explain features of human culture through direct correlation to physical environment "rest on fallacy" (1912/2001, p. 13). Nonetheless, he did define language as "a complex of symbols reflecting the whole physical and social background in which a group is placed" (1912/2001, p. 14) and that language is indeed "influenced by the environmental background of its speakers" (1912/2001, p. 14). In perhaps the most profound yet critiqued statement of the essay, Sapir wrote:

> The complete vocabulary of a language may indeed be looked upon as a complex inventory of all the ideas, interests, and occupations that take up the attention of the community, and were such a complete thesaurus of the language of a given tribe at our disposal, we might to a large extent infer the character of the physical environment and the characteristics of the culture of the people making use of it.
> (1912/2001, p. 14)

While the strong form of this statement attracted critics, it seems that in recent years this view has re-emerged and its message has become less controversial. The evidence of his influence on language ecology remains, and in perhaps the most comprehensive volume of essays on ecolinguistics, *The Ecolinguistics Reader: Language, Ecology, and Environment* (Fill & Mühlhäusler, 2001), Sapir's essay is the first included in the text.

The American southwest and languages of indigenous peoples of North America would also influence the work of C.F. and F.M. Voegelin and their collaboration with Noel Shutz Jr. (1967). Their publication in Dell Hymes' "Studies in Southwestern Ethnolinguistics" (1967) is of importance to the history of language ecology for its description of the languages used within a geographical area from a sociocultural perspective. This work moved beyond census-like reporting of number of speakers of a given language, a practice quite common of the period, to a much more in-depth analysis of the functional interactions between languages within an area and the complexity of interactions between the language varieties present. This sometimes overlooked precursor to the frequently cited work of Einar Haugen has an important place in the development of language ecology.

As do Couto writes in his history of the field, the concept of ecology of language was first produced in a 1970 talk by Einar Haugen at the Center of Applied Linguistics. Haugen coined the term *ecolinguistics* (do Couto, 2014) and his 1972 text *The Ecology of Language* is frequently marked as the beginning of modern ecological approaches to language studies. In his text, Haugen

(1972/2001) defined language ecology as "the study of interactions between any given language and its environment" (p. 325) and critiques biological, instrumental, and structural metaphors, asserting the ecology metaphor presents a more dynamic conceptualization of language and its interrelationship with the environments in which it exists. Within an ecological approach, Haugen charges that one must explain the context of the language but also report the effect the language has on the context. Thus, in Haugen's view, language ecology is characterized by reciprocity and interaction. Haugen also critiques many studies in language description for offering brief, and as he states, "perfunctory" (1972/2001, p. 324) information on the ecological environment in which languages are situated. He claimed the basic comments do little to actually explain the status and function of a language and argued that linguists should pay more attention to explaining much more comprehensively the ecology of a language. Though we noted Haeckel earns credit for the coinage of *ecology*, it appears Haugen receives the honor for *ecolinguistics*.

It is worth contextualizing briefly the context in which Haugen's ecology of language emerged. Only a few years earlier, Rachel Carson had captivated readers with her book *Silent Spring* (1962). Though not typically tethered to discussions of language and ecology, her text is in many ways an exemplar demonstration of how language use can reconfigure dominant conceptualizations of the environment while directing and inspiring readers to live more sustainable lives. Her work opened new spaces in the minds of her community of readers to think differently about the places they inhabit through her ominous portrayal of a spring without birdsong. Additionally, it does not seem incidental that only several years following the publication of her book that the United States held its first Earth Day and Europe celebrated its first Conservation Day. Indeed, many mark the publication of *Silent Spring* in 1962 as the beginning of the modern environmentalist movement in North America. And it was in this context in which Haugen's tethering of ecology and language emerged and which various research trajectories informed by ecological thinking soon sprang forth.

In the years following Haugen's work, scholars applied and extended Haugen's conceptualization of language and ecology to domains from linguistic diversity, language contact, to language planning and policy. However, most informing of the current tradition in ecolinguistics to investigate the role of language in normalizing and thereby perpetuating ecological degradation is work that questions whether linguistic patterns and features function within discourse to produce unsustainable relationships between humans and the environment (Steffensen & Fill, 2014). This discourse analytic strand of ecolinguistics is often tracked to M.A.K. Halliday's 1990 talk at the World Congress for the International Association of Applied Linguistics in Greece.

In his talk and subsequent publication of "New Ways of Meaning: The Challenge to Applied Linguistics," Halliday discusses features embedded within the English language in what he calls the "cryptogrammic fourth level" (1990/2001, p. 193) that operates beyond our conscious attention and functions to influence how we perceive the world. Halliday's argument asserted that "categories and concepts are construed by grammar, and thus, language is not an arbitrary system which represents and encodes pre-existing environmental realities" (p. 180). Thus, he forwards four features which construe the environment in ways he marks as unsustainable: (1) unbounded, non-count nouns present items as limitless, (2) the grammar of "good" as the grammar of "big" with grammar of "small" representing "bad," (3) inanimate objects are prohibited agency, (4) personal pronouns permitted only for animate entities. For Halliday, language is "at the same time a part of reality, a shaper of reality, and a metaphor for reality" (p. 184). This eco-critical stance toward language use continues to be a productive research space in ecolinguistics today; the corpus-assisted work emerging from this tradition will be more fully detailed in the following chapter.

From Haugen in 1972 to Halliday in 1990, the next key point in the discipline's emergence is *The Ecolinguistics Reader: Language, Ecology & Environment* in 2001—the edited volume included greater than twenty-five essays exploring the varied domains of language and ecology. Though the comprehensive collection reflected the breadth of the field and helped establish its standing, it also earned some criticism for its rather "broad notion of ecology" that would possibly "threaten a desirable unity of a field" (Gerbig, 2003, p. 93). While intellectually stimulating, variation in the research agenda was critiqued as a weakness for the emerging discipline. Such a multiplicity of research regimes has continued to be a source of critique for ecolinguistics, as some have felt that such diversity of application and approach has contributed to a lack of unity and coherence and an inability to create a unified mission amongst the community of scholars identifying as ecolinguists.

From 2001 to 2015, there were several noteworthy texts published in ecolinguistics, namely *Language of Environment, Environment of Language* (Mühlhäusler, 2003), *Framing Discourse on the Environment: A Critical Discourse Approach* (Alexander, 2009), and *Animals Erased: Discourse, Ecology, and Reconnection with the Natural World* (Stibbe, 2012). These have become core texts in the canon of ecolinguistics. However, as noted previously, ecolinguistics has faced critiques for lacking focus for the expansive and far-reaching ways in which ecology and language have been integrated and applied—ecolinguist Arran Stibbe commented in a 2014 article in the journal *Critical Discourse Studies* that ecolinguistics "is a divided area" and that the term "ecolinguistics" is "given to a range of different approaches and preoccupations" (p. 125). It is precisely this lack of cohesion and identity which made Stibbe's text *Ecolinguistics: Language, Ecology, and the Stories We Live By* (2015) such a valuable contribution to the field.

Stibbe's text (2015) brings together multiple theories and approaches to produce a unified ecolinguistic program. Reflecting Lakoff & Johnson's earlier work on the power of metaphors (1980), Stibbe's analysis aimed to go beyond the mental models present in the mind of single individuals to instead reveal the stories enmeshed across culture and society, particularly those stories which contribute to and perpetuate our current ecological crisis. These *stories we live by*, Stibbe argues, are realized through a variety of linguistic practices and are embedded deeply within language and culture. These stories can and must be revealed so they may either be resisted and subverted when shown to be destructive or promoted and encouraged when judged as positive. Importantly, the hegemony of the stories is demonstrated by their covert presence within discourses. In other words, these stories are not often explicit. Through highlighting these stories, e.g., economic growth is always positive, Stibbe argues we need new stories to live by and that ecolinguistics can help us shape these new stories rather than attempting the ambitious and likely impossible task of actually altering language. His book, thus, aims to analyze prevailing discourses, i.e., *the stories we live by*, while judging these discursive practices in relation to an ecosophy which values the lives of all species and promotes well-being. Most valuably, the book presents a comprehensive, theoretically grounded, and methodologically rigorous ecolinguistic framework that produces a coherence in purpose and approach critiqued as previously lacking in the field. Additionally, the text illustrated clearly the discipline's potential for producing important research, and many of the calls he makes for the investigation of language practices more broadly across discourse domains motivate the current text.

More recently, in 2017, a community of hundreds of international scholars agreed to a new definition for ecolinguistics and a revised mission for the International Ecolinguistics Association (IEA). Though some members of the community expressed displeasure with the narrowed focus produced by the definition and its concomitant mission, most agreed the specificity present in the revised mission statement and definition was desirable and necessary. The resulting definition from the IEA asserts that ecolinguistics "explores the role of language in the life-sustaining interactions of humans, other species and the physical environment" (ecolinguistics-association.org). Beyond this definition, the association forwards two key goals: (1) "to develop linguistic theories which see humans not only as part of society, but also as part of the larger ecosystems that life depends on" (2) "to show how linguistics can be used to address key ecological issues" (IEA). Though the scope has narrowed in some ways, ecolinguistics remains a rather interdisciplinary field.

And now the field moves forward with a growing scholarly community, a dedicated academic journal and ever more frequent publications in peer-reviewed journals, a growing number of undergraduate and graduate courses, and a thriving international conference. In Brazil, Hildo Honório do Couto and other scholars have developed Ecosystemic Linguistics (2017), an emergent branch of ecolinguistics that may be viewed as an elaboration of Haugen's original contribution. Additionally, Chinese ecolinguistics have forwarded an approach to ecolinguistics titled Harmonious Discourse Analysis (HDA) (Huang & Zhao, 2021). HDA integrates the theoretical framework of systemic functional linguistics with traditional Chinese philosophy in order to develop a context-sensitive, locally informed framework for application in non-Western settings.

Indeed, more points are certain to be added to the timeline as the field continues to grow and evolve in these turbulent ecological times with a mission as urgent as ever. As noted, other timelines and narratives are present and possible. This was only one story, and it is a story that captures, albeit briefly, the historical development of ecolinguistics. Some may view such attention to the field's genesis and growth as excessive or possibly unnecessary, but such historical accounts provide a sense of place, a lodestar to guide and offer direction to our work in this expanding and evolving discipline. Such an orientation will hopefully provide direction as others pursue ecolinguistic study and cultivate their own ecological thinking.

1.3 Corpus Linguistics

Corpus linguistics (CL) is the study of language through the analysis of large, principled, authentic, and often (though not without controversy) annotated collections of language. These fundamentals have become accepted features and qualities of CL over the decades since the development of the Brown Corpus, a one-million word corpus often considered as the beginning of modern corpus linguistics. In the years following this inception, corpus linguistics was largely focused on building ever larger collections of language for analysis. This attention to corpus creation would be advanced significantly in the 1980s and 1990s with digital scanning technology and the sudden explosion of data made available through the internet. A niche domain of linguistics suddenly gained prominence as the ability to create and analyze corpora became increasingly achievable. While early corpus work was largely confined to lexicography, suddenly CL was informing theoretical discussions and enabling statements about language use previously not possible with other methodological approaches. As affordances of CL continued to be identified, its contributions have proliferated in the past 20–25 years and researchers of various backgrounds and disciplinary orientations increasingly apply CL methods and techniques.

Most relevant for the purpose of this text is the integration of CL with discourse studies of both descriptive and critical orientations. Though the specific synergies and affordances of CL and discourse study will be detailed in the following section, it is first necessary to review the four fundamental features of corpus linguistics noted in the previous paragraph's definition of the field. These four qualities are central to the corpus linguistics enterprise, and, thus, are deserving of attention.

First, a fundamental mission of corpus studies is to uncover facts about language through the analysis of large collections of authentic language data that would most likely remain obscured and unnoticed through close reading, intuition, and introspection. While a systematic, manual coding and calculation of a particular linguistic feature or lexical item in a collection of texts is theoretically possible, the actual process without computational assistance would be exceedingly laborious, tedious, and time-consuming. Imagine conducting C.F. Fries' (1925) experiment in which he and his spouse manually documented and analyzed thousands of instances of *will* and *shall* in fifty English dramas written from 1560 to 1915, eighteen English dramas from 1902 to 1918, and another eighteen American dramas from 1905 to 1918. The amount of text that could be processed with such a method would be rather limited, and, in the digital age, insufficient. Thus, this quality of corpus linguistics for enabling the study of large collections of language is deeply significant. Admittedly, large is a fuzzy concept in CL and its threshold, i.e., number of words in a corpus, seems to increase annually. For instance, the collection of the corpora at

English-Corpora.org range in size from the 50-million word Strathy Corpus of Canadian English to the approximately 13-billion word News on the Web corpus. While on one hand the size of corpora has continued to grow, CADS researchers rather frequently compile specialized corpora of specific genres and/or texts that are typically much smaller than such general corpora. Sinclair famously states about corpora, "There is nothing beautiful about small" because with large corpora the "underlying regularities have a better chance of showing through the superficial variation" (2004, p. 189); however, specialized corpora, though perhaps small may yet be comprehensive, enable a targeted examination of particular registers, genres, etc. of language use and a recontextualization of data generally not possible in the analysis of output from massive corpora. Thus, it is not uncommon in discourse studies to employ corpora of only several hundred thousand words.

Size, however, must be coupled with careful considerations for corpus compilation, and thus, principled is the second keyword of corpus linguistics. For statements to be made about language use in a particular time period, a certain context, within a specific genre, etc., the corpus must be collected in a principled manner in order to be representative of the target domain so that one may advance valid claims about language use. Though a simple and transparent illustration, if one wishes to explore language use and development amongst second language writers of English, the researcher will need to carefully collect texts written by actual second-language writers. If a researcher aims to make claims regarding the presence/absence and use of a particular linguistic feature in a particular genre or discourse, the researcher must take great care in sourcing texts that indeed logically produce answers to the research question at hand. It is, thus, unsurprising that peer-reviewed articles in corpus linguistics and CADS offer extensive details regarding the compilation of the corpus. Often, a first question following many conference talks using corpus linguistic techniques implores the presenter to elaborate on the corpus compiled and analyzed in the study. If the construction of the corpus is in doubt, the findings will not be validated.

Reflected in the previous call for principled collection of source texts is the theoretical feature underlying the whole of corpus linguistics. Yes, a large, principled corpus in which non-obvious linguistics patternings may rise to the researcher's gaze are fundamental qualities of CL, but the unspoken value present in the statement is that the collected language must be authentic. Though now somewhat obvious and largely uncontroversial, it has not always been true that claims about language were based on actual language use from real language users in real social contexts. Instead, introspection and intuition about the potential of language and judgments of grammaticality rather than authentic language performance were the basis for language statements. CL, however, privileges the use of authentic language use, not researcher-contrived samples crafted to display an item or structure of interest for the researcher. As corpus methods have proliferated, the fallibility of introspection and intuition has been repeatedly highlighted, serving to further strengthen the data-driven approach of CL. Not only has intuition been called into doubt, one cannot generate intuitions about features and patterns of which they are unaware. For example, Tognini-Bonelli (2004) discusses the semantic prosodies of the adverbial near synonyms *largely* and *broadly*. In her corpus analysis, she notes *largely* typically occurs with a negative semantic prosody; in other words, it occurs when discussing undesirable events while *broadly* is used in positive contexts. Such mappings of semantic prosodies are one of the key affordances of corpus analysis.

A final feature and one of great importance for many types of CADS is the annotation of corpora with various tagging schema. The most common annotation schema applied are part of speech (POS) tags which enable more robust search syntax to allow greater focus on particular grammatical patterns of interest. For example, application of POS tags allows one to search for strings such as DET + ADJ + NN to identify all determiner + adjective + noun strings in a corpus or phrase searches to identify frequent entries in various slots of a phrase. TreeTagger and CLAWS are two frequently used POS tag schema and the two are often integrated in existing corpus software; TagAnt uses TreeTagger while Wmatrix integrates CLAWS. Similarly, semantic tags are also ascribed to lexical units in a corpus. In Potts (2015), she applies semantic tags in the analysis of the discourse of Hurricane Katrina while Poole (2016a) employed semantic tag analysis to identify common patterns of meanings produced in the texts created by two oppositional groups: an environmental activist group and a multinational mining corporation. Again, the annotations enable greater flexibility with the range of questions which may be asked of a corpus and language use. Though word-level annotations of POS and semantic meaning are the most commonly applied tags to corpus data, higher-order annotations are also possible. For instance, meta-tags above the level of the word can enable a researcher to focus on language production according to a range of sociolinguistic factors, e.g., gender, age, geographical location. One can also apply tagging schema to enable analysis of rhetorical moves, and researchers also develop their own project-specific tagging schema to enable the analysis of features not captured by POS and semantic tags.

While annotations provide certain analytic affordances, the ascription of tags is not without controversy. For those who view corpus linguistics as theory and thus possible of providing explanatory insights into language, the imposition of an a priori language model inhibits new insights from emerging from the data. Thus, for corpus-driven research, pre-existing models such as part of speech or semantic tags are not imposed on the data, thereby allowing potentially new understandings about language use in various contexts to emerge more organically. For example, Plappert (2017) identified keywords and the frequent patterns in which they appear in a corpus of articles from the journal *Nature Genetics* to demonstrate how an inductive corpus-driven approach enabled the identification of stance patterns which would not have been observed through corpus-based methods. Contrastingly, corpus-based studies apply a preexisting framework through which hypotheses are either confirmed or refuted and statements about language use forwarded. For instance, in much research on stance, researchers extract stance features of various types—e.g., modal auxiliaries, hedges, and boosters—compiled in lists from scholars such as Hyland (2005) and Biber et al. (2000). Such studies then examine the frequencies of these features in their target corpus and how their frequencies and functions may vary in relation to a reference corpus. Indeed, both approaches have value—it is not a simple either/or selection and which approach is selected depends on the project at hand. Though this discussion of the debate between corpus-based and corpus-driven has been brief, it hopefully illustrates an important issue within CADS of which researchers should be aware.

Further discussion and illustration of these core characteristics and the various analytic techniques of CL is present in subsequent chapters. These chapters also direct reader attention to key considerations of which researchers must be mindful when applying various corpus techniques.

1.4 Corpus-Assisted Discourse Studies

Corpus linguistic methods are increasingly applied for discourse analysis across language studies and social sciences, and in recent years, corpus methods have been adopted by researchers for investigations of various linguistic features across genres, registers, and discourses. As CADS has proliferated, the topics investigated have become exceptionally diverse. Areas that have received attention are political discourse (Conoscenti, 2011; Milizia, 2009, 2010, & 2012;

Partington, 2003; Partington & Morley, 2004), social issues such as immigration (Blinder & Allen, 2016; Fitzsimmons-Doolan, 2019; Incelli, 2013; Morley & Taylor, 2012), representations of Islam and Muslims (Baker, 2010; Baker, Gabrielatos, & McEnery, 2013), business and corporate communication (Hyland, 1998; Lischinsky, 2011; Poole 2016b), the language of extremism (Prentice, Rayson, & Taylor, 2012), and the language of news reporting of war (Kutter & Kanter, 2012). Other less-explored but nonetheless valuable and engaging studies report the discursive production of tourist locations (Jaworska, 2013), the discourse of tourism on the internet (Maci 2012a, b), English-only ideologies in the United States (Subtirelu, 2013), representations of feminism in the UK press (Jaworska & Krishnamurthy, 2012), investigation of legal language (Tabbert, 2013), as well as studies of communication in health and hospital settings (e.g., Maci, 2012c, d; Staples & Biber, 2014). Similarly, corpus-assisted studies within the discourse analytic strand of ecolinguistics has increased; as noted, this emerging body of research is detailed in Chapter 2.

It is beneficial to consider the theoretical rationale and the methodological affordances often cited for CADS in order to frame the analysis of subsequent chapters. Briefly, though CADS is attributed to the particular approach developed by Alan Partington and the research group at the University of Bologna, CADS here will be used as a superordinate term to classify the range of discourse studies applying predominantly corpus linguistics principles and techniques to the study of language use.

The rationale for a CADS approach to language and discourse study is reflected in systemic functional linguistics (SFL) and its conceptualization of language as a resource for meaning-making in social interaction (Halliday & Hasan, 1985). At the core of SFL is a privileged focus on the analysis of "authentic products of social interaction," i.e., texts (Eggins, 2004, p. 2); a similar preference for authentic texts is echoed throughout the literature of corpus linguistics. In SFL, language is viewed as a social semiotic system from which language users make meaningful selections from a range of linguistic choices. Each selection from the language system reflects and construes the values, beliefs, and worldview of the speaker/writer, as alternate and contrasting selections, which could equally have been selected, were not chosen. For example, one could produce either of the samples below:

a. Jaguars can be taken from the proposed mine area.
b. Jaguars will be killed in the proposed mine area.

The first sample (a) was written by the Arizona Corps of Engineers in a document discussing a potential open-pit copper mine in southern Arizona;

the second sample (b) was written by an environmental activist group in the same region opposing the proposed mine. The choice of verbs, *taken* or *killed*, demonstrates oppositional views toward a nonhuman animal species living in the vicinity of the mine. The modal auxiliary of the first grants permission to an unfortunate reality but one which nonetheless will occur without fear of punishment for such action is natural and legitimate. It naturalizes the legitimacy of an economic choice and reflects the hegemonic view that it is commonsense that an endangered species shall be pushed further to the brink in service to an economic project. To be clear, in this context, *taken* means killed, not relocated. Such fragmentation and obfuscation are not present in the second instance which more clearly conveys the brutal and tragic reality for the jaguar population of the Santa Rita Mountains if the mine is built. Both writers of these texts have access to the same language system, yet they choose rather divergent lexical items with each selection reflecting an underlying ideological view of physical spaces and human relationships with their nonhuman animal inhabitants.

In the Hallidayan view, meaning manifests and ideological stances are revealed through a language user's choices from a productive system when those choices are contrasted with equally possible selections not made. Each language user has access to a complex system of linguistic choices from which they make selections to fulfill various interpersonal and interactional needs. In such a constructivist Hallidayan view, these choices are made intentionally and function to realize one's construal of their reality. Such a stance on the function of grammatical and linguistic choices reflects the Foucauldian perspective which asserts the power of language and discourse for constructing reality and worldviews. In both perspectives, language choices provide a window into an individual's beliefs, attitudes, and values for no choice from the system is arbitrary and without meaning. As Eggins asserts, "no text is free of ideology," and all language use encodes ideological positions and values (2004, p. 11). This book does not perform fine-grained SLF analyses of text, but it is informed by the tenets of its theoretical program: language use is functional; language use is influenced by social and cultural context, and all choices from the language system are meaningful, i.e., no choice is arbitrary (Eggins, 2004).

The previous discussion of individual choices from the system should not obscure the factors both promoting and constraining language use experienced by speakers and writers. As corpus linguists have long argued and displayed through analyses, language users are primed to produce language patterns which they frequently encounter. Thus, while users have individual choice from the system, they are conditioned to produce the patterns which frequently occur in the prevailing discourse of their lived experiences. This reproduction of linguistic patterns thus naturalizes and perpetuates "commonsense assumptions" and dominant ideological belief systems shared by communities (Fairclough, 1989, p. 84). This highlights a key affordance of the CADS enterprise: the data-driven methodology allows researchers to identify frequent and salient patterns of language use that often operate covertly beyond our conscious awareness but which provide a lens to the hegemonic belief systems of a community of language users. This ability to identify and access prevailing discursive patterns provides insight into what Van Dijk terms *social cognition* (1990), the representations shared by groups of language users through engagement and exposure to discourse.

While not of immediate and obvious ecological relevance, one such pattern often discussed from recent immigration discourse in North America that highlights such naturalization of "commonsense assumptions" is the collocation of *illegal immigrant*. In corpus linguistics, a collocation is the habitual co-occurrence of two words. From a critical perspective, the frequency at which a collocation is used and encountered naturalizes the pairing in the minds of a community of language users, and over time the collocation becomes legitimized and unquestioned; thus, collocation analysis is a productive space for CADS. In this case, the collocation, *illegal immigrant*, is not especially frequent historically and has risen in use in the last 15–20 years in North America. When one selects the term *illegal immigrant*, they are eschewing other possible pairings, e.g., *undocumented immigrant*, and the perceptions which other pairings may construe and mediate. It is clear that the terms *illegal immigrant* and *undocumented immigrant* index quite distinct perceptions and ideological orientations and that various dispositions toward the group may cascade from this selection.

The power of corpus linguistics emerges from its ability to view "the incremental change of discourse" through such contrastive patterns on a macro scale (Baker, 2006, p. 13). Corpus linguistics, particularly diachronic study, enables analysts to see changes in frequency and function over time and can thus enable an unsettling of notions of normalcy and naturalness. Just as critical discourse analysis seeks to demystify language use, CADS can challenge perceptions of the normalcy of language use. As noted, individual choices made by language users reflect ideological orientations through selections of a grammatical structure or lexical item. However, CADS enables the researcher to view the "cumulative effect" of hegemonic discourses throughout a discourse community (Baker, 2006, p. 13). Such analysis beyond the level of the individual and the instance to the identification of community-shared, system-level patterns makes corpus linguistics and discourse studies rather well-suited partners.

CADS research can often be characterized as descriptive for it identifies lexicogrammatical features present in texts, genres, and registers and details how such features function in certain discourse communities. For instance, few areas have been so thoroughly explored within CADS than the written and spoken registers of academic discourse. Such work has extensively documented the lexicogrammatical patterns that imbue academic writing with interactional and interpersonal qualities (Biber, 2006; Gray & Biber, 2012; Hyland, 2005, 2010). Other work in the analysis of academic discourse has investigated the use of epistemic and attitudinal stance markers in undergraduate writing (Aull & Lancaster, 2014), graduate student theses (Charles, 2006), and experimental research articles (Hyland, 1996). Though such work does situate and interpret findings with respect to the specific social context under inquiry, it typically does not venture into a more critical space. This statement is not meant negatively for descriptive work has great value and has contributed significantly to our understanding of language use across a range of genres and registers. That said, in recent years the characteristically descriptive nature of CADS research has shifted toward more critical investigations of discourse. It is likely that register and genre-based studies will continue to dominate due to their varied applications and implications for lexicography, language pedagogy, etc. but there is increasing integration of CDS and CADS.

CDS conceptualizes language as social practice (Fairclough, 1989). Initially, such a definition does not significantly distinguish the approach from the aforementioned descriptive approaches which also typically situate discourses in the social and cultural contexts of production. While most simply, discourse analysis is "the analysis of text structure above the sentence" (Sinclair & Coulthard, 1975) or more simply "the study of language in use" (Gee, 2011, p. 8), this definition proves insufficient for CDS practitioners who view discourse analysis as much more than the study of "just language use" (Fairclough, 1992, p. 28). As noted, CDS defines discourse as "a form of social practice" (Fairclough & Wodak, 1997, p. 258). This broadened view of discourse as social practice asserts the constitutive quality of language to both shape and be shaped by discursive events, institutions, and situations. In such a critical orientation, identifying and describing language patterns is insufficient. Instead, CDS research seeks to address social problems through highlighting the "ideological assumptions" embedded within texts (Haig, 2001, p. 209) and which pattern throughout discourses to "sustain and reproduce the social status quo" (Fairclough & Wodak, 1997, p. 258). CADS is well-suited for the identification and analysis of such patterns and the ideological meanings they encode and (re)produce.

The potential for the integration of CDS and CADS was asserted in an oft-cited article from the critical discourse analyst Gerlinde Hardt-Mautner in the mid-1990s (Hardt-Mautner, 1995). In the opening paragraph to the article, she notes an obstacle to the primarily qualitative approach of critical discourse analysis when working with a large collection of texts. In her case study, she analyzed an ongoing debate in popular British press, yet due to a rather large amount of data, the application of qualitative CDS methods seemed limited. The most compelling affordance of CADS which supports its application with CDS is a product of two principles noted previously: corpora are large collections of authentic language. Corpus linguistics greatly increases the data available for analysis in comparison to the qualitative techniques of other discourse analytic methods such as CDS. This access and ability to process a much larger data volume mitigates the critique of subjectivity and researcher bias sometimes ascribed to CDS. While the quantitative measures of corpus linguistics do not fully limit the "cherry-picking" pitfall of CDS as asserted by Widdowson (2000, 2004), CADS does enhance the ability of researchers to make empirical statements about language use. Essentially, CADS enables the researcher to quantitatively measure the prevalence of a linguistic feature of interest in a discourse more broadly. While this statement seems to advantage the quantitative aspects of a corpus-assisted approach, CADS advances and indeed requires qualitative interpretation as well.

One of the enduring myths of CADS is the mistaken belief that it is an entirely quantitative endeavor. Certainly, CADS employs various statistical measures, but the analyst must still interpret the meanings of language use through careful interpretation of corpus data and understanding of the context of production. As Baker et al. (2008) comment, the distinction between the quantitative and qualitative in CADS is a rather "fuzzy boundary" as any quantitative finding must be interpreted qualitatively through a theoretical lens, leading to the potential formulation of new theories of language use (2008, p. 296). Similarly, Biber and colleagues comment, "a crucial part of the corpus-based approach is going beyond the quantitative patterns to propose functional interpretations explaining why the patterns exist" (1998, p. 9). The initial stages of CADS research are more quantitative in nature, but as the inquiry progresses, the work becomes more qualitative and context-sensitive (Baker and McEnery, 2015). Reflecting earlier work from Hardt-Mautner, Baker et al. (2008) identify the multiplicity of methods and techniques present in both CADS and CDS as they assert the "methodological synergy" of the two. In other words, the two approaches complement each other well with neither becoming "subservient" to the other (p. 274).

Importantly, and as others would also later note, the application of corpus techniques is not intended as a replacement for CDS methods but rather as a supplement, and the two techniques, qualitative and quantitative, "need to be combined, not played off against each other" (Hardt-Mautner, 1995, p. 2). CDS has never been a monolithic approach; instead, as stated by Wodak and Meyer, CDS is "multifarious, derived from quite different theoretical backgrounds, oriented toward different data and methodologies" (2009, p. 5). The "problem-driven" quality of CDS (Wodak & Meyer, 2009, p. 2) requires an interdisciplinary openness to investigate complex social phenomena (Is there a greater problem facing humanity than the climate crisis?). In a similar manner, Baker et al. (2008) note that CADS is not "uniform" and that researchers combine and deploy a range of techniques. Thus, the integration of corpus linguistic procedures to the CDS enterprise reflects both of the disciplines' methodological openness throughout their histories. As detailed in the next section, such methodological and theoretical openness and flexibility make their further application for ecolinguistic research quite seamless.

1.5 Ecolinguistics and Critical Discourse Studies

Informed by Baker and McEnery's assertion that all corpus linguistics is discourse analysis (2015), this text asserts a similar proposition: ecolinguistics is CDS. In the previous section, the increase in use of the collocation *illegal immigrant* may have been judged as irrelevant or tangential to the current focus on ecolinguistics and discourses of ecological importance. In contrast, an analysis and critique of the collocation would be representative of a CDS tradition that has a substantial record of research exploring how language functions to normalize, legitimate, and perpetuate mechanisms of power that further systems of oppression, exploitation, and inequality for marginalized peoples and groups. Such research has directly investigated representations of immigrants and immigration in the mainstream media of various national contexts. For example, O.S. Ana (1999) performed a metaphor analysis of a corpus of *Los Angeles Times* articles and discovered common metaphors depicting immigrants as animals, debased people, and burdens. More recently, corpus-assisted CDS has analyzed representations of refugees, asylum seekers, immigrants, and migrants in British media (Baker et al., 2008). The research of immigration discourse neither considers nor engages with the increasingly common cause driving displacement and immigration: the climate crisis. Between 2008 and

2016, Oxfam International concluded that approximately 22 million people were displaced as a result of climate change, and in the coming years, the World Bank estimates the displacement of approximately 150 million people from sub-Saharan Africa, South Asia, and Latin America due to climate chaos. UNESCO concurs and states that the effects of the climate crisis will significantly alter physical landscapes, leading to extreme pressures on natural resources, driving international conflict, and increasing immigration. These reports demonstrate the emerging reality that immigration and the climate crisis will increasingly be interconnected and that the "problems faced by oppressed groups are not just social but ecological, as climate change, biodiversity loss, resource depletion, and chemical contamination make it difficult for them to achieve wellbeing or even meet their basic needs for survival" (Stibbe, 2018, p. 497).

CDS aims to help people solve real-world problems and change their lived conditions, yet there are no more critical problems for humanity to solve than climate crisis and ecological devastation as both threaten the viability of humans as a species. As Stibbe asserts, "It is no longer enough to work towards an equitable society" when our current society is pushing forward on "a pathway to collapse" (p. 497). Humans are with greater frequency experiencing the consequences of the collapsing global ecosystem, and it is not particularly surprising that the peoples who are already marginalized, disempowered, oppressed, and exploited are the ones who also are most sharply affected by droughts, wildfires, rising sea levels, and myriad other ecological consequences. It is not the wealthiest and most powerful who are or will be the most significantly impacted by climate change. Though in time, the climate crisis, if not addressed, will touch all, those who are currently disadvantaged will be the ones who first suffer. While CDS has long aimed to create more fair and equitable societies, ecolinguistics contributes to this mission by also promoting the formation of more ecologically sustainable ones. Thus, a synergy of CDS and ecolinguistics is both well-equipped and indeed needed to critique the role of language in the present climate crisis while likewise contributing to the formation of a more ecologically sustainable future for all humans.

A case for synthesizing CDS and ecolinguistics extends to other species as well. As evident, the climate crisis is having clear and measurable effects on human life and well-being; however, the consequences are similarly severe for countless other species. While the peoples most impacted by ecological change most likely feel marginalized and without voice, nonhuman species are unable to protest the conditions of their endangerment and impending extinction, to fight against the warming and acidification of their waters and the shrinking of their habitats, to challenge their imprisonment in factory farms, to critique their representation in popular media, or to speak against the various forms in which they are marginalized and exploited. As CDS intends to give voice to marginalized humans and empower individuals and communities to challenge the systems contributing to their suffering, ecolinguistics seeks to also give voice to nonhuman species suffering from climate change, exploitation, pollution, habitat loss, etc. Research in this space has highlighted language practices which fragment and distance human animals from nonhuman ones. For instance, Singer (1990) notes that English language users say and eat beef rather than cow and pork rather than pig but also wear leather made from hides, not skin. Additionally, Stibbe (2003) details how the discourse of farming mediates human relationships with pigs and legitimizes their treatment and suffering while Freeman (2009) notes how farming discourses present nonhuman animals as commodities. Freeman (2009) further asserts that nonhuman animals are presented as empty vessels devoid of emotion while Gilbert (2019) critiques how farming discourse presents cows as poor mothers but farmers as the caring parent. Such work makes salient and observable the effects of discourse on our relationships with nonhuman animals and speaks to the value of CDS and ecolinguistics—the research on nonhuman animal representation continues in greater depth in Chapter 5.

Reflecting characteristics of CDS, ecolinguistics challenges the naturalization, legitimation, and (re)production of attitudes, dispositions, ideologies, and practices which are ecologically harmful and do not cultivate more ecologically sustainable ways of speaking, thinking, and being. Such language practices are embedded in discourses hiding in plain sight. For example, a 2018 article from National Public Radio (NPR), a reputable US public news agency that much of the public views as non-partisan, ominously reported the decline of Japan's birthrate and the resulting economic challenges it would produce for the nation. Encoded in the language of the article is an ideology of the naturalness and desirability of perpetual growth, an ideology Swedish climate activist Greta Thunberg labeled at the United Nations Climate Summit in 2019 as a "fantasy." This ideology, however, is so pervasive and dominant that in a period when we should be welcoming population plateaus and the consumption declines which result, we instead lament the loss of workers that would make Japan less competitive in the global market. Such a discourse reinforces a survival-of-the-fittest neoliberal world order that views nations as existing in a constant state of competition against each other. As Marc Fisher provocatively asserted, "It's easier to imagine the end of the world than the end of capitalism" (2009, p. 1). The

NPR article is reflective of Fisher's statement as no counter narrative or potential reality is given space as we seemingly lack the ability or interest to conceive what such an alternative world would look like. Not once does the article mention the positive environmental effects of the decline. The persistence of such an ideology and its reflection in language use is exactly the sort of pattern and practice that ecolinguistics seeks to challenge.

CDS and ecolinguistics aim to both reveal and challenge ideologies present in discourses; ecolinguistics simply aims to target those ideological apparatuses that perpetuate ecological degradation of various forms. Additionally, and quite importantly, CDS and ecolinguistics are well-suited to identify and promote discourses which are beneficial to the cultivation of ecological wellbeing and sustainability for all human and nonhuman animal species and the ecosystems in which they live. Through the critique of destructive discourses and the promotion of beneficial ones, CDS and ecolinguistics have the potential to make important contributions to the solving of real-world problems.

1.6 Corpus-Assisted Ecolinguistics

This chapter has asserted synergies, noted affordances, and made connections between multiple methodological approaches and theoretical frameworks. Thus, a brief summary on how these multiple orientations come together to inform the current project is necessary.

1. Corpus-assisted: This text specifically asserts the affordances of corpus-assisted discourse study for the analysis of discourses of ecological relevance. The collection of analytic techniques within CADS is well-suited for the identification of linguistic patterns operating beyond our conscious attention which function to normalize and perpetuate a complex of attitudes, ideologies, identities, practices, and dispositions regarding the environment and nonhuman animals that contribute to the climate crisis and related environmental crises.
2. Ecolinguistics: An ecolinguistic framework investigates the role of language in the climate crisis and ecological collapse while also contributing to the formation of more ecologically sustainable societies. It is critical for it challenges prevailing language practices that mediate relationships with the physical world and all of its inhabitants. Ecolinguistics aims to reveal and challenge language use which contributes

to continued ecological degradation while promoting language use which stimulates ecological well-being and sustainability.

And thus, corpus-assisted ecolinguistics draws from the methodological repertoire of CADS and the theoretical frameworks of ecolinguistics and CDS to enable an expanded ecolinguistic research enterprise for the study of language and its impacts, both negative and positive, on well-being and sustainability. This rationale and potential of this integrated framework is discussed and illustrated throughout this text.

1.7 Organization of the Text

The broad introduction to CADS and ecolinguistics provided here in this first chapter narrows to explore existing research in corpus-assisted ecolinguistics in Chapter 2. The review surveys research in the discursive representations of climate change as well as studies in representations of the environment and environmental issues in political, religious, and corporate discourse. The chapter also explores corpus-assisted studies of place, the discursive representation of nonhuman animals, and research exploring various eco-keywords and depictions of crises and disasters. Following this review of research, the chapter revisits the argument for an expanded scope for corpus-assisted ecolinguistics.

Chapter 3 presents a diachronic analysis of the evolving evaluations of the term *wilderness* across approximately two hundred years of English language use in the Google Books Corpus and the Corpus of Historical American English. The analysis identified the most frequent adjective collocates of *wilderness* from 1810 to 2010 and employed Kendall's Tau correlation coefficient to empirically evaluate the strength of the decade-by-decade increases/decreases in these frequent collocational patterns. The analysis revealed multiple shifting patterns in the representation of *wilderness* with varying evaluative framings increasing since 1950. This illustration displays the potential of diachronic corpus-assisted ecolinguistics, the framework of evaluation, and the collocation analysis method supported by Kendall's Tau correlation coefficient for assessing change in the representations of eco-keywords and other constructs of ecological relevance. As present in subsequent case studies, the chapter closes with comments on future research.

In Chapter 4, I present a corpus-assisted eco-stylistic analysis of Richard Powers' 2018 Pulitzer Prize-winning novel *The Overstory*. The study integrates ecolinguistics and stylistics along with the analytic techniques of CADS to explore how trees and forests become social, agentive, animate characters central to Powers' novel rather than background features serving as stage to human action. In particular, the analysis focuses upon the linguistic features which function to construe trees and forests as animate and agentive, thereby cultivating a human–nature interconnectivity ultimately beneficial to the development of more sustainable ways of being. Environmental fiction and nonfiction are critical spaces for inspiring and cultivating more ecologically sustainable attitudes, identities, and actions. As one character in *The Overstory* (2018) comments, "The best arguments in the world won't change a person's mind. The only thing that can do that is a good story" (Powers, 336). This power of stories to inspire change and action motivates this chapter's analysis and discussion.

Chapter 5 diverges in its design and method for it analyses a rather small, specialized corpus of newspaper articles concerning nonhuman animal escapes. This investigation looks at wordplays such as puns and how they function within these news stories to minimize and trivialize the suffering of the animals by eschewing objective journalistic practices in favor of a farcical, entertaining treatment of these events. This illustration demonstrates the value of corpus-assisted discourse study in cases where access to copious data may not be available for a variety of reasons. Further, it argues that emergent, beneficial discourses can be identified and promoted through corpus linguistic techniques.

Chapter 6 draws inspiration from the spatial humanities and geographical information systems in its geographical text analysis that explores references to and representations of place within environmental communication. CADS has explored a range of linguistic features and their functioning within discourse; however, it has much less frequently considered the places mentioned in texts/corpora, what functions these place name references serve, and how these places are discursively represented. This chapter looks at the place name references within specialized corpora of texts centered around the protection and conservation of several iconic places in the United States. And finally, the conclusion offers closing remarks on the potential of corpus-assisted ecolinguistics and suggests numerous research trajectories which may be pursued.

2

Corpus-Assisted Ecolinguistics

2.0 Introduction

This chapter reviews the body of research integrating the theoretical framework of ecolinguistics and the methodological techniques of CADS. The chapter is divided into sections corresponding to the primary domains in which studies have been performed. These categories are climate crisis discourse, representations of nonhuman animals, political and corporate discursive treatment of the environment as well as secondary, i.e., less explored, areas such as discourses of disasters, representations of place, and studies of ecology-relevant key terms such as *green* or *sustainability*.

For this overview, it was necessary to establish criteria for inclusion and exclusion as much research has been produced that explores climate crisis communication, representations of nonhuman animals, etc. from a range of disciplinary orientations across the humanities and social sciences. As valuable and insightful as this research may often be, it is generally not included in this chapter for it does not meet the criteria of corpus-assisted ecolinguistics listed below. The criteria applied for inclusion are:

1. The study compiles a specialized corpus or analyzes an existing publicly available corpus to answer a research question of relevance to the aims of ecolinguistics; however, the study may neither explicitly mention nor implement ecolinguistics as its framework.
2. The study analyzes a linguistic feature or features (e.g., pronouns, metaphors, modality, nominalization, passivization, transitivity, etc.) and investigates its/their functioning within the target discourse for normalizing and (re)producing either positive or negative ideologies, beliefs, attitudes, or practices regarding the physical world and/or its diverse human and nonhuman animal inhabitants.
3. The analysis applies techniques (e.g., collocational analysis, cluster analysis, keyword analysis, semantic tag analysis, etc.) from corpus linguistics

and CADS to aid in the analysis of the linguistic feature or a complex of features within the target discourse.

The range of studies reviewed in this chapter conforms to these guiding criteria to varying degrees; in other words, not all of the included research fully aligns with and reflects each of the characteristics closely. There are certain studies that are clearly forwarded from an ecolinguistics framework and apply robust corpus techniques to the analysis of particular linguistic features; however, there is great variance amongst the studies as each reflects the three criteria somewhat differently. It is worth noting that many studies excluded from the current review are those emanating from media and communication studies. Though many of these studies do compile specialized corpora of various sorts, these studies typically do not perform detailed linguistic analysis of grammatical features and/or lexical items nor do they explore the functions of these features within discourse. Thus, while media and communication studies have been undeniably productive in the study of climate crisis communication in particular, these studies (with a few illustrative exceptions) are largely absent from the following review. Similarly, other discourse analysis studies relevant to ecolinguistics were excluded for they do not apply techniques common within CADS. Again, these studies clearly have value but are beyond the purview of the current focus on corpus-assisted ecolinguistics.

2.1 Corpora

Before proceeding with the review of research in corpus-assisted ecolinguistics, it will be useful for some readers to first include a brief discussion of the various types of corpora compiled and studied in CADS. The following list provides a brief description of the primary corpus types.

1. A **general corpus** (sometimes referred to as a **monitor corpus**) is a large corpus often with tokens in the hundreds of millions or even billions. Such corpora are generally compiled of a range of text types from newspaper articles, movie scripts, academic texts, television sitcoms, magazines, etc. and are intended to provide a broad and comprehensive view of general language use—the moniker monitor corpus reflects the frequent application in the monitoring of language change. Perhaps the most popular general corpus is the Corpus of Contemporary American English (COCA) (Davies, 2008–). This corpus contains approximately 1 billion words balanced for each year from 1990 to 2019 across eight registers of

language use. Similar to the COCA, the British National Corpus (BNC) (Davies, 2004) includes 100 million words from 1991 to 1995 while the Strathy Corpus of Canadian English (Davies, 2012) is comprised of 50 million words. At times, a general corpus is used as a **reference corpus.** In these cases, a node corpus—the corpus under investigation—is compared to the typically much larger reference corpus to identify variation of language use; the BNC and COCA are frequently employed as a reference corpus in CADS.

2. A **diachronic corpus** enables researchers to explore language change over time by compiling corpora with time as the guiding factor. Time can be conceived broadly as in the Corpus of Historical American English (COHA) (Davies, 2010–) which stratifies the corpus into increments of decades from 1810 to 2010. Though one may imagine a diachronic corpus to represent larger periods of time similar to the COHA, corpora may be arranged according to any time parameter from decade, year, month, week, etc. For example, in Carvahlo's (2005) study of climate change discourse, the corpus is arranged in three time periods from 1985 to 2000 while Fusari (2018) investigates the evolving representations of the term *animal* over the past 100 years in the Strathy Corpus. The manner in which time is operationalized varies.

3. A **specialized corpus** is one constructed in a manner which enables a focus on research questions on language use in specific genres, registers, texts, discourse domains, etc. For example, in previous research, I compiled a corpus of blog posts from an advocacy group opposed to the construction of an open-pit copper mine in southern Arizona and a second corpus of press releases from the multinational mining corporation aiming to build the mine (Poole, 2016a, 2017b). Though the corpora were small (each was fewer than 100K words), they enabled me to ask and answer targeted research questions about the language use of the two oppositional groups engaged in the public debate about the potential construction of the massive copper mine. Another example of a specialized corpus is the approximately 30,000-word collection of transcripts from the documentary series *Life* compiled by Sealey and Oakley (2013). Researchers in CADS often compile and analyze specialized corpora in order to answer focused questions about particular genres, texts, or discourse communities.

These corpus types may initially appear marked by clearly defined boundaries but that is not uniformly true as researchers exploit corpora in various ways. It is quite possible and indeed somewhat common for a corpus to reflect qualities of the various types. For example, the COCA is most commonly viewed as a general corpus for its large size and the number of registers included. Yet, the functionality of the corpus enables users to explore language use diachronically over the thirty-year period represented by the corpus. Similarly, one could target a specific sub-register, e.g., fiction, and then narrow further to children's literature; thus, the analyst could then be said to be studying a specialized corpus. When considered holistically, COCA is perhaps best judged as a general corpus, but it can be queried for a range of investigations. Despite the fluid boundaries, a general understanding of these primary corpus types is useful as researchers must select whether to use existing public corpora or compile novel, specialized ones for their investigations.

2.2 Climate Crisis Discourse

The discourse of climate change has been frequently investigated through CADS methods and techniques. These studies have displayed the value of data-driven corpus linguistic techniques for exploring and understanding how climate change is discursively represented and construed in various discourse spaces. This research is aided by the accessibility of digital texts and the relative ease at which large purpose-driven, specialized corpora may be compiled through the use of media aggregators such as LexisNexis, web crawlers like Bootcat, and computational techniques employing programming scripts to scrape texts from targeted websites. The requisite data needed for such corpus-aided investigations is readily obtainable. An additional contributing factor is the technical simplicity of identifying and extracting revelatory data for such terms as *climate change* and *global warming*. This is not intended to imply that research in this domain is simplistic, for researchers perform complex and varied analyses to a range of discourse sites from blogs to user comments as well as newspaper articles and corporate reports. The transdisciplinary reach of the climate crisis motivates significant scholarly attention with an increasing number of studies using corpora as data and corpus linguistic techniques as their method.

Within research of climate crisis discourse, one particularly productive and insightful research space compares the discursive treatment of the crisis in the media of various national contexts. This work is often conducted in communication, media studies, and journalism through theoretical lenses and analytic approaches common to these disciplines such as topic modeling, frames theory, or content analysis amongst a variety of others. In one particularly illustrative example, Schmidt et al. (2013) investigate newspaper coverage of climate change communication across twenty-seven national contexts. Indeed, the study displays qualities of corpus linguistics in its principled and comprehensive approach to data collection; their corpus included more than 150,000 newspaper articles from 1996 to 2010. Studies such as this one typically examine and measure attentional focus offered to the crisis through analysis of frequency data of certain terms in various national media outlets and how these terms and their use evolve diachronically. In other words, these studies report how frequently *climate change* or related terms are mentioned in national media and how those mentions either increase or decrease over time. Though Schmidt and colleagues survey media across nearly thirty national contexts, other works, e.g., Boussalis, Coan, and Poberezhskaya's (2016) diachronic analysis of climate change discourse in Russia, investigate attentional focus more narrowly and deeply within one nation's media coverage. However, research in this tradition largely eschews linguistic analysis that maps and interprets form-to-function relationships in a discourse analytic and ecolinguistic manner.

While some work in this space was excluded due to the absence of linguistic analysis, much remains. Indeed, the first two studies to discuss bridge the space between communication studies and CADS through collaborations by noted scholars from these fields. For example, Grundmann and Krishnamurthy (2010) integrate their disciplinary orientations quite effectively in their exploration of trends in news reporting regarding the frequency of the terms *climate change, global warming*, and *greenhouse effect* in a corpus of newspaper articles from 1980 to 2007 in the United States, the United Kingdom, France, and Germany (2010). Though initially this study may seem similar to Schmidt et al. (2013), this study provides greater analysis of lexical items and their meanings and functions within the discourse. In the study, the researchers observed an increase in climate change reporting in all four countries with the greatest rise around 2005 with more reporting on the topic occurring in France and Germany. In the United States, the discourse mostly reflected scientific framing of the crisis while the three European nations focus on political responses aimed at mitigation. In a sense, the US news media seemed to still be discussing and debating the veracity of the science while the other nations had accepted the data and proceeded to discussions of how to mitigate and address. Interestingly, in the United States, there was a clear difference between the use of *global warming* and *climate change* as *global warming* was viewed as dramatizing and occurred in contexts of threats and fights while *climate change* was framed and discussed with more natural causes.

In a similarly designed study but with greater application of corpus linguistic techniques, Grundmann & Scott (2012) again explore the terms *global warming, greenhouse effect,* and *climate change* in the media of the United States, the United Kingdom, France, and Germany but from 2000 to 2010. In contrast to the previous study of a similar collection of national media corpora, this study performed cluster, collocation, and keyword analyses to more deeply explore the discursive framing of climate change. They observed varied and evolving levels of urgency and skepticism in the discourse of the four nations with Germany showing greater initial urgency while the United States and France displayed greater visibility of skepticism. They also noted that although attentional focus in the media may not be fully predictive of the nature of the political action toward addressing a crisis, their findings display that media reporting generally aligns with degree of political action within each national context. These labels for *climate change* continue to evolve, and as the reader has likely observed, this text often opts for *climate crisis* for a more accurate depiction. This is a contentious space with selection of a term often indexing various ideological orientations. Even recently, US Secretary of Finance Steven Mnuchin at the Davos 2020 Climate Summit asserted *climate change* to be misleading and inaccurate, suggesting instead we use the term *environmental issue* (Long, 2020). Mnuchin's framing is clearly problematic.

While the previous projects were largely descriptive in nature, other studies have pursued an additional stage of analysis by offering critical evaluations and interpretations of language patterns within their broader socio-historical contexts in a manner reflective of CDS. As noted in the previous chapter, ecolinguistics and CDS share many characteristics and aims, and thus, it is unsurprising that CDS and ecolinguistics have been integrated and applied in the discursive production of climate change in national media. An exemplar of such work is Carvahlo (2005) and its investigation of the evolving representations of climate change in three UK newspapers from 1985 to 2000. The study reports changes in representations illustrated with researcher-selected samples to display various discursive representations of the crisis.

Beyond comparisons of variation in national coverage in generally mainstream media outlets, representations of climate crisis have also been explored in blogs, user comments, and institutional reports. One rather noteworthy offering in this space is a study from Koteyko, Jaspal, and Nerlich (2013) which investigated online user comments from *The Daily Mail*, a popular London-based newspaper, added by users both before and after the so-called Climate Gate Controversy of 2010 in which greater than 1,000 emails from the University of East Anglia's Climate Research Unit were stolen and manipulated by climate change skeptics to suggest that global warming was a hoax (Carrington, 2011). While media discourse can be viewed as reflecting macro-level institutional communication, online user comments provide insights into how "lay people" engage with such a complex and evolving issue (Koteyko et al., 2013, p. 74). In their study, they explored the frequent topics discussed in the forums, how the nearly 5,000 total comments differ before and after Climate Gate, and also how climate science is represented throughout the discourse. Their construction of corpora representing both before and after the event made possible a keyword analysis to identify salient terms of each period. It is important to note that within corpus linguistics, a statement that a term is a keyword is not simply saying it is important and frequent. More precisely, a keyword is a lexical item that occurs in one corpus (the node corpus) at a frequency that is statistically significant in comparison to a second corpus (the reference corpus). In other words, the frequency in the node corpus was greater than one would expect when compared to a reference corpus and measured by either significance, effect size, or both—keyness/keyword analysis is discussed in greater detail in Chapter 4. Thus, the Koteyko and colleagues, study focuses on those salient items whose variation in use is statistically divergent. Such a quantitative procedure enables the researcher to focus attention on the most distinctive items of a subcorpus, and in this study, it allowed the researchers to view the divergence in the user comments from before and after Climate Gate. The technique displayed how user comments discussed scientists in generally negative semantic contexts but also how the focus on climate science differed at the two points in time.

With a similar focus on user comments, Collins and Nerlich (2015) use semantic tag analysis to explore user comments attached to articles regarding climate change in *The Guardian*. The authors assert that climate crisis debate is rather heterogeneous and that comment spaces are typically quite polarized despite their intention to foster public interaction and deliberation. The use of semantic tag analysis enabled the identification of key themes present within the comments. Briefly, a semantic tag is an annotation applied to words in a corpus to mark their general semantic category. For example, the commonly used UCREL Semantic Tag Analysis System (USAS) (Piao et al., 2015) applies tags such as *I: money and commerce, L: life and living things, T: time* as well as many others to all the words within a corpus. In this study of user comments, terms present in the semantic categories of weather (e.g., *climate, weather, snow*), temperature (*warming, warm, heat*), and science (*scientists, science*) were the most common but terms invoking evaluations of truth (*evidence, fact, true*) and also cause and effect connections (*effect, cause, due to*) were frequent.

Displaying the usefulness of corpus-assisted contrastive analysis, Fløttum and Dahl (2012) perform a contrastive analysis of the United Nations' Human Development Report from 2007–8 and the World Bank's World Development Report from 2010; both focused on the challenges of the climate crisis and policy actions to be considered and taken in order to mitigate its consequences on global populations. In the study, they explored stance markers that produce various epistemic, deontic, and attitudinal meanings, e.g., modal auxiliaries such as *may, might, can,* and adverbials such as *simply, clearly, obviously,* to explore in the reports both who is talking about climate change and how they are doing so. Essentially, the authors investigate how two influential international organizations tell contrasting climate crisis stories to legitimate and support their varying policy decisions and actions. Amongst their findings, the analysis revealed variation in how the organizations appealed to authority to support their policy positions and actions. Interestingly, the World Bank used a much higher frequency of deontic modals such as *must* and *should*. The greater frequency of such modals of obligation indexes a greater urgency and emphasizes the necessity that proposed actions be urgently completed to a degree that was not similarly present in UN report.

Of greater corpus size but with a similar comparative approach, Nerlich and Koteyko (2009) compared one corpus of thirty-three newspaper articles with a second corpus of fifty-four blog posts to explore the word *carbon* and its R1 collocates, e.g., *carbon footprint, carbon finance, carbon credits, carbon indulgence, carbon offsetting*, in order to study the rapidly changing related discourses of climate change. Such compound words with *carbon* as the node have greatly increased in recent years. As an aside, it is hardly coincidental that many studies employ such contrastive analytic techniques. As noted in Chapter 1, the salience of a pattern is likely best interpreted in comparison to its use and frequency to a second corpus of similar texts or a general corpus. Such variation can provide insights into the values, belief system, and ideological apparatus of a community. In a sense, highly frequent terms index what is important and valued by a discourse community. For the Nerlich and Koteyko (2009) study, the analysis of carbon compounds generally and the compound *carbon indulgence* in particular reveal how cultures evolve and adapt in relation to environmental events. Profoundly, they assert that the changes in the compounds, the creativity in the language system, and the multiple ways the compounds create meanings in various contexts are "indicators of trends in human thinking and behaving toward climate change" (p. 352) and provide a means to understand how various groups frame climate change.

In a subsequent and related study, Koteyko (2010) further explores collocations with the node *carbon* to investigate climate change discourse but also the discourse of climate change mitigation efforts and strategies. Methodologically, this study is rather comprehensive in its application of corpus linguistics techniques through its concordance and collocational analysis procedures. Though the study investigates similar collocations as the study discussed in the previous paragraph, there is a greater emphasis on semantic associations. The corpus was a collection of approximately 82,000 RSS feeds in which seventy-nine collocations with *carbon* as node were then extracted and analyzed. In the data, a category of carbon collocations with scientific terms and displaying a neutral semantic prosody were common, e.g., *carbon sequestration* and *carbon sink*, as well as *carbon* with collocates from finance and economics such as *carbon economy* and *carbon cost*. In contrast, while the semantic prosodies with scientific associations were largely neutral, compounds such as *carbon credit* and *carbon tax* often occurred with rather negative semantic loadings as evident through terms such as *backlash, failings, problems*, and *criticism* which were often present in the concordance lines. In other instances, such pejorative terms as *stupid, useless*, and *pathetic* were deployed. A third group of what the author terms popular carbon compounds, e.g., *carbon footprint* and *carbon calculator*, were also present. The prevalence of such features reflects that awareness of the climate crisis is not resigned to institutions and governments but is also present at the individual level. Such analysis is valuable for it displays how climate crisis discourse patterns across many social levels and domains, highlighting the "complex discursive processes underlying the social construction of climate change" (Koteyko, 2010, p. 669).

A rather novel and intriguing study in this space explores representations of the future in climate change blogs. In the study, Fløttum, Gjesdal, and Gjerstad (2014) compile a corpus of approximately 1.5 million blog posts from 3,000 blogs related to climate change. In the analysis, the focus was specifically on terms salient to discussions of the future, e.g., *future, threat, danger*, and *must*; they performed concordance and cluster analysis of such terms using Antconc (Anthony, 2020) to explore the varying representations of the future. They identify nine categories which are then organized into superordinate classes of "doom and gloom" and "bright future" (p. 220). Perhaps defying expectation and intuition, they note a greater presence of positive framings of climate change and its potential effects on nature and humanity. The authors comment that a discourse of hope and emotion may actually promote greater action and change than messaging of fear and danger.

One final and rather distinct corpus study of climate crisis discourse compares texts from a religious figure, the Pope, and a science organization, the National Aeronautics and Space Administration (NASA). Though such a pairing may at first seem incongruous, the comparison affords insights into how religious and scientific texts differently depict climate change, characterize human responsibility for the crisis, and forward solutions for mitigating its effects. For the religious text, Castello and Gesualto (2019) analyze the encyclical letter, *Laudato Si*, and compare it with science updates posted on the NASA website—both were approximately 40K words. Through a semantic and keyword analysis, the study reveals how the influential religious text focuses upon topics such as ecology, humanity, physical context, and a divine force with issues often framed in relation to the importance and urgency of time. Additionally, the papal letter focuses on human and social relations and consistently conveys a need for heightened awareness and care of the environment while also expressing a story of interrelatedness of ecological and human well-being, a message the authors judge quite positively.

Studies of climate crisis discourse have been the most numerous within corpus-assisted ecolinguistics. These studies offer valuable insights into this contested, fluid, and emergent discourse space and studies should continue to explore evolutions in how institutions, governments, and individuals discursively depict the crisis and its myriad consequences.

2.3 Representations of Nonhuman Animals

Corpus studies exploring human and nonhuman animal relationships frequently explore and critique linguistic patterns that reflect human perceptions of nonhuman animals and how such language use may perpetuate a range of harmful attitudes and actions. Discursive patterns reflect prevailing human conceptualizations of nonhuman animals while also often obscuring the suffering experienced by nonhuman animals often as a result of human actions. For example, humans regularly eat ham sandwiches or charbroiled steak—we do not name these meals pig flesh sandwich or charbroiled cow flesh—we instead apply modified terms that commodify nonhuman animal flesh as products in order to distance ourselves from the sentient beings that were slaughtered (Singer, 1990; Stibbe, 2012). Such seemingly mundane and innocuous linguistic patterns facilitate a distancing between humans and nonhuman animals that occludes and naturalizes nonhuman animal suffering. For an additional example, the Environmental Protection Agency in their review of a proposal for a massive open pit copper mine in Arizona uses the verb *take* when discussing the jaguars of the region. The agency chose not to use the term *kill*, an ostensibly accurate description as the agency was essentially licensing the murder of jaguars, instead opting for the euphemistic *take*, a verb that commonly collocates with such positive lexical items as *care*, *break*, and *picture*. More recently, in a letter in the *New York Times* during the period of the COVID-19 pandemic in the United States, the chief financial officer of Tyson Foods wrote that due to the pandemic, the company may have to *depopulate* more than 1 million nonhuman animals. The selection of *depopulate* rather than *kill* plainly hides the horrific reality of murdering more than 1 million nonhuman animals. Even in the company biography, they assert they are a "protein-based food company," obscuring the fact that the protein they reference is the flesh of sentient beings as well as commodifying nonhuman animals for their end product as meat.

Discursive representation of nonhuman animals such as those in the aforementioned samples has naturally garnered much attention within discourse studies broadly. As with the previous discussion of climate crisis research, this area has also received extensive attention across the disciplinary spectrum but for understandably a longer period than more recent climate crisis study. Though the climate crisis is a largely recent phenomenon, many philosophers, social scientists, and scholars have long pondered human and nonhuman animal relationships; for example, Descartes in the 1600s restricted consciousness to humans alone and asserted nonhuman animals to be machines. Within corpus-assisted ecolinguistics, studies in this area have explored both large corpora, e.g., Frayne (2019) employs both the massive Google Ngram corpus and the Corpus of Historical American English (COHA), as well as smaller, specialized corpora, e.g., Sealey and Oakley (2013) study a corpus of approximately 30,000 words from the nature documentary series *Life* in order to explore representations of nonhuman animals in the popular series. These two display the poles with many studies falling at various points along this continuum of corpus size. As a collection, the studies in this area pursue rather detailed linguistic analysis and form-function mapping, and thus, are more closely aligned with corpus-assisted ecolinguistics than the communication studies of climate crisis discourse detailed in the previous section.

The approaches applied and research questions answered have been diverse, but variation in pronoun use and how pronoun choice reflects and reproduces prevailing construals of nonhuman animals have been frequent targets of research in this space—this literature is reviewed more comprehensively in Chapter 6. Pronoun use and variation provide clear examples of how language choices index human and nonhuman animal relationships, and thus, it is unsurprising that rights advocates have long problematized the application of pronouns *it*, *its*, and *which* for objectifying and removing agency and animation from nonhuman animals. It hardly seems hyperbolic to argue that the use of such depersonalized pronouns depicts animals as objects for human exploitation. In one now well-known anecdote, the editor and reviewers for Jane Goodall's seminal study of chimpanzees demanded she revise her submission and remove all instances of *he*, *she*, and *who* when referring to chimpanzees in favor of *it* and *which*. She refused and years later wrote in her memoir: "Incensed, I, in my turn, crossed out the *its* and *which* and scrawled back the original pronouns" (as cited in Giamo, 2016). Though Goodall may have won this particular case, the most recent publication manual from the American Psychological Association (2020) prescriptively advises the use of *who* for humans and the relative pronoun *that* or *which* for nonhuman animals and inanimate objects.

Several studies serve as useful exemplars for corpus investigations of pronoun use. In one of these offerings, Gupta (2006) focused specifically on the discourse of fox hunting and how patterns of *who* and *which* in texts related to fox hunting are used to refer to the nonhuman animals involved in the hunt: *foxes*, *hounds*, and *horses*. Gilquin and Jacobs (2006) similarly focus on the use of relative pronouns, yet they widen their focus to a list of more than 900 nonhuman animals. Employing the 100-million word British National Corpus, they extract 738 sentences which produce a pattern of *nonhuman animal + who/whom*. They observe that nonhuman animals rarely occupy the subject position in the sentence structure, i.e., agency is removed, and that the relative pronoun *who* occurs with negative semantic loads as frequently as it does in more positive patterns. In a later study of a smaller specialized corpus, Sealey and Oakley (2013) explore pronoun use but extend attention to the verbs which most frequently follow the pronoun; they also investigate the use of lexical items *so* and *to* in an attempt to explore the degree of intention and desire extended to nonhuman animals within the *Life* nature documentary series. The researchers concluded that pronoun selection serves to humanize nonhuman animals and that *so* is frequently used to display intent of actions pursued by the nonhuman animals.

In a related study, Goatly (2002) applies a systemic functional grammar (SFG) approach to investigate representations of nature on the prestigious, reputable, and purportedly objective BBC World Service. In the study, Goatly compiles a corpus of 2.5 million words collected in 1990–1 from the BBC. His study moves beyond semantic choices to choices of lexicogrammar that instantiate representations of nature for the nearly 140 million listeners. Asserting a weak-form of the Whorfian Hypothesis, he argues that language "predisposes us to perceive, think, and act in certain ways, and makes it more difficult to perceive and think in alternative ways" (p. 2). Such a statement is essentially the defining statement of ecolinguistics—the way we speak about nonhuman animals and the physical world influences how we think and therefore how we act. In adherence to its SFG alignment, the study applies a transitivity model which assigns roles of actor, process, affected, and circumstance to clausal elements. In the analysis, concordance lines of various categories of nonhuman animals (*insects, birds, land animals, aquatic animals*) are extracted as well as other lexical items from nature (*water, land and landscape, weather, disease*) with the role of each coded for semantic role (e.g., actor in transitive clause, patient affected, actor in intransitive clause). His study illustrates that on the BBC there are "frames of consistency" (p. 20) and that the BBC consistently presents nature as acted upon rather than actor and that nature is generally presented as having agency only when viewed as hostile to human life, e.g., disease and earthquakes. He argues that the consistency of the representations affects cognition and how individuals perceive and think about nature and concludes that "linguistic representations can both induce action or be used to justify it" (p. 25).

In recent years, a research collaboration titled *People, Products, Pests, and Pets* with partners at Lancaster University and Kings College London compiled a corpus of approximately 9 million words and 4,500 texts[1] of various types to explore discursive depictions of human and nonhuman animal relationships in contemporary language use in the United Kingdom. Impressively, the corpus contains texts from ten domains, including broadcasts, food websites, journals, legislation, focus groups, and interviews. Though publications and findings from the collaboration continue to emerge, some analyses have been published. For example, a study from Guy Cook (2015) explores the erasure of animals in daily life and the discursive tension between traditional/speciesist and non-traditional/non-speciesist language use in the interviews of sixteen spokespersons for organizations connected to animal/nonhuman animal issues. More recently, Cook and Ancarno (2019) analyzed *taste* and its collocates across various text types in the corpus through an innovative three-dimensional discourse analysis approach which triangulated data from interviews, focus groups, and the balance of the corpus compiled for the project. Their study explored how individuals rationalize and support their choices to eat or not eat the flesh of nonhuman animals. Some individuals rationalized their practice of eating organically raised animal products while opposing the industrial factory farming operations and the cruelty which they associate with the industry. Other individuals reflected a prevailing discourse of human exceptionalism that legitimates their consumption choices while others firmly reject all consumption of animal flesh for moral, ethical, and/or environmental reasons. Yet, many occupy places between these positions. Ultimately, the study highlights the powerful nostalgia-based, taste-driven justifications people offer to explain their choices in the face of ethical and environmental arguments against meat consumption.

An additional study emerging from the *People, Products, Pests, and Pets* collaboration explores the degree of animacy conferred to nonhuman animals as reflected in verb use following a mention of a nonhuman animal in the journal article subcorpus (Sealey, 2018). In the analysis, the verb *were* in passive structures (*were + past participle*) followed the naming of a nonhuman animal in slightly more than 70 percent of all instances; thus, in most instances nonhuman animals were patients being acted upon by other forces rather than agents initiating actions. Patterns such as *were fed, were housed, were kept, were collected, were observed,* and many others reflect the patient status of nonhuman animals as receivers of action from their human counterparts. In other words, nonhuman animals are rarely the doers and actors but instead receivers of the actions of their human counterparts. Additionally, even in the non-passive constructions, nonhuman animals were still resigned to largely passive roles as their naming followed verbs that semantically framed their action as a receiver of human action, e.g., *ate, consumed,* and *received*. An additional analysis in the study expanded the scope of the inquiry to the full corpus beyond the journal article subcorpus. For this part of the investigation, Sketch diff, a function within the corpus tool Sketch Engine which displays a word's collocational behavior, was employed to explore the naming terms *dog/s, cow/s, bird/s, fish,* and *bee/s*. Reflecting earlier findings, again nonhuman animals were discursively presented rather passively and in contexts emphasizing their perceived usefulness to humans.

The nonhuman animal studies previously discussed are generally synchronic in nature, but diachronic research on the changing representations of nonhuman animals over time has also been conducted. Two noteworthy projects that pursue such diachronic corpus-assisted analysis are Fusari (2018) and Frayne (2019). In the former, Fusari analyzes the single word *animal* and its evolution from 1921 to 2011 in the 50-million word Strathy Corpus of Canadian English. The study of 100 years of language use displays a consistent discursive practice to separate human and nonhuman animals along with patterns of metaphors which present humans as rational and nonhuman animals as irrational and dangerous. The data also displays emergent trends in the discourse to represent nonhuman animals with greater compassion, e.g., *companion animal*. However, the use of such phrasings as *companion animal* also reinforces hierarchical relationships as it places animals on a deictic cline from important and therefore spatially or metaphorically close to humans on one pole and unimportant and thus distant on the other. Ultimately, the diachronic analysis shows the pervasive and enduring notion of human–nonhuman animal dichotomies within language use and hierarchies that locate humans in a position of status and dominion.

While Fusari (2018) explores the evolving uses of one term, Frayne (2019) is more expansive in its diachronic analysis of 134 species names (both the singular and plural) in the COHA and the Google Ngram viewer from 1800 to 2000; both the COHA and Ngram Viewer exceed the Strathy Corpus by many millions of words. The Frayne study is unique in corpus-assisted ecolinguistics as it explores how cultural and technological change is reflected in the relative prominence or absence of key terms historically. In other words, the study asks whether references to nonhuman animals have changed in the past two centuries as industrialization and urbanization have proliferated. The data suggests that indeed correlation is present between rural population decline and frequency of species references. Additionally, while the frequency of species reference declined so too did the level of sentiment in which nonhuman animals were represented.

These diachronic studies from Fusari and Frayne are noteworthy, for their analysis highlights the evolving representations of nonhuman animals over many years of language use. Such diachronic work illustrates the semantic changes which lexical items can experience while also challenging notions of an objective linguistic code that captures an existing truth. Seeing changes in phraseological and collocational patterns highlights the dynamic influence of socio-cultural contexts on language use. While synchronic studies provide important insights into community and cultural beliefs and attitudes toward nonhuman animals and the natural world at a defined point in time, diachronic studies illustrate the contentious and fluid nature of meaning and language use and demonstrate how representations of and relationships with nonhuman animals are dynamic and emergent. Diachronic studies are revelatory and important for they challenge and dispel notions that existing constructs are somehow natural, normal, and inherent. Chapter 6 further explores the discursive representation of nonhuman animals in prevailing discourse.

2.4 Corporate and Political Discourse

Analyses of corporate discourse within ecolinguistics have typically investigated the linguistic practices which corporations employ to obscure their roles and responsibilities for ecological harm in a process referred to as greenwashing (Plec & Pettenger, 2012) as well as how corporations discursively present themselves as caring environmental stewards and partners invested in sustainable development. As Greer and Bruno (1996, p. 11) comment, corporate leaders seek to protect and expand markets "by posing as friends of the environment"—ultimately, major corporate polluters simultaneously proclaim to be environmental protectors. To illustrate such discursive maneuvering, business-talk in statements such as "Mistakes were made" and "Emissions increased 5%" shows how speakers hide their agency and diffuse responsibility. In the first sample, the passive construction obscures the agent guilty of the transgression—who made the mistake? Such a statement could be deployed to mask responsibility for a toxic chemical release into a local waterway, shirk responsibility for the release of harmful pollutants into the atmosphere, or diffuse blame for an oil spill in public waters. In the latter, the euphemism *emission* seems less negative than its near yet rather negative synonym *pollution* while the process of nominalization again allows the responsible stakeholder to be erased from the message—the nominalization allows the author to avoid ascription of explicit agency for the actor releasing the pollutants. Such patterns in corporate discourse are prevalent and ecolinguists have attempted to reveal and challenge.

In studies of corporate discourse, multinational oil and gas corporations have received much scrutiny. In one such study, Richard Alexander (1999) investigated communication of British Petroleum through an ecolinguistics lens. In the study, he analyzed a speech from the chief executive officer of BP titled "Our common journey," identifying a number of salient lexical items such as we, *our*, *against*, and a*im* in the texts. In the speech from BP's CEO, Alexander asserts the patterning of *we* conceals causality for environmental degradation by diffusing responsibility and spreading need for action broadly. Such a tendency for corporate communication to diffuse accountability broadly while obscuring their own offending actions has been noted in numerous studies. Additionally, as noted with greenwashing in the previous paragraph, BP presents itself as compassionate environmental steward while erasing the ecological degradation that their actions produce.

The case of the Deepwater Horizon Oil Disaster—BP and others euphemized and minimized by labeling it a *spill,* but *disaster* is more accurate—in the Gulf of Mexico prompted increased attention toward corporate crisis communication in relation to environmental catastrophes. Immediately following the Deepwater Horizon Disaster, Alexander (2013) analyzed messages from BP. In the study, Alexander explored a specialized corpus of approximately 35K words containing press releases from BP from April to July of 2010 in addition to a 12K word corpus of text from BP's "Gulf of Mexico Restoration" webpage. In the press releases, BP only uses the word *disaster* once, opting instead nearly 100 times to label the event an *incident*—such an obvious reframing that explication seems unnecessary. Similarly, the word *spill* is used greater than 200 times, making it one of the most used lexical items in the releases. Consistently, BP attempts to downplay the severity of the disaster and distance itself from responsibility, and in one line it even states, "It is simply too early—and not up to us—to decide who is at fault." Though nominalizations and agentless constructions enable such deflection of accountability, this statement does so quite explicitly. Also revealed in the analysis is the prominence of metaphors of war within the press releases invoked through such framings as *attack, kill, deploy, launch,* and *target* as well as multiple phrasing of attacking and fighting on various fronts. Such war metaphors possibly evoke nationalistic sentiments and stifle various forms of dissent and critique. Though Alexander's work has typically analyzed rather small corpora of sometimes only one short text (e.g., the 2008 study of one article from *The Economist*), his work is noteworthy for he is one of the first researchers to integrate CDS, ecolinguistics, and corpus techniques for the study of texts of ecological relevance, and his text, *Framing Discourse on the Environment: A Critical Discourse Approach* (2009), occupies a key space in the canon of ecolinguistics.

While the previous studies explore corporate communication in the aftermath of a major environmental catastrophe, other research investigates the rhetorical waters corporations must navigate in messaging intended to inspire stakeholder confidence while likewise appearing to be responsible corporate entities mindful of and contributing to ecological well-being. In one such study, Lischinksy and

Sjolander (2014) explore a 125 thousand word corpus of press releases from Swedish companies, extracting and analyzing various eco-relevant terms such as *sustainability*, *green*, *ecology*, and *climate*. They concluded that although such eco-keywords were frequent in corporate messaging, the terms often occurred in isolated contexts with little or no textual elaboration. Essentially, the company presented itself as sensitive to ecological concerns but core messaging offered little substantive focus to actual sustainability efforts. In a similar study exploring the inclusion/exclusion of environmental concerns from corporate communication, Lischinsky (2015) analyzes a corpus of fifty sustainability and environmental reports. While the previous study explored a range of eco-terms, this investigation explored the term *environment* and its collocates in addition to analysis of the term's transitivity operations and syntactic roles. As seen elsewhere, the eco-relevant word was frequent yet marginalized with a restricted range of participant roles and never in agentive positions. Interestingly, Lischinsky (2015) asserts that texts present corporations' environmental actions as "philanthropic," seemingly expecting praise and recognition (p. 555).

The political forum is a critical space in which understandings of the environment and environmental issues are shaped and produced, yet political discourse has not been extensively studied in corpus-assisted ecolinguistics. That said, several ecolinguistics studies of political discourse have been pursued. In one such study, Bevitori (2015) analyzes *environment* and *green* in US presidential State of the Union addresses from 1960 to 2013. In this diachronic analysis, the researcher explores these terms through a systemic functional linguistic framework to uncover how the representation of the environment has evolved over fifty years of presidential discourse. In an earlier study and with a smaller collection of State of the Union addresses, Bonnefille (2008) merges discourse analysis with cognitive linguistics in a study of metaphor and metonymy patterns within the speeches of US president George W. Bush between 2001 and 2008. In the study, the researcher illustrates how greenwashing practices are employed to communicate and conceptualize climate change in popular political discourse. The analysis displays how "talking green" is consistently coupled with economic frames and how environmental responsibility is discursively joined with economic growth as if economy and environment occupy a "single domain of experience" (p. 53). And perhaps most interestingly, the research notes that the president's speeches are "greener" (p. 55) in years where oil prices are higher. In other words, the urgency for cleaner energy and greater environmental responsibility is a function of global economic realities rather than climate change concern.

The illustrations that follow in Chapters 3 through 6 do not explore corporate or political discourse but these spaces indeed merit continued and expanded attention from corpus-assisted ecolinguistics.

2.5 Eco-relevant Terms, Disasters and Crises, Places, and Other Studies

Corpus studies in previously reviewed domains such as climate crisis and corporate communication are easily categorized and grouped with numerous related studies. However, there are many studies that do not fit so comfortably into one designated space and do not have immediately identifiable partners. Such variation is not surprising given the interdisciplinary qualities of CDS, CADS, and ecolinguistics. Each of these disciplines, though discipline may not be a particularly accurate term as each employs such varied methods and approaches, has explored a range of social problems and their reflection and reproduction in discourse. This section introduces other literature that productively integrates CADS and ecolinguistics beyond the typical categories previously discussed.

2.5.1 Eco-relevant Terms

Within corpus-aided ecolinguistics, key ecological terms such as *green, sustainability, vegetarian,* and s*ustainable development* have been explored. In one such study, Bevitori (2011) investigates the discourse of *green* and its related word forms (e.g., *greening, greens, greenwashing, greeny,* etc.) in two specialized corpora: one a 3.5 million word collection of newspaper articles from six major media outlets in the United States and the United Kingdom in 2007 and a second of blog posts and responses from a thirteen-month period spanning 2009–10. Though corpus studies often perform collocational analyses of salient terms, Bevitori extends this traditional collocational analysis technique by also applying a semantic domain analysis. The study displays the high frequency at which semantic domains of energy and technology, politics and policy, and lifestyle and behavior are similarly associated with the various green terms in the US and UK press. For blogs, there is a greater frequency of energy and technology frames realized through terms such as *wind, solar,* and *nuclear*. The semantic frames enacted in contexts of *green* in the blogs diverged, however. While *green* and its variations occur frequently in reference to business and economic interests with "negative overtones of opportunism" (p. 15), the term occurs in more positive evaluative frames in the blogs.

As Bevitori explores *green*, Mahlberg (2007) examines the phrase *sustainable development* in a 150 thousand word corpus of 211 articles from *The Guardian* in 2002. As is often the case in corpus and discourse studies, texts were collected and analyzed which reference an important international event or include particular seed words (web crawlers operate by searching for and collecting online texts that include researcher-selected seed words). In this study, this organizing event that drives text collection was the World Summit on Sustainable Development in Johannesburg, South Africa. In the corpus, there were approximately 350 samples of *sustainable development* which were then categorized into eleven functional groups. In the data, there was a preference for the now-common phrase to occur in contexts in which *sustainable development* was referenced aspirationally as a goal for nations to be working toward. However, the phrase appears in numerous semantic domains and often displays specialized, evaluative meanings depending on the section of the newspaper in which it is used. Studies such as Mahlberg's highlight the various meanings words and phrases may display and the importance of context and register on meaning creation and interpretation.

An additional study exploring a set of eco-relevant lexical items is a diachronic analysis of the terms *vegetarian*, *vegan*, and *plant-based* from 1944 to 2008 Google Search, Google Scholar, Google Trends, and the Google Books Ngram Viewer. As the authors note in their opening statement, "Language both reflects and promotes change in societies" (Jacobs et al., n.d., p. 1). Such a statement reflects the evolving nature of cultural and social norms and conventions and the affordance of CADS for enabling insights into the reciprocal, dynamic relationship between language and culture. In this study, the authors detail the history of the terms and their emergence into the lexicon through an analysis of these words in a set of Google tools: Search, Trends, Scholar, and the NGram Viewer. Interestingly, the data shows that the term *vegan* now exceeds *vegetarian* in use while *plant-based* appears almost exclusively in academic discourse. Although *vegetarian* has been largely consistent in its use throughout recent decades, there is a marked increase in frequency of *vegan* over the past ten years. Such studies illustrate shifting cultural practices and a greater awareness of dietary choices.

The most expansive of such eco-relevant key word studies is Wild et al. (2013) and their analysis of greater than 100 environmental terms from one massive 1.5 billion word web corpus and three smaller, specialized corpora all compiled from sources in the UK. In their study, they illustrate patterns that reflect nature as distinct and separate from humans and also how nature is depicted as a commodity for economic exploitation. The study also identifies patterns that reflect a range of attitudes, both negative and positive, but also feelings of fear and anxiety regarding the environment. Though these findings and others from their work are indeed worthy of review and reflection, the value of their study also stems from the detailed descriptions of their methodological techniques and analytic approach. Their methods account for the critiques often offered against CDS—a lack of rigor, replicability, and transparency—and corpus linguistics—decontextualized and descriptive with little critical interpretation. Their corpus compilation method and complementary application of automatic and manual analysis integrating the affordances of CDS and CADS are deserving of a careful review by all seeking to do corpus-aided work in this space.

2.5.2 Disasters

Environmental disasters and crises such as hurricanes, pollution, and ozone depletion have also been investigated in corpus-assisted ecolinguistics. In one such study, Bednarek and Caple (2010) analyze the evaluative meanings in article headings and captions in tandem with the featured images of forty news stories from *The Sydney Morning Herald* of Australia. The article is unique in its integration of ecolinguistics literature and theory with both an SFL and CDS approach for multimodal analysis. While the appraisal framework (Martin, 2000) is extensive, the study focuses upon ATTITUDE and its sub-system of appreciation. The primary finding displays how language play in the headings and captions mitigate the reader's perception of the seriousness of the situation. While the playful headings may engage readers with an environmental text they otherwise would not have read, the authors claim the practice is inappropriate for its presentation of serious environmental issues as trivial. Also exploring news reporting of major weather-related events, Potts, Bednarek, and Caple (2015) compile a 36 million word corpus of newspaper reporting in the United States on Hurricane Katrina. They perform a complex of techniques from collocation analysis to part of speech and semantic tag analysis to explore how Hurricane Katrina was discursively constructed in the media while illustrating how CADS "can help reveal how phraseologies, figurative devices, and rhetorical strategies" contribute to maximize the newsworthiness of an environmental disaster (p. 169).

Studying a different sort of environmental disaster, Liu and Li (2017) analyze and compare the variation in how *smog* is depicted in English-language newspapers published in China as well as internationally. They compile a corpus of greater than 500K words from the English-language *China Daily* and three international newspapers. Pursuing a keyword analysis (reference corpus: BNC), the study compares the top 100 keywords from the two sites. The authors interpret the keyword lists through a frames approach; in other words, the keywords are sorted into categories of problem, cause, consequence, and solution in efforts to evaluate discursive divergence between the two corpora. Most notably, for the China-based English language publication, *smog* is framed benignly as fog and as simply a temporary weather condition, with the actual causes of the condition backgrounded and erased.

Andrea Gerbig (1997) and her analysis of ozone discourse hold a unique position within corpus-assisted ecolinguistics—her book-length treatment of the discourse of ozone depletion is likely the most detailed corpus-assisted analysis of an environmental issue. In her analysis of ozone discourse, she displays the attempts by various stakeholders to construe their view of the ozone crisis; each interest group uses language in a manner conforming to their worldview and reflective of their view of reality. She writes, "there is no extralinguistic, objective reality" as meaning is socially constructed (p. 34). The texts from the groups do not record existing realities but reflect the social structures and understandings that are actively mediated by language use. Gerbig states that because the two primary groups in the ozone issue "value aspects of ecological facts and economic consequences differently" (p. 34), they display divergent linguistic patterns in the texts they produce. Though many studies are lexical in nature, the primary analytical focus of her study is the grammatical realizations of agency, causation, and responsibility through features such as ergative, reporting, and attitudinal verbs. For ergative verbs, Gerbig notes how their patterning in texts reveals agency, or avoidance of agency, and the who/what that control various ozone-related processes. Gerbig writes that ergative verb use obscures agency through "blame avoidance" (p. 163). In analysis of reporting verbs, she comments that variation in reporting verbs reflects which element of the issue is most concerning and deserving of attention for a particular group while attitudinal verbs show how each group encodes opinions to the issue. At several points, this text has expressed the value of comparison; Gerbig forwards a similar claim: "Frequency of use can only be interpreted as a value which is relative to the values found in other texts" (p. 197). This comment reflects why the use of reference corpora for facilitating contrastive analysis is common practice in CADS.

2.5.3 Place

Keith Basso's *Wisdom Sits in Places: Language and Landscape among the Western Apache* (1996) is an iconic, ethnographic account of the dynamic and inseparable interrelationship between people, cultures, and places. Though the piece is an anthropological study, its influence on language ecology generally and ecolinguistics specifically seems undeniable and echoes of Basso inform ecolinguistics work in this space. Most notable amongst ecolinguistic studies of place are Donal Carbaugh's chapter in *The Ecolinguistics Reader* on the competing discourses of Mount Greylock in Massachusetts (2001) and a second from Carbaugh and Rudnick (2006) on the contrasting naming and storytelling practices of Blackfeet and non-Blackfeet guides in regards to the Blackfeet Reservation and Glacier National Park in the state of Montana in the United States. These ethnographic studies are insightful for understanding how groups differently depict physical spaces, the historical and cultural meanings reflected in naming, and the importance of such depictions in the meaning-making process of groups. As Carbaugh and Rudnick assert, "to name a place, or to refer to a place, is to make a move in a cultural political game" and the manner by which a person refers to a place produces a particular view of that place. While Carbaugh and Rudnick (2006) analyzed the contested nature of "the park" and "the reservation," my corpus study (Poole, 2016a) of the Santa Rita Mountains and Rosemont Mine in southwest Arizona noted the oppositional stances cascading from labeling the potential mine as either *project* or *proposal*. For the mining corporation, *project* framed the mine as inevitable, a seemingly foregone conclusion not worthy of attention, where the oppositional party exclusively deployed *proposal* to index the mine as far from finalized with time for action remaining.

In related research, I extended this place-based work through an integration of corpus linguistics and geographical information systems (GIS) (Poole, 2017b). As has been displayed, corpus linguistics is well suited for reporting what is in a text/corpus, how many times the feature occurs, and how this frequency of use diverges from elsewhere, but it can also be applied to gain insight into where, i.e., the actual physical places with latitudes and longitudes, is being discussed and how such places are discursively produced. Spatial and digital humanities, as displayed through the work of Ian Gregory and Andrew Hardie (2011), can benefit from such GIS-corpus linguistic integrations. As their work and mine have displayed, the use of GIS and corpus linguistic techniques enables one to visualize the places discussed and also the semantic meanings frequently attached to them. In my earlier work, I detailed how the press releases from a multinational mining corporation and a local activist group reference a divergent list of physical places. While the mining corporation invokes governmental and financial centers in a rhetorical attempt to gain authority and credibility, the environmental group consistently references physical places to be transformed irrevocably by the potential mine project. Even when the mining corporation mentions the possible Santa Rita Mountain location of the mine, they do so in semantic frames which construe the mountains for the resources which lay ready for extraction and exploitation and the economic wealth to be produced along the way. In contrast, the activist group frames the places as sites of beauty in a discourse that promotes care and stewardship.

Corpus-assisted ecolinguistics informed by GIS offers great potential yet to date remains largely unexplored. While my work explored one particular place-based concern, there is ample opportunity to expand study in this domain to other relevant and contested places. Chapter 5 provides a case study for such an integration of corpus-assisted ecolinguistics and GIS that builds upon previous research in this space—a more comprehensive review of place and the attention it has received in discourse studies is offered in Chapter 5.

2.6 Expanding Corpus-Assisted Ecolinguistics

This review of corpus-assisted ecolinguistics to-date reflects the potential of corpus-assisted analyses of a wide range of discourses of ecological relevance. The scope of ecolinguistics is indeed expanding, yet corpus-assisted ecolinguistics has space for growth. Historically, the majority of corpus-assisted ecolinguistics has explored mainstream, popular media communication of climate change. This is indeed understandable as explicit environmental communication is common and general public awareness of climate change is growing, yet the stories that reflect and reproduce our ecological consciousness are embedded more broadly throughout prevailing language use. As Castello and Gesualto assert, "All discourses about ecological issues and those which have some impact on the environment are worthwhile objects of analysis for ecolinguistics" (2019, p. 122). This statement reflects the direction and aims of the current text and echoes earlier sentiments from Richard Alexander and Arran Stibbe (2014). In their collaboration, they argue that ecolinguistics has generally pursued the analysis of ecological discourse—in other words, it has focused primarily on environmental communication. Similarly, corpus-assisted ecolinguistics has largely been corpus-aided analysis of environmental communication. Yet, as they assert, ecolinguistics can realize a broader scope of inquiry to become ecological analysis of discourse rather than primarily analysis of ecological discourse. And yes, corpus-assisted ecolinguistics too can pursue a more expansive approach and explore discourses through an ecolinguistic lens rather than limiting its purview to environmental communication. With such a purpose in mind, the following case studies of Chapters 3–6 illustrate corpus-assisted analysis of ecological discourse but also attempt to expand the scope of corpus-assisted ecolinguistics.

3

A Corpus-Assisted Diachronic Analysis of Representations of *Wilderness*

3.0 Introduction

The ecolinguistic enterprise is grounded in the fundamental notion that "perceptions of nature are mediated through the language and that in turn such perceptions and lifestyles feed back into the structure of discourse" (Mühlhäusler, 2003, p. 12). Though it is worthwhile to present explicitly this central theoretical foundation, this statement and the orientation to language use and analysis are easily modified and extended to whatever domain the critical discourse analyst aims to explore, whether that be racism, sexism, classism, etc. and their patterning in language use. Extending this Mühlhäusler principle, diachronic analysis of language use reveals how perceptions of and attitudes toward nature are not static, objective renderings of a pre-existing and given reality but rather dynamic and emerging representations reflecting a range of evolving attitudes, beliefs, and ideologies held by individuals and shared by communities. Thus, as this chapter asserts and illustrates, corpus-assisted diachronic analysis provides great potential for ecolinguistics, as such investigations enable one to challenge present day language use popularly imagined as inherent, objective, and normal regarding the environment, nonhuman animals, and other constructs and issues of ecological relevance. Such insights into evolving discursive depictions of eco-relevant constructs as reflected through diachronic data analysis provide direct evidence of the evolving nature of meaning and allow ecolinguists to challenge and question contemporary discursive practices that transgress our broadly shared ecosophies grounded in wellbeing and sustainability.

In the corpus-assisted ecolinguistic illustration of the present chapter, the evolving representation of *wilderness* as displayed in changes in evaluative adjective collocates is explored. The investigation analyzes changes in representations of the term *wilderness* in US discourse over a 200 year period from the early 1800s to the 2000s. Indeed, North Americans have long had a complex relationship with wilderness. In early American literature such as *The Scarlett Letter* (1850), the wilderness was a treacherous, dark place where evil and temptation lurked. Similarly, in Arthur Miller's *The Crucible* (1953) which fictionalized the Salem Witch Trials of the late 1600s, the wilderness was represented as the devil's territory where transgressive deeds were done. These ominous, foreboding depictions of wilderness evolved as the United States expanded westward and became entranced and inspired by the writings of Muir, Walden, Thoreau, and others. Their depictions of the splendor and beauty of wild spaces prompted Americans to re-imagine wilderness and move beyond earlier notions of a foreboding, ominous nature. A wilderness once popularly conceived to be savage and godless suddenly was transformed to a place where the divine could be best approached and experienced (Cronon, 1996). More recently, it seems our popular conceptualizations of wilderness depict a government-designated place of pristine beauty, largely untouched by humans, existing for weekend camping trips and hiking adventures away from the hustle of modern urban life. Yet, as Cronon (1996) provocatively asserts, such a conceptualization of wilderness as a distant, remote, and wild place to be visited, preserved, and curated as a museum of natural history problematically separates humans from the natural world all around them. And as recent research has displayed, the impact of humans in the Anthropocene is greater than imagined; thus, the idea that wilderness is somehow untouched and preserved in some ancient, primitive form seems rather suspect if not wholly inaccurate. Thus, this chapter explores the term *wilderness* to investigate the changing perceptions of and toward nature in the North American context in order to better understand how these evolving evaluations reflect our mediated relationships with place and nature.

This chapter investigates *wilderness* and its evolving representations in popular American discourse through the analytical apparatus of corpus-assisted ecolinguistics. By doing so, it aims to provide quantitative evidence of the shifting relationships and perceptions of *wilderness* while also illuminating the potential of corpus-assisted diachronic ecolinguistics, the framework of evaluation, and the collocation analysis method supported by Kendall's Tau correlation coefficient for empirically assessing the strength of diachronic language use trends. The chapter opens with discussions of diachronic CADS and additional relevant diachronic studies within ecolinguistics. Following these reviews, the corpora investigated, the method applied, and the statistical analysis technique employed are discussed. Finally, evidence of the evolving evaluations of *wilderness* as well as possibilities for future research are presented.

3.1 Diachronic Corpus-Assisted Discourse Study

Diachronic corpus-assisted discourse study (D-CADS) merges corpus linguistics, sociolinguistics, and historical linguistics, and though it is not an altogether new domain of inquiry, it is perhaps fairly characterized as a somewhat "nascent discipline" when considering its more recent focus on how social, political, and cultural changes are reflected in language use (Partington, 2010, p. 83). That said, corpus linguists have certainly been investigating language change for some time. For example, the Brown Corpus, a trailblazing corpus of the 1960s, inspired similarly balanced corpora, e.g., the Lancaster-Oslo Bergen (LOB) Corpus of the 1970s and the Freiburg-Lancaster-Oslo Bergen (FLOB) of the 1980s; these three corpora have been productively employed in diachronic studies. Additionally, the 1.5 million-word Helsinki Diachronic Corpus of English Texts released in 1991 is noteworthy for the investigations of Old, Middle, and Early Modern English it has made possible and the Archer Corpus of Historical English Registers has similarly facilitated numerous insights into language change. However, in the years since Partington's statement of the field's emergent status, D-CADS has expanded from its historical focus upon the emergence or decline of particular grammatical features over rather broad time periods to more narrow analyses of discursive changes in certain discourses in recent history to explore topics of social interest as reflected in language use.

Diachronic analyses have most frequently focused upon the emergence or decline of grammatical features. For example, Smith (2001) analyzed the previously mentioned LOB and FLOB corpora to explore how use of the progressive aspect has changed over time. Additionally, Johansson (2002) investigated prepositions in Middle English, Mair (2002) analyzed changing patterns of verb complementation in Late Modern English, Hoffman (2002) explored the emergence of complex prepositions over a 300-year period, Leech (2002) compared the frequencies of modal verbs between British and American English, Millar (2009) narrowed more specifically to changes in modal verbs in the TIME Magazine Corpus from 1923 to 2006, while Hilpert and Gries (2010) reported the movement in English third-person singular present tense suffixes from Late Middle to Early Modern English (2010). Each of these studies employed large corpora to display changes of specific grammatical and/or lexical items over a specified time period. These studies at times offered claims for why such changes appeared, but critical observations of these trends and their cultural, political, and social implications and/or motivations were generally left unexplored.

One productive space for diachronic analysis has been the exploration of changes within science writing. Such studies have often centered around analyses of grammatical and lexical features in attempts to challenge the prevailing understanding that imagines science writing to simply report an objective, external reality. In this domain, diachronic studies have identified discursive changes that reflect the interpersonal, social, and rhetorical qualities of the register of science writing. In one such corpus-assisted analysis, Atkinson (1999) documented the transformation of science writing from its initial emphasis on authorial presence and narrative style to a contemporary preference for abstractness and information density. This diachronic change was highlighted through a multidimensional corpus-driven analysis of the publications of the *Philosophical Transactions of the Royal Society of London* from 1675 to 1975. More recently, diachronic changes in the use of stance markers—grammatical and lexical features that reflect attitudes and judgment of a writer/speaker to the propositional content of a message (Biber & Finegan, 1989)—across four academic disciplines (applied linguistics, sociology, electrical engineering, and biology) were explored (Hyland & Jiang, 2016). In the approximately 50-year period, changes were observed in the realization and frequency of stance features in academic research writing, which the authors conclude provides evidence of the evolution in "traditional knowledge construction practices" (p. 269). While many studies in this space have looked at broad discursive changes in science and academic writing, Poole, Gnann, and Powell (2019) explored the evolving construction of knowledge regarding one specific cellular phenomenon: chemotaxis—the movement of cells. Their work noted evolving discursive representations of the phenomenon as the community moved toward consensus in regard to their shared understanding of cellular motility.

The aforementioned studies are relevant to the present endeavor as they display the various sites of and approaches to corpus-assisted diachronic analysis, yet of greater interest are those which explore language change and how such change reflects broader cultural and societal shifts or attitudes toward particular contemporary social issues—it is this space which Partington evaluates as "nascent" (2010, p. 83). In one such study, Baker (2011) investigated changes in use of common words in British English from 1931 to 2006 through an analysis of the Brown Corpus family. Baker noted an increase in the use of *children,* as well as other words, across the three periods, suggesting that the increase in use may be attributed to evolving constructions of gender in British society and a "shift in cultural priorities" (p. 75). The Baker study is of particular value as it implements and evaluates a variety of statistical measures for conducting such diachronic research. Ultimately, Baker (2011) determined the coefficient of variance is well suited for such diachronic investigation—the statistical measure applied in this illustration, Kendall's Tau correlation coefficient, is discussed later in the chapter.

Relatedly, Shi and Lei (2020) track shifts in use of six LGTBQ labelling words (*homosexual, gay, lesbian, bisexual, transgender,* and *queer*) within approximately 200 years of language use in the United States as captured within the Corpus of Historical American English (COHA). Through a computational word-embedding technique, they generate data that displays the "semantic neighbours" of each term over the time period and the points at which new neighbors emerge while others recede (p. 34). They observe a shift in the collocates with *gay* at several points in history. First, from the 1860s to 1960s, collocates of *gay* generally reflect and produce a positive semantic prosody in such words as *merry, blithe, cheerful,* and *mirthful*. As the 1980s commenced, the neighbors become increasingly negative as reflected in terms *promiscuous, incest,* and *antigay*. However, terms emerging in the early 2000s reflect a shifting and more positive discourse through terms such as *rights* and *legalized*. Their method demonstrates a data-driven procedure for exploring semantic shifts of certain terms as reflected in co-occurrence patterns, but their discussion also, and importantly, is of value as they move beyond sharing descriptive findings as they incorporate relevant social events and developments into their contextualization of the changes and interpretation of their findings.

In a similar study, Wilkinson (2019) explored representations and erasure of bisexuality—a sexual identity less frequently represented in popular media—in the UK press from 1957 to 2017. Though the methodology differed from the more computational approach of the aforementioned study from Shi and Lei (2020), it is grounded in a similar rationale which posits that lexical items that frequently collocate with a node item, in this case *bisexual,* reflect how the group is represented and perceived within a discourse community. The corpus-based critical discourse analytic approach of Wilkinson thus explores both the representation and misrepresentation of bisexual identity to illustrate how media depictions of marginalized and/or minority groups shape how these groups are perceived. Interestingly, the study discovers a "temporal displacement" which frames bisexuality consistently in the past tense (p. 264). Such a discursive representation is argued to remove the agency of bisexual people and limit their existence as social actors. In other words, the sexual identity of bisexualism is erased. Of relevance to the present project is the theoretical rationale of the corpus-based critical discourse approach. Such an approach is supported by the notion that how a phenomenon, entity, or proposition is consistently represented reflects how it is broadly perceived by a discourse community. The present illustration aligns with this theoretical rationale. In other words, the collocates of *wilderness* over the period analyzed reflect how the construct is perceived, thereby influencing how people subsequently act toward and in relation to it.

Other research has similarly explored issues of social and cultural interest and their discursive representation in the media. In one such study, Partington (2012) analyzes the discourse of anti-Semitism in the UK press through a comparative analysis of corpora representing 1993, 2005, and 2009. Partington comments that it is "clear and unsurprising" that the newspapers uniformly evaluate anti-Semitism negatively through the frequent use of terms such as *vile* and *racist*, yet variation is evident (p. 68). In the earliest sub-corpus, anti-Semitism was referenced as if in history through language use generally conveying worries in the potential rise of anti-Jewish sentiment due to the rise of various nationalist movements in Europe. However, the historical view of 1993 takes a more urgent "here-and-now" tone in 2005 (p. 71). The data also importantly displays how the frequency of a term/entity may remain largely unchanged even while experiencing quite clear discursive changes. In a somewhat related study, Marchi (2010) investigated lexicalizations of the construct of *morality* in the UK press in the English Language Newspaper Corpus in the years 1993 and 2005. In the study's analysis of various terms of *morality* and their collocates, the study discovered lower frequency use of such terms in 2005 than in 1993. The collocation analysis also revealed that *ethical* most frequently occurred with collocates and contexts indicating a sort of human control (e.g., behavior, inventions) while *morality* most often was framed in terms of religion and identity.

Finally, Fitzsimmons-Doolan (2019) explored diachronic change in the discourse of immigration in the United States in corpora of online comments on the topic of immigration education collected in the years 2009 and 2016; the 2009 sub-corpus includes nearly 900 user comments totaling approximately 150,000 words while the 2016 sub-corpus consisted of greater than 1,000 comments and 50,000 words. Additionally, the study employed a reference corpus of comments drawn from the *New York Times* and *The Washington Post*. The reference corpus enabled the generation of keyword lists for the corpora of the respective time periods which was then extended through a qualitative analysis of the keywords in context and the coding of these key lexical items. Emerging in the 2016 data were seven themes not present in the 2009 comments. These seven emergent themes framed immigrants with an "overwhelmingly negative focus" (p. 112). The study has clear relevance for the present work as it displays how diachronic corpus-assisted discourse analysis enables insights into the evolving nature of discursive depictions of entities and propositions and the suitability of corpus analysis for exacting such discoveries.

This brief review illustrates a social turn in diachronic CADS while also displaying the affordances of a corpus-assisted approach to diachronic studies of ecological relevance. As noted, corpus linguistics has long explored historical change in language, but it has often done so through investigations of the emergence or decline of certain grammatical and/or lexical features over broad expanses of time. Evident in more recent work is greater attention to changes in the discursive representations of entities of social, political, and cultural interest within a more contemporary time frame. This chapter extends this attention to areas of ecological interest and asserts that diachronic analyses of entities and/or constructs presented and perceived as natural and given in prevailing discourse can help challenge the generally unquestioned status of such framings. This affordance of diachronic analysis offers great potential for ecolinguistics.

3.2 Diachronic Studies in Ecolinguistics

Diachronic studies in ecolinguistics have been fruitfully but infrequently pursued. The exemplar studies to be reviewed survey language change in relation to environment-relevant issues across varying time periods and also in particular contexts. For Bonnefille (2008), the temporal period under investigation is the eight-year US presidency of George W. Bush through an analysis of a specialized diachronic corpus consisting of the eight State of the Union addresses (SOTUA) he delivered while in office. Applying a cognitive theoretical framework (Lakoff & Johnson, 1980), the study focuses upon the potential power of the discursive and rhetorical framing of climate change in the addresses and the possible effects such framings have on listeners. Intriguingly, in attempts to answer why some years seemed "greener" than others (p. 29), the study concluded that the emergence of green narrative frames was directly impacted by rising global oil prices. As Bonnefille summarizes: "the more expensive the oil barrel gets, the greener the SOTUA is" (p. 55). Consistently, the important addresses dually engage the economics of increased energy prices with a desire for more sustainable energy solutions—clean energy is syntactically coordinated within a discourse of economic growth. In other words, clauses typically begin with an economic framing, e.g., "keeps America's economy running," "step up domestic oil production," followed by a coordinator and a closing green frame, "to keep

America's environment clean," "in environmentally sensitive ways." Through such coordination, economy and environment are discursively joined and "seem to naturally belong to a singular domain of experience" (p. 53).

Bevitori (2015) similarly explores US presidential discourse and the changing representations of the environment; however, she does so across a broader timeframe: 1960–2013. Thus, her analysis captures construals of the environment from the administration of John F. Kennedy to Barack Obama for a total of eighty-five addresses. The study demonstrates evolving depictions of environment and illustrates that meanings of environment are not "fixed and stable" but indeed vary according to a complex of factors (p. 129). Reflecting similarly interconnected framings, the study shows how environment, energy, efficiency, and conservation are joined discursively—in other words, the story of the environment is generally framed along with economic considerations. Bevitori's integrated use of qualitative and quantitative methods provides "robust data" into how meanings evolve diachronically (p. 129).

Moving beyond the political sphere, evolving representations of environmental interest have been explored more broadly. In one intriguing study published in *Weather*, Grant and Walsh (2015) attempt to complement existing research reporting physical data of climate change from indicators such as glacial melting and increasing global temperatures with social data derived from a corpus. In essence, the study aims to demonstrate an emergent social awareness of climate change reflected in language use that supports and possibly even precedes scientific recognition of the climate crisis. Employing the massive Google Books Corpus, the researchers track the emergence of climate change-related n-grams to investigate whether there is actual linguistic evidence of the awareness of climate change before the crisis became such a frequent topic through analysis of such terms such as *unseasonal, cyclone, hurricane, flood*, and many others. The researchers assert that widespread, mainstream awareness of climate change did not emerge until the 1980s. However, their study did discover evidence of such social awareness of climate change in the data through increasing mentions of climate-related weather events prior to 1980. As the authors state, their findings are totally "unconnected with the traditional physical forms of data" used to assert climate change and can thus provide additional compelling evidence of climate change (p. 197). Though this study may not strictly meet the criteria presented for corpus-assisted ecolinguistics in Chapter 2, its value and insight are undeniable. Such complementary social data of an emergent climate change awareness well before the crisis became so omnipresent in prevailing discourse, and unfortunately politicized in some national contexts, demonstrates broad human recognition of climate change and its myriad consequences in people's lives.

Of even broader scope, Frayne (2019) analyzes references to species in the Google Books Corpus and the Corpus of Historical American English. This study is of particular interest for it illustrates how language change reflects "shifting meanings and values within a society or culture" as diachronic lexical variation reflects cultural change (2018, p. 331). Rather comprehensive in scope, the study explores whether the frequency and manner of references to species have changed in the past 200 years. Reflective of the Grant and Walsh study, Frayne similarly pursues a culturomics approach as the study posits a decline in knowledge of the natural world as reflected in fewer mentions of references over time in the corpus will correlate with increases in urbanization and industrialization. The study discerned a "devolution" (p. 344) in species references throughout the twentieth century in the US data, though similar findings were not noted in the British data. Additionally, aspect-level sentiment in species mentions declined over time. In closing, Frayne asserted that corpus-assisted ecolinguistics is "a promising approach to understanding the Anthropocene" (p. 345), a position clearly shared within this text.

In a study somewhat similar to Frayne's analysis of species references, Jacobs et al. (n.d.) track the use trajectories of the dietary terms *vegetarian*, *vegan*, and *plant-based* to display trends in dietary habits and practices from 1944 to 2008. The analysis explored the use of these terms across multiple Google platforms: Search, Scholar, Trends, and the NGram Viewer. They discover that the term *vegan* has overtaken *vegetarian* across several of the Google platforms employed in the analysis. For *plant-based*, the attention offered was greatest in academia; in other words, it was most frequently used in Google Scholar. However, *plant-based* and *vegan* meet at a rather fuzzy boundary and are often employed in divergent contexts—*vegan* occurs in discussions beyond food, e.g., fashion, personal cosmetics, while *plant-based* is constrained to food-only contexts. The study posits that such rise in the use of *vegan* and *plant-based* may reflect increased environmental awareness and greater attention to health concerns as well as increased concern for the well-being of nonhuman animals. Such studies are valuable as they can display people's changing attitudes and practices and the emergent ecological identities to which people are perhaps shifting, thereby influencing the practices of the food industry and others.

These studies demonstrate the insights that can be provided through diachronic corpus-assisted ecolinguistics. The changing discursive practices as reported in these studies reflect the evolving and ever dynamic relationship between humans and the natural world. While the analysis in the present chapter reflects evolving understandings of a salient eco-keyword, *wilderness*, numerous explorations of our understandings of ecologically relevant terms and constructs are possible.

3.3 Evaluation and Collocation Analysis

The present chapter performs its diachronic corpus-assisted ecolinguistic analysis through a collocation analysis procedure underpinned by the framework of evaluation—thus, both collocation and evaluation deserve discussion before proceeding to the analysis. Though briefly discussed elsewhere in the text, a more thorough treatment of collocation is presented in this section. Firstly, a collocation is defined most directly as "combinations of words that habitually co-occur in texts and corpora" (Brezina, 2018, p. 67). The word under investigation is the node and its collocates are those with which it co-occurs frequently. Such a mechanistic definition may not fully reflect the importance of this feature of language use, yet this essential reality of the recurrent patterning of language in discourse is central to the corpus linguistic enterprise. In an often-cited quotation in discussions of collocation, Firth (1968) stated, "You shall know a word by the company it keeps"; this assertion has become the "informal definition of the collocational relationship" (Brezina, 2018, p. 67). For corpus linguistics, Firth's statement captures the reality that "important aspects of the meaning of a word are not contained within the word itself, considered in isolation, but rather subsist in the characteristic associations that the word participates in" (McEnery & Hardie, 2012, p. 123).

The investigation, identification, and interpretation of collocations and other patterns of co-occurrence within corpora and discourse is a common and productive research endeavor, though how collocation is defined and thus investigated does vary. For some, collocation is constrained to two lexical items occurring in immediate adjacency to one another (e.g., *the vast wilderness* with *wilderness* as node and the premodifier adjective *vast* as its collocate). More common, however, is an expanded conception of the parameters of co-occurrence. From this broader view, a node has collocates beyond immediate word-to-word adjacency. In other words, collocates may appear in a span or window within close textual proximity—the span in such an approach is generally four words to the left of the node and four words to the right with the common shorthand being 4L-4R. The present investigation takes this broader view of collocation, as it explores adjective collocates in the 4L-4R collocational window of the node under analysis: *wilderness*.

Collocations are typically identified quantitatively through the calculation of various association measures (see Brezina, 2018 for detailed discussion of these various measures), though qualitative analysis of concordance lines of the node word has value in certain contexts for identifying collocates. For example, corpus-assisted language teaching pedagogy often tasks language learners with analysis activities that require identification of common patterns of use. However, quantitative procedures for identifying collocations are standard within CADS, for the application of statistical measures facilitates an empirical evaluation of the strength of the bond between the lexical items. Such bondings are of interest to discourse analysts broadly but are points of interest for critical analysis as well. For example, in the opening chapter, the collocation *illegal immigrant* was briefly discussed. This pair illustrates how such collocational bondings reflect and reproduce ideological orientations toward an entity, topic, or construct of interest. In the North American context, this collocation has increased in frequency to the point where it now seems normalized in the discourse with the pairing rarely questioned or critiqued. Even proponents of progressive immigration policies use the collocation in their own language even though it seems clear that the collocation frames the discourse of immigration in a manner counter to their progressive aims. The collocation, which has a relatively short history in US discourse, persists and attempts to replace with *undocumented immigrant* or other lexical choices have largely been unsuccessful. This collocation of *illegal* + *immigrant* reflects, normalizes, and perpetuates an orientation to immigrants and immigration of which certain perceptions and actions become unfortunate yet unsurprising. In other words, if the dominant discursive construct depicts *immigrant* as *illegal*, then, and quite sadly, it seems thus unsurprising that walls, fences, cages, and militarized response would be the outcome of such representational tendencies. This sample illustrates the ideological beliefs that are present and perpetuated within collocations and reflects why collocation as linguistic phenomenon draws the attention of many critically oriented analysts, including ecolinguists. The investigation of collocation through an ecolinguistic lens holds value as it provides insights into how various ecology-relevant constructs are discursively evaluated.

As noted, this illustration couples collocation analysis with the framework of evaluation. Evaluation is "the expression of the speaker or writer's attitude or stance towards, viewpoint on, or feelings about the entities or propositions" about which a person is speaking or writing (Thompson & Hunston, 2000, p. 5).

In Stibbe's ecolinguistic framework, evaluation is presented as particularly important to ecolinguistics for it reflects whether individuals perceive "an area of life positively or negatively" (2021, p. 81). He couples evaluation with the related systemic functional grammar framework of appraisal (Martin, 2000) to gain insight into the "stories in people's minds" regarding domains of ecological importance. Stibbe states that patterns of evaluation "that run across large numbers of texts within a culture are too widespread to gather a representative sample to analyse," and thus, investigations may pursue "prototypical instances of the pattern across different discourses and areas" (p. 81). This qualitative approach to investigation and identification yields samples of evaluative patterns that the analyst may then assess in relation to their ecosophy. In one sample presented, Stibbe explores the appraisal patterns present for the term *convenient* in addition to several other exemplar lexical items. For *convenient*, he notes that *convenient*, not *inconvenient*, is the unmarked and positive term of the pair operating broadly within an appraisal pattern of CONVENIENCE IS GOOD. As judged against his operating ecosophy, he argues that such a pervasive pattern within prevailing discourse that presents convenience as an "aspirational goal" has implications for creating a more sustainable system.

Similar identification and interpretation in relation to his ecosophy extends to patterns such as SUCCESS IS GOOD and SMALL IS BEAUTIFUL. For the latter, he reviews the efforts of E.F. Shumacher in his book *Small Is Beautiful* (1973) to counter the more pervasive evaluation of LARGE IS GOOD. As Stibbe notes, *small* is "the negative, marked term in the language system" whereas its inverse *large* is almost uniformly evaluated positively. Though such an evaluation is not inherently problematic, when the pattern is reproduced and extended it becomes "ecologically damaging at the point when an increase in size (whether of a meal, an intensive farming system, or an economy) consumes extra resources without creating any extra benefits" (p. 83). Additionally, as societies adopt and apply this frame, it causes distortions in how individuals and groups organize and understand the world. LARGE IS BEAUTIFUL then extends to GROWTH IS GOOD, thereby normalizing and reproducing an economic world order that looks to metrics such as Gross Domestic Product or Gross National Product as measures of national health and progress. Such measures obscure the ecological degradation underlying such an artificial measure. For example, in this perverse economic system, the Deepwater Horizon Oil Disaster of the Gulf of Mexico actually contributed positively to US gross domestic product.

Stibbe's application of evaluation diverges from the manner in which it has been implemented in CADS, however. Though his analysis is prescient and insightful, a corpus-assisted methodology is able to contribute positively to the identification and interpretation of such evaluation patterns in discourse. Indeed, the introspective manner in which he arrives at patterns that are potentially problematic in relation to his ecosophy is worthwhile, and his selection of prototypical samples to support his claims is compelling. However, evaluation as an analytic framework for corpus-assisted analysis of language use in particular domains has been pursued frequently and has displayed utility for enabling insight into the values, attitudes, and beliefs of various discourse communities. The following reviews a selection of this corpus-assisted research of evaluation, and though the examples are not drawn from ecolinguistics, the implementations of such a corpus-assisted, data-driven approach to the study of evaluation are illustrative of how this technique will be implemented in the forthcoming analysis.

Corpus-assisted studies in this space generally operationalize the previously included definition and approach to evaluation as forwarded by Thompson and Hunston (2000). Beyond this definition, Thompson and Hunston enumerate three functions of evaluation. One of these, and the one most applicable to the present case study, is the function of evaluation to "express the speaker or writer's opinion, and in doing so to reflect the value system of that person and their community" (2005, p. 6). Though both elements are important, for the present study, the latter clause's assertion that evaluation reflects the values of a particular person or community is of particular interest from an ecolinguistic perspective. From such an orientation, analyzing patterns of evaluation in discourse provides a window into the value system of a community—CADS is perfectly suited in the identification of such patterns whether synchronically or diachronically.

In one such corpus-assisted study of evaluation, Hewings (2004) analyzes the language of evaluation of more than two hundred reviews written by peer reviewers to submissions to a journal in applied linguistics. The corpus spans approximately three years and includes approximately 160,000 words. The corpus-aided approach analyzed both the entities evaluated and their most frequent adjective collocates. Put more simply, Hewings analyzes the things the community frequently writes about and how these things are represented. For example, approximately 20 percent of the total entities evaluated were related to the actual product through lexical items such as *article*, *manuscript*, *contribution*, and an additional entity class through words such as *statement*, *assertion*, and *position*. Of greater interest to the present study are the semantic classes of evaluative adjectives collocating with these entities. The most frequent semantic class were positive evaluations of *interesting, original, innovative*, etc., and negative evaluations such as *tedious, uninteresting*, and *uninspiring*. Other semantic classes reflected values of suitability, comprehensibility, accuracy, and importance. Fortanet (2008), Hyon (2011), and Luzón (2012) also explore evaluation in the academic register. Fortanet analyzed evaluative language in peer review referee reports while Hyon similarly explored evaluative lexis in letters of retention, promotion, and tenure with Luzon pursuing much the same but in academic weblogs. Each of these studies illustrates how analysis of evaluative language provides insights into the discourse communities which produce and consume these texts.

Corpus-assisted studies of evaluation have been pursued in business communication as well. In one such study, Poole (2017a) constructed a specialized corpus of letters to the shareholders from corporations in the Fortune 500 index. This study first identified the most common evaluative adjectives in this important persuasive genre—corporations rhetorically attempt to convince current and future stakeholders of the financial good standing of the organization and its potential for further financial gains in the coming year. In the study, the most frequent evaluative adjectives and their common noun collocates (e.g., *new* + *opportunity, strong* + *performance*) were analyzed in order to reveal the entities the discourse community values as well as how these entities are evaluated. Some of the most frequent adjectives were *new*, *important*, and *strong* while the most common nominal entities were *growth*, *performance*, and *results*. The semantic classes of evaluative adjectives and their noun collocates "present an optimistic view of a seemingly inevitable future of success and growth through the confluence of positively-weighted and temporally-oriented evaluative entities and adjectives" (Poole, 2017a, p. 48). Though this study was synchronic in nature, it further demonstrates the insights made possible through the investigation of evaluation in discourse.

The importance of these corpus-assisted studies lies both in their methodological approach and theoretical framework. First, for the methodological approach, these studies demonstrate how evaluation can be productively investigated through a corpus-assisted method which identifies frequent propositions and their collocations. Although these studies were synchronic in design as each explores evaluation at essentially one point in time with no attention to diachronic change, an elaboration of evaluation patterns across time periods would enable insights into how an entity such as *wilderness* is variably depicted across decades. Secondly, these studies demonstrate the insights made possible into community attitudes, values, and beliefs through an analysis of evaluation in texts from said community. This chapter applies similar logic: values, perceptions, attitudes, and beliefs regarding an entity or proposition may be evidenced through a corpus-assisted analysis of the language use of a community of speakers/writers when invoking and evaluating said entity. The present illustration exhibits how evaluations of the important socially constructed entity of *wilderness* have evolved diachronically as well as how traces of ecological understandings are evident in emergent language use patterns operating in its discursive space. The case study thus demonstrates how such changes in evaluation patterns are revelatory of the complex of prevailing attitudes and beliefs operating within a discourse community. In ecolinguistics, researchers can operationalize evaluation in explorations of various entities and propositions of ecological relevance while judging these prevailing evaluations against their individual ecosophies. This illustration will do just that in its investigation of *wilderness* and the evaluations through which it has variably been represented in popular US discourse.

3.4 Corpora and Kendall's Tau Correlation Coefficient

The analysis presented in this chapter employs two large English reference corpora, the Google Books Corpus accessed through the Google Ngram Viewer site and the Corpus of Historical American English (COHA). Each corpus serves a valuable purpose in the illustration. First, the Google Books Ngram Viewer allows one to search the massive Google Books Corpus, and though this corpus lacks the degree of granularity of other reference corpora, for the present study, the resource allows one to visualize broadly the trends in evaluation as reflected in adjective collocates with the node *wilderness* over various time periods. It should be noted that only the sub-corpus of books published in the United States was used. The second corpus, the COHA, consists of approximately 400 million words of American English from 1810 to 2010[1] accessible through an interface that offers much greater functionality than the Google Ngram Viewer. The COHA is comprised of greater than 100,000 individual texts balanced with genres from non-fiction, fiction, magazine, newspaper, and, more recently, television and movies. Searches in the COHA were completed to identify and extract the top 100 adjective collocates across the approximately 200-year span of the COHA. Further details on the COHA and its construction are available on its homepage.

The collocation data of *wilderness* (specified to capture only adjectives in the 4L-4R window) collected in COHA provides a list of the most frequent adjective collocates co-occurring with the term as well as its raw frequency and per million rate for each decade at which the collocation occurs. Though a qualitative analysis of these evolving evaluative patterns in which the term appears by decade would be revealing, an additional statistical measure was applied here to empirically evaluate the strength/weakness of the decade-by-decade variation in these pairings. The Kendall's τ (henceforth, Tau) correlation coefficient provides such a measure, as it makes possible the statistical evaluation of the strength of diachronic language use trends, thereby enabling a closer empirical inspection of language use across time (Hilpert & Gries, 2009).

The calculation of Kendall's Tau yields a value between -1.0 and +1.0 with a rather straightforward interpretation. When the Kendall's Tau value nears 0, the correlation is weak and no trend is present; in other words, the feature exhibits irregular rises and falls across time periods with no discernible trajectory of use. As values approach -1.0, the correlation is strong yet negative, meaning the feature under analysis is decreasing in use over time. Finally, as values approach +1.0, the correlation is strong and positive, indicating that the item is increasing in use over time. In other words, when the Kendall's Tau correlation coefficient approaches +1.0 or -1.0, "the passage of time correlates perfectly with an increase or decrease in frequency" (Hilpert & Gries, 2009, p. 390). If an item's frequency fluctuates yet overall there is an increase in use, the value will be positive but not approaching 1. Similarly, if an item generally decreases yet experiences "peaks" and "troughs" over time (Gabrielatos et al., 2012, p. 1), the value will be negative but not approaching -1.0. Though scrutiny of data can provide insight into language use trends, the statistical evaluation made possible through Kendall's Tau correlation coefficient enables the analysis of the strength of trends of evaluations with the node words. This does not suggest that this illustration is strictly quantitative, as all CADS research offers qualitative interpretations. For the calculation of Kendall's Tau, the per million rates of each collocation across all decades were used. In other words, Kendall's Tau was operationalized by decade with the per million rate for each decade included in the calculations. Briefly, per million rate rather than raw frequency is used as the sub-corpora of each decade are not uniform in size. A Kendall's Tau measure was calculated for the 1810–2010 span but also for the period from 1950 to 2010.

3.5 The Evolving Evaluations of *Wilderness*

The analysis begins with a review of the broad use trends with *wilderness* in the Google Books Corpus. The data yielded through an *adjective + wilderness* search in the Ngram Viewer provides initial evidence of the changing representation of the node term. As Plate 1 displays, the top 10 most frequent adjectives paired with *wilderness* gain their status as common evaluative collocates largely due to their high frequencies in the 1800s. At the turn of the century in 1900, the frequencies of these top 10 evaluative items are all on declining trajectories before each stabilizes at a low-frequency level as the 1900s proceed.

In these top 10 adjective collocates, several evaluative patterns are discernible. First, *vast*, *great*, and *unbroken* generally convey a positive evaluation pertaining to the immense size of the imagined *wilderness*. It is unsurprising that throughout the 1800s *wilderness* would be regularly attached to such grandiose framings as the American West remained largely unknown to the settlers of the newly formed United States. Indeed, in the first half of the century, many of the western states as now demarcated were still labeled as territories and had not yet gained statehood. For example, California was not granted statehood until 1850 and Utah was not added until 1890. Thus, evaluating this region through frames of size and grandeur reflects the awe and wonder the frontier conjured in this period. Though this evaluative framing is positive, it is revealing that these qualities ascribed to *wilderness* become less frequent as time passes. There is a possible conclusion that as these settlers of European descent moved West, denuded the land of its forests, transformed the land into farms and towns, and generally took dominion of the land, there was simply less need and fewer opportunities to describe the rapidly changing landscape in such expansive terms. Over the decades, wilderness spaces, as originally and popularly imagined, in the United States became less vast, less great, and less unbroken, and thus the exigency to describe these natural spaces as such declined.

In contrast to the previous positive evaluations of size are the items producing a more negative, even foreboding, framing: *desolate, barren, savage, dreary*, and *pathless*. As true with the positive evaluative features, these negative items similarly peaked in frequency in the first half of the 1800s and decreased quite noticeably in the following century. It is similarly revealing that these collocates experienced such a decrease in use across this approximately 200-year period. Indeed, these frequent evaluative patterns declined, but it is also possibly true that language users in this context simply were not evaluating *wilderness* with much frequency. In other words, they had a reduced need to talk and write about *wilderness*. As earlier studies have displayed, the evaluative adjectives invoked by a community are revealing but equally insightful are the entities and propositions receiving such consistent evaluative focus for these are deemed worthy of attention by speakers and writers of the community. An additional search in the Google Books Corpus indicates that the frequency of *wilderness* began a rather precipitous decline at approximately 1850 and did not rise again until the middle of the following century. Thus, language users seem to evaluate the term differently across the time periods, but they also use the term less frequently until its post–Second World War resurgence.

To the negative items specifically, these evaluations of *desolate*, *barren*, and *savage* are reflective of early American attitudes toward *wilderness* as discussed by environmentalist William Cronon (1996). These foreboding representations are rather dominant through this period and reflect US American culture's fearful view of wilderness spaces. These three evaluative terms unambiguously produce a negative semantic framing, reflecting a view of *wilderness* as lacking inherent and intrinsic value. In other words, without the presence of European settlers, the spaces were imagined as desolate and barren, ostensibly waiting for development to take place. Modern scientific understandings of *wilderness* would strongly disagree with such a characterization of wild spaces as empty, bleak, and lifeless, instead viewing such places as complex, vibrant ecosystems teeming with activity and life— just not human life. Such negative discursive evaluations make unsurprising the ecological devastation wrought on the American landscape of this period. If an entity indeed possesses such negative traits, then it only seems logical that one would seek to remove the features reflective of such characteristics. Through such processes, one could potentially bring some anthropocentric sense of order to the space, and what was once imagined as seemingly without value could become ordered farms and new settlements mapped in a perfect grid across the frontier.

These negative evaluations often operate within contexts that reference and allude to religion and religious faith. For example, these natural spaces are framed negatively as *desolate*, *barren*, *savage*, etc. for there was perceived to be an absence of God in these spaces. Most reflective of these religious undertones is the collocate *savage*. Indeed, the term's denotation produces meanings of fierceness, uncivilized and uncontrollable, but it also construes godlessness for an uncivilized person of the time is one without Christian faith. Thus, wilderness spaces, evaluated with this framing, are imagined as godless spaces beyond human control where evil and temptation are present. Similar religious connections are present with other lexis. In an early instance in the COHA of *desolate wilderness,* Cox (1817) writes, "Infinitely better had it been for him to have accompanied Abraham to Mamre, or even to have lived in a retired and desolate wilderness." Similar juxtapositions that function to frame *wilderness* in such religious contexts occur commonly in the 1800s with the Garden of Eden framed for plenty and abundance, but wilderness oppositely depicted as barren and desolate.

The remaining two items on the list are not overtly evaluative in a binary positive/negative sense, but they are nonetheless intriguing from an ecolinguistic perspective as they index a human–nature relationship. *Western* displays an unsurprising trajectory. In a phrase that captured American imagination and reflected its ideal for westward growth, Horace Greeley delivered the following well-known statement: "Go west, young man, and grow up with the country" (1865). The statement was even included in US passports for many years alongside notable quotations from John F. Kennedy, Martin Luther King Jr., George Washington, and others. The western wilderness was at the heart of the American imagination, yet as the western frontier was settled and transformed by peoples of European descent, there was no more *western wilderness* remaining to discuss—it was in rapid decline. That western wilderness so romanticized in US culture would be reproduced on the big screen and persist in American consciousness, but its actual existence was shrinking. Again, it is unsurprising that as an entity or proposition becomes smaller and/or less common that it would be less frequently discussed and evaluated. The final collocate for discussion before proceeding to the COHA data is the adjective *American.* Though this item could be seen as neutral, its appearance also reflects a changing human–nature relationship through its labelling of national boundaries on natural spaces. Such labelling of nature creates a relationship of human dominion and ownership as it ascribes national boundaries upon physical place. As will be discussed in chapter 5, referencing and naming of places are not arbitrary acts.

In Plate 1 displaying data from the Google Books Corpus, the immediate L1 adjective collocates were displayed—the restricted immediate adjacency definition of collocation as previously discussed. However, Table 1 broadens to include the top fifty adjectives within a 4L-4R collocational window across the 200-year period captured in the COHA. The most frequent evaluative adjectives collocating with *wilderness* from 1810 to 2010 in the COHA include the same evaluative lexis as the Google Books Corpus. It is worth noting that COHA includes multiple registers of language use of American English (e.g., fiction, magazines, newspapers, non-fiction, as well as television and film from recent history), in contrast to the Google Books Corpus, which, as its title reflects, only includes published books.

As with the Google Books Corpus, *vast* and *great* are the most frequent evaluative adjectives with each depicting the expansive quality of wilderness. Review of the COHA data reveals many of these high-frequency items are largely concentrated in the first century of the corpus, as *national* and *American* appear to be the only items of the top 15 whose frequencies are largely attributable to post-1950 increases in use. Present in the top 50 are numerous items that evaluate *wilderness* in more negative terms: *howling, old, savage, lonely, tangled, dreary, barren*, in addition to several others.

Table 1 Top 50 4L-4R adjective collocates of wilderness 1810–2010

Rank	Collocate	Frequency	PM
1	vast	132	0.33
2	great	111	0.27
3	howling	90	0.22
4	western	76	0.19
5	wild	73	0.18
6	new	64	0.16
7	remote	63	0.16
8	little	57	0.14
9	American	52	0.13
10	old	47	0.12
11	savage	41	0.1
12	other	40	0.1
13	solitary	39	0.1
14	northern	37	0.09
15	national	36	0.09
16	unbroken	36	0.09
17	lonely	35	0.09
18	trackless	35	0.09
19	alone	32	0.08
20	long	32	0.08
21	silent	32	0.08
22	tangled	32	0.08

23	unknown	32	0.08
24	dreary	30	0.07
25	white	30	0.07
26	whole	29	0.07
27	barren	28	0.07
28	green	28	0.07
29	dark	27	0.07
30	pathless	27	0.07
31	boundless	26	0.06
32	desolate	26	0.06
33	very	26	0.06
34	wide	26	0.06
35	Indian	25	0.06
36	rough	25	0.06
37	true	25	0.06
38	deep	24	0.06
39	full	23	0.06
40	primeval	22	0.05
41	far	21	0.05
42	virgin	21	0.05
43	distant	20	0.05
44	only	20	0.05
45	perfect	20	0.05
46	strange	20	0.05
47	human	19	0.05
48	southern	19	0.05
49	unexplored	19	0.05
50	big	18	0.04

Plate 1 and Table 1 report the most common evaluative adjectives across the time period but do not reveal which evaluative framings are rising or falling. The Kendall's Tau correlation coefficient in the following tables does provide such information. As noted, strong correlations approach +1.0 and -1.0. In such an expansive period, there will be many fluctuations in use with uniformly positive or negative growth across decades and centuries perhaps rare. However, the adjective collocates in Tables 2 and 3 display generally positive growth for the respective time periods.

Table 2 Evaluative adjectives increasing in use 1810–2010

Collocate	Kendall's Tau
national	0.674
federal	0.645
pristine	0.555
designated	0.513
high	0.414
central	0.397
empty	0.395
huge	0.379
large	0.366
big	0.35

Table 3 Evaluative adjectives increasing in use 1950–2010

Collocate	Kendall's Tau
southern	0.894
native	0.856
true	0.745
designated	0.745
empty	0.701
remote	0.69
new	0.602
moral	0.602
thick	0.602
solitary	0.577
high	0.577
American	0.552
national	0.552
pristine	0.552
alone	0.545
Canadian	0.501

At the top of the list of Table 2 are collocates reflecting a legal status for wilderness areas across the United States. Though *national* appears in the top 20 most frequent collocates previously presented in Table 1, *federal* falls well outside the top 50. In fact, *federal* does not appear with *wilderness* in the COHA until nearly the 1950s. This emergence of these two terms perhaps foreshadows the U.S. Wilderness Act of 1964 which would identify and designate lands for federal review and preservation. The emergence of *national* and *federal* is connected with *designated*, which appears as the fourth item displaying positive growth. Since the first wilderness space was officially created in the 1960s, greater than 800 federal wilderness areas have been designated for federal control. *National, federal,* and *designated* and their growth reflect an emergent post–Second World War environmental consciousness which only expanded following the publication of Rachel Carson's *Silent Spring* in 1962, celebration of the first Earth Day in 1970, and the public viewing of The Blue Marble image in 1972.

These lexical items of *national, federal,* and *designated* reflect a growing interest both in the US general public and in the US federal government to protect and conserve wilderness spaces, and though laudable and worthy, such a practice of designating some natural spaces as worthy of preservation and others unworthy possibly contributes to "the environment is out there" social understanding. While we choose to grant protected status on natural spaces we imagine to be untouched and untrammeled by humans, we perhaps grant ourselves license to not value and not appreciate the environment all around us from our backyards to our neighborhood park. In a sense, these designations of certain spaces as protected and others as not worthy perfectly illuminate the Mühlhäusler maxim provided in the opening paragraph, as through language, spaces are either granted or denied status and, thus human engagement with nature is mediated. Through such designations, human perception and action in relation to these spaces is influenced and shaped. Simply think of the entrance sign to any national park or wilderness area—on one side of the sign certain actions are possible and permitted while on the other side they are forbidden and even illegal—this all occurs through language, and thus, language mediates how we engaged with these spaces.

Pristine is an additionally intriguing item experiencing growth, and one that per recent findings made possible through light detection and ranging (LIDAR) as discussed later in Chapter 6 on geographical text analysis seems flawed at best and problematic at worst. The item's semantic loading is overtly positive as it typically collocates in the COHA with other positive evaluative lexis such as *beauty, pure, freshness,* and *perfect*—to be evaluated as pristine is clearly desirous. As reflected in its denotation, language users attach meanings of unspoiled, clean, and untouched to entities evaluated with the term. Interestingly, notions of pristine are not attached to *wilderness* in the COHA until 1960. Intuitively, one may imagine this evaluation would have been invoked in the preceding century when North American wilderness was seemingly to a greater degree pristine. Yet there is not one instance of *pristine* in the collocational window of *wilderness* until the following sentence from a 1969 issue of Christian Science Monitor: "For years the National Audubon Society and National Parks Association have worked to preserve the nation's only subtropical wilderness in its pristine state." Though the collocate does not appear with *wilderness* in the data of the 1980s, which is why the only moderate correlation, it otherwise trends positively from 1969 to the present.

As the previous analysis indicated a post-1950 emergence of several evaluative items, an additional Kendall's Tau statistic was calculated for the period 1950–2010—this data is included in Table 3. Though several items appear on the lists for both periods, there are also several divergences—the discussion omits *southern* as this use, as evident in concordance line analysis, identified geographical areas of wilderness spaces, e.g., wilderness of southern Indiana, wilderness of southern Utah. To continue, *pristine* appears on both lists and is joined by evaluations of *empty* and *remote*, which both are pertinent to discussion of *pristine* in its depiction of *wilderness*. In concordance lines of *empty*, this characteristic is framed as desirous for it speaks to the absence of humans in these spaces. Wilderness moves from depictions of size and traits of barrenness in the 1800s to framings of pristine and emptiness in the later 1900s. In essence, it is pristine for it is empty of humans due to its remote locations far from suburban/urban population centers.

Additionally related to conceptualizations of pristine is the framing produced by *true*. While *true* does collocate with *wilderness* in the 1800s, the meanings are distinct. In 1841, the first sample in the COHA, the passage states "true children of the wilderness"; in 1848, there appears "true tales of the wilderness"; in 1878, there is an instance of "true citizen of the wilderness." In the 1920s, the attachment of *true* in contexts of wilderness does not evaluate the people present in the wilderness but an actual quality of *wilderness*. In the 2000s, the collocation appears at its most frequent across the COHA in instances such as *you'll find true wilderness experience, the Boundary Waters has true wilderness, the Anaconda-Pintler wilderness remains true*. Again evident are the reflections of a wilderness/environment-out-there framing that possibly fractures humans from environment—are spaces not officially designated wilderness false, not real? It appears there is a growing tendency of humans to seek to experience *true wilderness*—one that is empty and pristine. Perhaps therein lies a nascent human recognition that natural spaces are declining.

Evaluations of size are again present in *huge* and *large*, yet these are qualitatively distinct from *vast*, *great*, and *unbroken*. For the former, these terms convey a boundedness that is not present in the latter. For example, in the COHA, *big* most commonly collocates with the nouns *man*, *house*, *eyes*, and *business* while *huge* pairs with *eyes*, *man*, *room*, and *hand*. These nouns are tangible and easily imagined; they are not so grand in size that they are difficult to conceive. In contrast, *vast* appears with *majority*, *amount*, *number*, and *numbers*—items that seem rather vague and poorly defined in comparison. Thus, yes, the designated wilderness spaces of recent US history are huge and large, but they are neither vast nor unbroken in the grander sense of the 1800s. Thus, while language users still evaluate wilderness frequently for size, the manner in which they do so has shifted.

Many items displaying the strongest negative correlations in Table 4 were also some of the items previously mentioned for their high frequency. The negative evaluative patterns displayed in the Google Books Corpus visualization and in the COHA frequency list are also evident here. However, as the Kendall's Tau measure displays, many of these items are on the decline. It seems reasonable to suggest that the decline of such negative lexis in the evaluative frame of *wilderness*

Table 4 Adjectives decreasing 1810–2010

Collocate	Kendall's Tau
distant	-0.754
western	-0.714
desolate	-0.638
barren	-0.616
wide	-0.608
rude	-0.572
savage	-0.568
dreary	-0.565
solitary	-0.56
boundless	-0.56
very	-0.554
weary	-0.552
howling	-0.536
rough	-0.528
tangled	-0.509

is a positive discursive trend that reflects an emergent environmental ethic. Such evaluations of wilderness as *desolate, barren, savage, dreary, howling, rough*, and *tangled* represent wilderness as a foreboding space of little if any intrinsic value. These evaluative terms hold negative prosodies which then construe wilderness with similar negative perceptions. For example, *howling* most often collocates with *wind, wolves, dogs, mob, storm, night, and gale*—the negative evaluative loading is quite clear.

These items decreasing across this span contrast quite clearly with the aforementioned items on the rise. The items generally on decline from 1810 to 2010 are more negatively loaded: *distant, desolate*, and *barren*. While increases were present with the use of *remote*, its near synonym *distant* was on the decline, further reflecting the linguistics maxim that no words are truly synonymous. Investigation of these near synonyms reveals divergence in their application. For *distant*, the common entities with which it collocates are *sound, time, future*, and *thunder*. These entities feel elusive, abstract, and difficult to tangibly grasp and experience. In contrast, the entities evaluated by *remote*, following its most common and perhaps obvious partner *control*, feel qualitatively more tangible and achievable: *part, corner, country, areas, places*. It seems *wilderness* is decreasingly imagined in such abstract terms as time and future, but it is instead viewed as more easily defined and imagined regardless of how remote it may still be.

In relation to previous discussion of a changing conceptualization of size, it is intriguing but unsurprising to see the term *boundless* appear on the list. It seems expected that as wilderness spaces are increasingly designated and brought under the control of federal agencies that depictions of wilderness as boundless would decline as, quite literally, they are now bounded. What was once popularly imagined as existing without limits is no more. Following two instances of *boundless wilderness* in two works in fiction in the 1920s, the collocation is not attested again in the COHA. A similar discussion could be had with *wide*; the last pairing of *wide wilderness* is in the early 1940s as the sample from 1998 refers to the width of a trail through the *wilderness*.

To close the analysis, the evaluative adjectives from 1950 to 2010 were also investigated with particular attention to those decreasing in use. The items declining in this period produced some rather strong negative correlations with *savage* scoring one the strongest Kendall's tau figures of all items in all time periods. Multiple items which were not present on the list for declining items from 1810 to 2010 do, however, appear in this more recent period. For instance, *big, old, bare* appear to sharply decline in this period while *good*,

Table 5 Adjectives decreasing 1950-2010

Collocate	Kendall's Tau
savage	-0.856
big	-0.788
old	-0.775
bare	-0.701
rough	-0.602
dreary	-0.577
distant	-0.577
good	-0.577
sweet	-0.577
dangerous	-0.548
dead	-0.548
surrounding	-0.548
full	-0.501

sweet, dangerous, and *dead* follow similar downward trajectories. *Old* was actually in the top 10 most frequent evaluative adjectives appearing with *wilderness,* yet its frequency, after some fluctuation in the late 1800s, steadily declined and even disappears in the 1970s. However, Table 5 generally reflects the declining use trajectories as noted in Table 4 for the period from 1800 to 2010 as many of the items previously identified continue their decline in this recent time period.

3.6 Conclusion and Future Research

Diachronic corpus-assisted ecolinguistics enables researchers to unsettle and challenge prevailing language practices that contribute to ecological degradation. Such diachronic work highlights "that our reality is not something ready-made and waiting to be meant—it has to be actively construed" (Halliday, 1990/2000, p. 179). Herein lies the power of diachronic research to illuminate the dynamic, emergent qualities of language, thereby enabling individuals to challenge contemporary language use practices that many likely view as objective and natural. The illustration provided in this chapter alone displays how popular conceptualizations of *wilderness* have evolved in US discourse. These shifts away from characterizations of *wilderness* as *savage*, *barren*, and *desolate* are indeed positive discursive movements. Yet other patterns which perhaps on first viewing appear similarly positive may be critiqued for fragmenting humans from the environment. As people begin to conceptualize natural spaces worthy of protection and preservation as "out there" far from modern urban/suburban life, other spaces conversely may be viewed as less true, less pristine, and thus less worthy of attention. Such romanticization of a distant wilderness as untouched and untrammeled reifies those protected spaces as worthy of conservation while rivers, lakes, mountains, and more beyond those confines do not receive such positive sentiment and conservation. Yes, we should protect the spaces "out there"—this is not to argue that we should not. However, we should be mindful of language practices that function to further solidify human fragmentation from the natural world.

There are numerous potential research sites of ecolinguistic interest that could be pursued through diachronic corpus-assisted ecolinguistics. While this illustration analyzed the evolving representations of *wilderness*, various other eco-keywords could be similarly interrogated. Such studies could pursue research aims akin to Grant and Walsh's study (2015) investigating linguistic indicators of an emergent climate change consciousness. We now have ample and overwhelming evidence of pervasive ecological crisis, yet skepticism toward the science of the climate crisis persists, particularly in the United States but elsewhere as well. Ecolinguists could further provide answers to Grant and Walsh's guiding question: "Can we buttress this physical data with social evidence?" (2015, p. 195). Further research could similarly employ a quantitative corpus-assisted analytic method but with greater attention to qualitative interpretations of the discursive patterns of salient entities. Such work could uncover the latent traces of human recognition of climate change and ecological degradation embedded within language use.

Such diachronic study should not be constrained to analysis of perhaps obvious eco-keywords such as wilderness, forests, water, and air. Indeed, investigations of these terms would likely reveal evolving attitudes, ideologies, and dispositions toward these entities, yet other features beyond eco-keywords specifically could be explored. For example, studies could explore emergent discursive features that reflect social practices either harmful or beneficial for sustainability and well-being. Such studies could explore, for instance, the discourse of disposability in modern consumerist culture and other similar topics that while not of immediate ecological relevance either challenge or promote practices, attitudes, and identities that are ecologically beneficial or problematic.

In closing, it feels apropos that a popular and critically acclaimed novel of 2020 was Diane Cook's dystopian narrative *The New Wilderness*. In the novel, she presents a suffering world transformed by the climate crisis in which people are fleeing overpopulated cities in hopes of forging a new life in, as the title suggests, a new wilderness—the novel served as an inspiration for this chapter. From savage, barren, and desolate as well as vast, great, and unbroken in the 1800s to more recent evaluations of national, federal, and designated and true, empty, and pristine, wilderness has been variably imagined and evaluated in US discourse. The scientific evidence of the climate crisis and its myriad consequences on ecosystems around the world suggests that a *new wilderness* is indeed forthcoming.

4

Corpus-Assisted Ecolinguistics for Literary Texts: A Keyness Analysis of Richard Powers' *The Overstory*

4.0 Introduction

In discussions of the climate crisis, Covid-19, or any other number of issues, policy makers, scientists, and activists frequently and rationally assume that if individuals are provided comprehensible and factual information, they will consequently understand the crisis at hand more completely and thus amend beliefs and actions accordingly. In regard to the climate crisis, the expectation is that if the public is presented the data, they will be persuaded to act in a more ecologically responsible and sustainable manner. This assumption is termed the Information Deficit Model (Suldovsky, 2017), for it assumes that the primary obstacle to motivating action and influencing belief is insufficient access to relevant information by the general public.

Unfortunately, and to the dismay and consternation of many, there is now ample evidence that resolving the information deficit regarding the clearly human-made causes and increasingly severe effects of climate crisis does little to persuade many people of the gravity of the ecological crisis. Thus, we are left to ask: If knowledge reached through rigorous scientific research and disseminated broadly in varied and accessible forms does not compel people to amend beliefs and actions, how are people to be convinced to act in more ecological ways? Perhaps a statement from a character in *The Overstory* holds the answer: "The best arguments in the world won't change a person's mind. The only thing that can do that is a story" (Powers, 2018, p. 336). It is a recognition and hope in the power of stories that motivates the present chapter and its focus on environmental writing.

In this chapter, the scope of corpus-assisted ecolinguistics is expanded to the study of literary texts. Unsurprisingly, corpus analysis has been conducted on literary texts—this area of study is referred to as corpus stylistics for it integrates the methods of corpus analysis with the theoretical framework of stylistics. Corpus stylistics seeks answers to many types of research questions of literary interest, but, and this is observation not critique, its inquiries are not pursued from an ecolinguistics orientation. Ecolinguistics has at times explored literary texts as well, yet this work has focused primarily on shorter works of poetry with no attention, to my knowledge, extended to longer literary texts of clear ecological relevance. This chapter, therefore, asserts and briefly illustrates the potential of research at the interface of corpus stylistics and corpus-assisted ecolinguistics in a period where environmental writing broadly and climate crisis fiction specifically are widely acclaimed and increasingly popular.

The chapter first discusses the importance of environmental writing and the primary types of texts in this space. It then introduces corpus stylistics and asserts a rationale for corpus-assisted ecolinguistics to pursue research of literary texts. To illustrate this integration of corpus stylistics and corpus-assisted ecolinguistics, the chapter presents a keyness analysis—a CADS technique soon explained—of Richard Powers' Pulitzer Prize-winning novel, *The Overstory* (2018), before closing with a discussion of avenues for continued research of literary texts.

4.1 Environmental Writing

When one thinks of environmental writing, they likely recall such classics of environmental non-fiction as Rachel Carson's *Silent Spring* (1962) and its profound role in stirring an environmental movement in North America in the 1960s and challenging a development-at-all-costs ideology; perhaps no other modern environmental text has been so widely influential. Others may point to early American classics like *Nature* (1836) or *Walden* (1854) from naturalists Ralph Waldo Emerson and Henry David Thoreau or the collection of essays by Aldo Leopold in *The Sand County Almanac* (1949) in which he promotes a land ethic philosophy for how humans can sustainably coexist with nonhuman animals, plants, and the land. These authors urged readers to reconceptualize their relationships with the natural world, and their writings moved many North Americans to reimagine a nature full of awe and splendor rather than a dangerous and tempting wilderness (Cronon, 1996). While these aforementioned writers and their well-known non-fiction works are environmental in topic and aim, literary works of fiction similarly engage with environmental themes, although their ecological messaging is typically not as explicit.

In the canon of North American fiction, John Steinbeck's *The Grapes of Wrath* (1939) occupies an esteemed status, and his enduring classic—the novel begins with dust storms in a US Midwest devastated by destructive farming and land-use practices and closes with a severe flood resulting from the same—is considered "one of the most significant environmental novels of the century" (Demott, 1992, p. xix). Just as ecology and ecolinguistics today speak of interrelatedness, unity, interconnectedness, and reciprocity, Jim Casy, one of the novel's characters, succinctly expresses a philosophy reflective of ecology: "There was the hills, an' there was me, an we wasn't separate no more. We was one thing." (Demott, 1992). This deep ecological awareness is woven throughout Steinbeck's American classic. Though Steinbeck's text and others have been analyzed through an ecological lens in environmental humanities, ecolinguistics broadly and corpus-assisted ecolinguistics has not extensively explored this space.

As concern for and attention to climate crisis and its causes and effects rises, the number of texts either overtly or covertly utilizing climate crisis as an imaginative device has likewise increased. In Trexler's *Anthropogenic Fictions: The Novel in Times of Climate Change* (2015), he identifies approximately 150 climate-related novels alone—a number which has certainly grown in the years since the publication. One aim of ecolinguistics is to identify and promote discourses, or *stories to live by* (Stibbe, 2015), which imagine and present alternative and more sustainable ecological futures. Thus, it seems prudent to look to environmental writing in the burgeoning literary spaces of environmental fiction and environmental non-fiction for such discourses that could inform and shape the emergence of greater ecological consciousness.

From climate crisis fiction to environmental non-fiction, the popularity of multiple forms of environmental writing has expanded, and it is now common to see texts with obvious environmental relevance on best-seller lists. The following section illustrates the diversity of environmental writing in its discussion of four genres of environmental writing: environmental non-fiction, new nature writing, climate fiction, and speculative fiction. Though this list is not exhaustive and the classification is admittedly subjective, the discussion details the numerous sites in which corpus-assisted ecolinguistics can be productively applied in this space.

4.2 Genres of Environmental Writing

The first genre, environmental non-fiction, is accessible, science-driven writing intended for a broad general audience. Perhaps no better exemplar exists than Bill McKibben's *The End of Nature* (1989). The text, first published in 1989, is considered the first book-length work written on the climate crisis for a general audience. It is clear and accessible prose packed densely with scientific information, yet the data and detail do not overwhelm for the book does not read as academic research of the type found in scholarly journals. Instead, it cogently and deliberately details the severity and immensity of the climate crisis while promoting awareness and issuing a call to action in its readership. McKibben has continued to write in this space and has more recently published the best seller *Falter: Has the Human Game Started to Play Itself Out* (2019)—a bleak but ultimately hopeful look at the state of the planet thirty years following *The End of Nature*. Other examples of this genre are Naomi Klein's *On Fire: The Burning Case for a Green New Deal* (2019), Elizabeth Kolbert's *The Sixth Extinction: An Unnatural Extinction* (2014), and Fred Pearce's *The New Wild: How Invasive Species Will Be Nature's Salvation* (2015). These books confront readers with the tragedy of climate-driven species loss, argue passionately for transformative policy, and look for solutions to species loss in at times unexpected places. Similar aims are pursued in evolutionary biologist E.O. Wilson's trilogy *The Anthropocene Epoch* whose final offering, *Half-Earth: Our Planet's Fight for Life* (2016), boldly forwards a goal of preserving half of the Earth for nature's resurgence.

A related yet markedly distinct genre, New Nature writing (MacFarlane, 2013) retains the presence of scientific information and precision of previously reviewed environmental non-fiction yet offers rich and evocative memoir-style descriptions of everyday encounters with nonhuman animals and the natural world. Coined by Robert MacFarlane to describe an emergent style of writing in the United Kingdom, he asserts that New Nature writing "is distinguished by its mix of memoir and lyricism and specializes in delicacy of thought and precision of observation" (p. 66). As reflected in this description, New Nature writing is typified by a prose style steeped in awe and wonder for the beauty and complexity of nonhuman species and the natural world in hopes of possibly stirring an ecological awakening within the reader. Importantly, the prose of new nature writing does not recount a thrilling scene of a lion chasing an antelope across the open savannah or a dramatic moment where a crocodile lurches from the water with jaws agape typical of high-budget National Geographic or BBC

Earth productions. Instead, new nature writing captures the overlooked and seemingly mundane moments such as a sparrow's daily visit to a backyard garden or a butterfly fluttering through a gentle breeze. In Michael McCarthy's *The Moth Snowstorm: Joy and Nature* (2015), the author inspires a greater awareness of the natural world through a poignant memoir of moths and butterflies joined with tragedies of his youth and personal life, Elizabeth Tova Bailey's *The Sound of a Wild Snail Eating* (2016) tells of her observations of a snail during a period she was bedridden with illness, and David Abram's opening chapter to *The Spell of the Sensuous* (1997) offers accounts of spiders weaving a web, ants marching, and birds in flight. A hopefulness for a stirred ecological consciousness is reflected in McCarthy's closing chapter aptly titled "A new kind of love" and its dance of the butterfly and George Monbiot's inspiring opening passage to *Feral; Rewilding the Land, Sea, and Human Life* (2013) named "A Raucous Summer," an allusion to Carson's *Silent Spring* (1962), and his impassioned call for new sort of environmentalism.

New Nature writing is unique and important for it makes prominent "the interconnections between nature and human beings" (Bunting, 2007, as cited in Stibbe, 2015, p. 31). These texts challenge prevailing resource-driven perceptions of nature and nonhuman animals which commodify and assign worth based on human-centric economic valuations. Though prevailing discourse rarely attributes intrinsic value to the nonhuman world, New Nature writing subverts the ideological apparatus that perpetuates human dominion over the natural world and the many species which inhabit it. Thus, rather than unwittingly and implicitly promoting discourses that normalize and perpetuate a hierarchy rooted in dominion and exploitation, New Nature writing inspires readers to be more conscious of their place in the world and to see the beauty in daily encounters with nature rather than romanticizing the faraway national park or remote wilderness reserve.

The division between New Nature writing and environmental non-fiction is not uniformly transparent, and one may critique the categories and the labels applied here. This text places environmental non-fiction and New Nature writing as opposing poles on a shared continuum. Texts which reflect a more journalistic, information-rich, science-driven presentation gravitate toward the environmental non-fiction pole while the more lyrical and poetic prose reflective of New Nature writing moves toward the other end of the spectrum. For example, McKibben's *The End of Nature* (1989), Klein's *On Fire* (2019), and Wallace-Wells' *The Uninhabitable Earth* (2020) with their copious detailing of climate change data are rather data-driven in their approach while Abrams' *The Spell of the Sensuous*

(1996), Monbiot's *Feral* (2013), and McCarthy's *The Moth Snowstorm* (2015) qualitatively feel more poetic and lyrical. Passages indeed exist in McKibben's text that are lyrical and expressive; for example, the book's final paragraphs evocatively recount his experience on a clear August night watching the Perseid meteor shower woven seamlessly with a quotation from naturalist John Burroughs and a brief excerpt from Milton's *Paradise Lost*. And similarly, New Nature writing often offers precise scientific information within its largely poetic delivery. Nonetheless, the genres provide different reader experiences, although their ultimate rhetorical aims for greater ecological awareness are shared.

The subjective messiness of genre categorization continues with the next two types of environmental writing: speculative fiction and climate fiction. For the former, it would be inaccurate to say that speculative writing is broadly environmental in focus. In fact, speculative fiction ranges across a number of genre types such as science fiction, horror, fantasy, alternative histories, supernatural, as well as many others, and treatment of environmental concerns is not constant or even especially common across these sub-genres. Of interest to this brief review are those texts within speculative fiction which depict dystopian apocalyptic and post-apocalyptic worlds in which climate crisis provides an interpretive and critical lens for understanding the narrative and the world it builds. One exemplar, or perhaps three, of this genre is the Southern Reach Trilogy comprised of the novels *Annihilation, Authority*, and *Acceptance* (2014) by Jeff VanderMeer, an author dubbed the "weird Thoreau" in *The New Yorker* (Rothman, 2015). At the heart of each text is a mysterious and dangerous region of the United States called Area X which nature has reclaimed and which causes disappearances, suicide, and disease to the humans who enter. Fiction such as VanderMeer's in which a vengeful nature punishes humanity is at times referred to as eco-horror.

The popularity of VanderMeer's eco-science fiction trilogy was shared by Max Brooks' *War Z: An Oral History of the Zombie War* (2006) and the subsequent film adaptation. In the novel, the author explores a world plagued and terrorized by zombies through a collection of interviews with characters from various backgrounds, e.g., soldiers, doctors, teachers, government officials, and many more. In eco-horror such as the Southern Reach Trilogy and *World War Z*, "nature strikes back against humans as punishment for environmental disruption" (Rust & Soles, 2014 p. 509). While speculative fiction serves as platforms to critiques of many social issues such as racism, classism, and capitalism, it also at times creates "a stage for addressing some of the negative impacts humans have had on their environment" (Murray & Heumann, p. 100).

Schneider-Mayerson and Bellamy argue that speculative fiction offers "great promise" for "the very act of imagining the future enables a radical departure from the trajectory of the present" (2020, p. 3). Importantly, speculative fiction provides "critical perspectives on the present and remind us of the infinite possibilities of life on Earth, as well as the ways that we might bring some of them into being" (Schneider-Mayerson & Bellamy, 2020, p. 3).

As with environmental non-fiction and New Nature writing, speculative fiction and the final genre to be discussed, climate fiction, share some features while diverging elsewhere. The distinction presented here delineates the two by the degree to which climate change is present as an imaginative device. As previously noted, VanderMeer's trilogy and Brooks' *World War Z* do not explicitly mention climate change. Even in Margaret Atwood's *Oryx and Crake* (2003) and its post-apocalyptic world, climate crisis looms but never enters the text explicitly. This is similarly true in Emmi Itäranta's dystopian *Memory of Water* (2012), in which the protagonist, Noria Kaitio, a tea master in an occupied Scandinavian Union, must survive in a world where water is frighteningly scarce and rationed by an occupying force. Such speculative futures as Atwood's and Itäranta's enable readers to imagine "the probable alterity of future inhabitants of Earth," allowing audiences to traverse "a first step in meeting the obligation to change our culture, our selves" (Schneider-Mayerson & Bellamy, 2020).

While speculative fiction at times presents futures that seem fantastical (e.g., Atwood's world in *Oryx and Crake* is populated by pigoons, rakunks, and wolvlogs as well as a group of genetically modified humans named crakers), climate fiction more directly presents cautionary narratives of a worrisomely recognizable and immediate future transformed and devastated by climate crisis and ecological collapse. For example, Marcel Theroux's *Far North* (2009) and Nathaniel Rich's *Odds against Tomorrow* (2013) are imagined worlds that feel eerily probable for readers. In Theroux's novel, the main character, Makepeace, and her family move to northern Siberia for the region is the only livable area remaining in an overheated, depleted, and burning world plagued with war. In Rich's novel, New York City and much of the US eastern seaboard experience a devastating climate crisis-induced scenario of a droughts, rising ocean levels, and a powerful hurricane, leaving the protagonist, Mitchell Zukor, to traverse a destroyed and flooded Manhattan to then emerge into a chaos of refugees struggling to survive. For many readers, scenes from *Odds against Tomorrow* may conjure memories of climate disaster films such as *The Day after Tomorrow* (2004) or actual real-life events such as Hurricane Katrina in New Orleans in 2005 and later the flooding of Houston as a result of Hurricane Harvey in 2017.

Each of these genres of environmental writing is a critical site for cultivating ecological awareness and promoting more ecologically sustainable identities and actions. The functions of environmental nonfiction and New Nature writing to educate and inspire are indeed valuable. Yet, of equal, perhaps even greater, importance are the alternative possible futures presented in speculative and climate crisis fiction. These texts enable readers to reflect upon and deeply consider the "trajectory of the present" and the course which our practices are leading the planet (Schneider-Mayerson & Bellamy, 2020, p. 3). Critical discourse studies and ecolinguistics are well equipped to explore this literary space; however, the two have infrequently investigated domains where positive discursive practices are potentially emerging, instead opting more commonly to identify and challenge language use which perpetuates systems of oppression and inequality—clearly a laudable aim.

As Stibbe's ecolinguistic framework asserts, discourses of environmental importance may be categorized along three parameters: 1) *negative discourses* which perpetuate ecological destruction 2) *ambivalent discourses* which superficially appear to cultivate ecological sustainability and well-being but which reproduce practices and beliefs that lead to ecological harm, and 3) *positive discourses* which identify, praise, and promote language use that cultivates well-being and sustainability. Most of the illustrations in this text highlight negative linguistic practices which conflict with an ecosophy of sustainability and well-being for all. In contrast, this chapter explores a site of positive discourse where a deeper ecological consciousness is cultivated. Environmental writing is an ideal site where beneficial discourses which may contribute to more sustainable ways of being may be identified and subsequently promoted. Corpus-assisted ecolinguistics paired with corpus stylistics provide the theoretical apparatus and the methodological toolkit for exploring texts in this space.

4.3 Corpus Stylistics

Though now quite familiar with CADS, this chapter presents an analysis of literary texts inspired by corpus stylistics—a related yet distinct field of inquiry. As this book has consistently displayed, ecolinguistics is a rather interdisciplinary endeavor with researchers drawing from many disciplines and approaches in this problem-oriented venture. Stylistics is similarly interdisciplinary, and thus, an approach which integrates (corpus) stylistics and (corpus-assisted) ecolinguistics feels a suitable and promising union. Corpus stylistics both informs and inspires the forthcoming analysis while also providing an opportunity for the expanded scope of ecolinguistics imagined in this book; therefore, a review of the field and its scholarship, albeit brief, is relevant and necessary.

Firstly, stylistics is the linguistic analysis of style in language with aims of providing insights into "how the linguistic choices evident in a text contribute to the overall meanings and effects of that text" (McIntyre & Walker, p. 16). As Fischer-Starke asserts, the goal of stylistics is "to decode literary meanings and structural features of literary texts by identifying linguistic patterns and their functions in the texts" (2010, p. 2). While stylistics traditionally has been pursued primarily through qualitative inquiry and close reading, corpus stylistics adds a quantitative dimension through the application of corpus techniques to the analysis of both fiction and nonfiction texts. Defining corpus stylistics as merely the analysis of literary texts through the use of corpus techniques is insufficient for some scholars in this space. These scholars alternatively present corpus stylistics as "the application of theories, models, and frameworks from stylistics in corpus analysis" (McIntyre & Walker, 2019, p. 15).

Corpus stylistics employs the techniques applied in corpus-assisted discourse studies to offer statements such as how certain linguistic features and their presence in a text foreground or background certain meanings or how particular patterns contribute to characterization within a text or in the work of a particular author. For instance, Vincent and Clark (2017) perform a keyword analysis of Anthony Burgess' dystopian novel *A Clockwork Orange*. The analysis identified and described the distinguishing lexicogrammatical features of the constructed language, Nadsat, which the protagonist/narrator Alex and his gang of *droogs* speak in the text. Similarly, Culpeper (2002) conducted a keyword analysis of Shakespeare's *Romeo and Juliet* to ascertain character-specific language patterns which function in the characterization of the two iconic lovers. In a later study, Culpeper applied a similar keyness methodology but instead focused upon the analysis of semantic frames to explore use of metaphor in Romeo's language use (Culpeper, 2009).

While the above studies focused on one primary text, other projects have looked more broadly at the style of particular authors across their work. For example, Fischer-Starke (2010) presented a monograph-length corpus stylistic analysis of the prose of Jane Austen in which she compiled and analyzed a corpus of six Austen novels (*Emma, Mansfield Park, Northanger Abbey, Persuasion, Pride and Prejudice*, and *Sense and Sensibility*). Guiding Fischer-Starke's text is her attempt to answer two critical questions of corpus stylistics: "1. Can literary insights into the data that have been published be reproduced by using corpus linguistic techniques in the analysis? 2. Is it possible to gain new insights into the data by using new analytic, that is, corpus linguistic techniques?" (Fischer-Starcke, 2010, p. 11). For the first, she answers affirmatively by illustrating how previous statements regarding intertextual references within *Northanger Abbey* were replicated by her keyword and concordance analysis. Such replication highlights the value of quantitative, corpus-assisted approaches to the analysis of literary texts for it displays the ability of corpus methods to reach similar outcomes as earlier research. Such confirmations add strength to previously forwarded claims, but, and perhaps most importantly, they also illustrate the potential of corpus stylistics to reliably and accurately answer larger and more complex research questions in the future. To the second question, she also answers positively as she demonstrates how corpus techniques aid in the identification of frequent phrases and how these phrases function to characterize people and places. These affirmations display the value of corpus stylistics.

Perhaps the most public and accessible display of the usefulness of corpus stylistics is the online CliC Dickens Project (Mahlberg et al., 2016). The free, online tool enables students, teachers, and researchers to analyze fifteen novels of Charles Dickens, another twenty-nine novels of other authors from the nineteenth century, a collection of children's literature from the period, as well as several other works specially requested by CliC users. As the name of the project indicates, much of the research emanating from the project has focused on the style of Charles Dickens. In one of her many studies of Dickens, Mahlberg investigated the distinguishing features of Dickens' novel *Bleak House*. In the piece, Mahlberg asserts the value of corpus approaches to stylistics is its ability to "make an important contribution to the investigation of the interplay between conventional, idiosyncratic and creative patterns of language use" (Mahlberg, 2007, p. 224). She expands upon her study of Dickens' much more comprehensively in a monograph-length exploration of Dickens' novels. In the text, she applies techniques such as cluster analysis to explore aspects of characterization in dialogue and character speech. Though readers may intuit a certain Dickensian style, Mahlberg's corpus stylistic approach enables the researcher to quantify such intuitions and reveal facts about language and literature that have largely remained hidden from observation (Mahlberg, 2013, p. 1).

Corpus stylistics research is expanding, and readers interested in this domain are encouraged to explore further as this review provides only a limited report of the emerging discipline. Though admittedly brief, for the purposes of the current chapter, the overview suffices as an orientation to the subsequent analysis. It is also worth noting that some may assert that the analysis this chapter pursues and illustrates is not corpus stylistics proper for it does not fully apply the "theories, models, and frameworks from stylistics in corpus analysis" (McIntyre & Walker, 2019, p. 15). This claim has partial validity. That said, the subsequent illustration is indebted to and informed by corpus stylistics, and though it may not adhere to this definition fully, its approach and analysis reflect qualities of corpus stylistics and recognition of this fact seems prudent. As the chapter illustrates, an integration of corpus-assisted ecolinguistics and corpus stylistics for the study of literary texts of ecological relevance produces a promising research space for scholars of both domains.

4.4 Ecolinguistic Analysis of Literary Texts

The sort of corpus-assisted ecolinguistics of literary text pursued in this chapter is rare but not wholly novel in its approach and aims. Indeed, ecolinguistic analysis of literary texts has been compellingly illustrated in explorations of Native American literature (Bringhurst, 2008), Japanese Haiku poetry (Stibbe, 2012), and the poetry of Emily Dickinson (Zuo, 2019). These studies aimed to identify patterns within these respective discourses that reflect and produce heightened ecological awareness and sensitivity. As Stibbe notes, when such beneficial discourses are identified, it is possible they may be "adapted and incorporated across a wide range of areas of life" (Stibbe, 2015). Similar identification of beneficial discourses is possible through corpus-assisted analysis of literary texts, yet, as has been noted, this research space has received little attention.

The study which most comprehensively incorporates the techniques of CADS with ecolinguistics is Andrew Goatly's (2004) comparative analysis of the poem *The Prelude* by William Wordsworth to one issue of *The Times* of London; his rationale for use of only one issue of *The Times* is its comparable size to Wordsworth's poem. Goatly asserts that English construes the world in a manner which is incongruent with modern science and ecological thinking, and he details several instances where the grammar of English could be shifted to construct a more ecological worldview. For instance, he argues that we can reconstruct experiences present in clauses of mental experience to actors in material processes:

1. We noticed the river.   →   *The river arrested my gaze.*
2. We love the forest.   →   *The forest touches my heart.*

He also highlights how we can reconfigure relational processes into material ones in a process he terms "activation of tokens" (p. 201):

3. *There are five trees in the valley.* → *Five trees stand in the valley.*
4. *There is a boulder on top of the hill.* → *A boulder tops the hill.*

Similarly, he illustrates how positioning a location circumstantial as an actor produces an utterance which presents participant and location as interrelated participants in an event.

5. *Ants are crawling all over the bed.* → *The bed is crawling with ants.*

A final item highlighted are ergative verbs—verbs which may alternatively function as both transitive and intransitive. Using the example "the door opened," he illustrates how the energy for the action originates in the door. If such ergative potential were extended to "so-called inanimate things" in nature, then they would be construed with greater agency and animacy. In one provocative suggestion, he questions whether the increase in ergativity in the English-language system over the past 100 years is actually grammar's "adaptive response to the insights of modern scientific thinking?" (p. 201).

In the corpus-assisted analysis, Goatly identifies a beneficial discourse within Wordsworth's poem that construes nature as active, animate, and alive. In one portion of the analysis, the clauses featuring elements of nature were analyzed using a framework that ranked participants from most to least powerful. For example, an actor in a transitive clause is able to affect other entities, and thus, it is coded as powerful. In contrast, when the natural element is coded as goal of the process it is coded as powerless, i.e., it is acted upon by the power of the subject. In the language of *The Times*, nature is depicted as passive and inanimate. With this framework, Goatly asserts that nature is "twice as active" in *The Prelude* than in *The Times*. For example, in the poem, nature often is presented as sayers (able to send messages and affect others) and experiencers (conscious of and responsive to stimuli). In *The Prelude*, Goatly notes multiple instances of nature speaking and sending message while such actions by nonhuman animals are not present in *The Times*. In the instances where nonhuman animals are speakers in *The Times*, it is done so comically and without sincerity. Wordsworth also construes bodies of water as sayers, e.g., a river murmuring and talking. Thus, in the poem, nature and animals are construed as communicators able to express meaningful messages of which humans should be receptive. Similarly, landscapes are presented as actors in ways which are absent from the newspaper discourse with pastures dancing and mountains embracing. In *The Times*, when animals are experiencers, it is typically suffering which they are experiencing, e.g., "Tube drivers ran over injured dog."

The identification of the beneficial discourse embedded within *The Prelude* and its contrastingly negative depictions of nature and animals in *The Times* is an illustrative and valuable investigation. Stibbe (2015) comments on the insight of Goatly's analysis of Wordsworth's writing but also notes that many forms of environmental writing are produced by cultures around the world, asserting that such discourses may be explored in culturally respectful, sensitive, and appropriate ways to possibly identify more ecologically sustainable forms of language use. With the potential for corpus-assisted ecolinguistic analysis of literary text demonstrated by Goatly's study, the dearth of work in this domain feels somewhat surprising. Eco-critical readings of texts are not uncommon, and it would certainly be possible to find examples of literary critiques of climate change fiction, speculative fiction, and other literary forms engaging with environmental topics, themes, and questions. The types of environmental writing previously described in the chapter have been studied in other areas of the humanities, particularly ecocriticism, but corpus-assisted ecolinguistics has a unique potential to contribute to research in this space. Ecolinguistics has explored shorter works such as haikus, poems, and short stories, but it has not analyzed literary novels of ecological relevance through a corpus-assisted approach. The analysis to follow, thus, aims to display the potential for an expanded corpus-assisted ecolinguistics which explores literary texts to identify and promote beneficial discursive practices.

4.5 Methods

4.5.1 Constructing the Corpus

This analysis investigates *The Overstory* (2018) by Richard Powers. The novel was a *New York Times* bestseller and was awarded the 2019 Pulitzer Prize for Fiction—along with its clear environmental relevance, this popular appeal and critical acclaim are key factors in its selection for the present case study. The novel explores the experiences of a collection of characters, their deep relationships with trees, and their activism to save forests of North America.

The text is divided into four sections (Roots, Trunk, Crown, and Seeds) with the narrative joining the lives of the core human characters and their awakening to the beauty and complexity of trees and the natural world. Importantly, and as the analysis will subsequently display, trees also become central characters within the novel.

It was necessary to create a corpus of *The Overstory* by Richard Powers as no digital copy is publicly available. Often researchers in corpus stylistics source digital texts from online repositories such as Project Gutenberg, but this was not possible for this recently published text. It should be noted that research ethics and respect for copyright are a considerable ethical concern in the compilation of corpora. In respect for copyright, the use of excerpts from the text is limited in this chapter, no long passages from the texts are included, and the corpus is solely used for research purposes and is not available to others. These guidelines are in adherence with copyright law in the United States and abide by the notion of fair dealing. Fair dealing permits the use of short excerpts of text for non-commercial purposes (McIntryre & Walker, 2019).

At approximately 500 pages, the corpus construction process was admittedly tedious and time-consuming. This reality presents a notable barrier to such research, and any person seeking to manually create a corpus from a full-length text should be aware of this significant time required to scan and manually clean the text; depending on various factors, e.g., length of text and quality of scanner, the process can take tens of hours to complete. In the first phase, the full text, page by page, was scanned with a high-resolution scanner. Next, the scanned pages were processed using the Tesseract OCR engine. Though Tesseract is a quality tool for such a task, a significant amount of manual cleaning of the txt files was nonetheless required. After cleaning the corpus, it was tagged for part of speech with the CLAWS Tagger and annotated for semantic meaning with the USAS tagger within the WMatrix platform. Its final size was 179,135 tokens. And finally, the fiction sub-corpus of the Corpus of Contemporary of American English (COCA) (Davies, 2008–) from 2000 to 2012[1] was used as the reference corpus for the study. The reference corpus was approximately 48 million words.

One additional comment regards the not uncontroversial application of the term corpus for the digitization of a single text. Typically, corpus linguists conceive of a corpus to be a representative sample of language use comprised of many texts that is studied in order to make statements about language in a particular register, genre, etc. or in language use broadly. However, one key affordance of corpus study is the ability to make statements on language use that are generally beyond the reach of other methods. Corpus linguistics enables one to *see* patterns of language that are generally not discernable by close reading. In this sense, the digitized, annotated, and searchable version of *The Overstory* may be viewed as a corpus for the observations made would not be possible through other approaches.

4.5.2 Keyness Analysis

Keyness analysis is a corpus analytic technique which compares linguistic items in a node corpus (the corpus being investigated) to a larger reference corpus in order to identify those features which occur at a rate significantly and meaningfully greater or lesser in the node corpus than would be expected given their frequencies in the reference corpus. At times in this text and even this chapter, this approach has been termed keyword analysis for it specifically focused on the analysis of lexical items. However, as Gabrielatos notes, keyness can be investigated for other types of linguistic units as well, and thus, referring to the technique uniformly as keyword analysis is "restricted and restricting" (2018, p. 228).

As noted, a keyness analysis identifies the linguistic items, whether syntactic, semantic, or lexical, in the node corpus through a comparative analysis with a reference corpus. Word lists reporting raw frequency of a particular word or tag are useful for some purposes, but a keyness analysis provides greater insights into the "aboutness and style" of a corpus or text by identifying the features of the node corpus that distinguishes it from a reference corpus (Scott & Tribble, 2006, p. 55). For example, the frequency list of lexical items in *The Overstory* includes *the, a, of, and, to, in he, she, her,* and *his* near the top of its list. Though useful for certain inquiries, this list provides little information into the distinguishing linguistic features of Powers' text. Indeed, it is quite probable that all novels would have a nearly identical list of high-frequency lexical items. In contrast, as later displayed in Table 6, the keyness list of lexical items gets to the heart of the matter much more directly and effectively, as it identifies those lexical items that are notably more frequent in Powers' novel than in fiction writing generally. That said, the resulting keyness list is reflective of the ways that the node and reference texts are similar or different in terms of time, register, topic, etc. In other words, the selection of a different reference corpus would yield a different keyness list, and researchers should be mindful of the reference corpus employed when implementing the technique.

In keyness analysis, a log likelihood statistic is likely the most commonly employed measure of statistical significance. As the log likelihood measure is a

Table 6 Keywords in *The Overstory* (sorted by BIC)

	Keyword	Frequency: *Overstory*	Frequency: Fiction	BIC	Log_L	Log_R
1	Mimi	234	263	1,918.37	1,936.07	7.91
2	Neelay	142	0	1,573.08	1,590.78	138.70
3	tree	412	7,482	1,417.91	1,435.61	3.89
4	Adam	264	2,398	1,236.49	1,254.19	4.89
5	trees	384	8,090	1,217.37	1,235.07	3.68
6	Douglas	157	473	1,037.18	1,054.88	6.48
7	Maidenhair	67	3	708.13	725.83	12.56
8	Watchman	74	145	532.21	549.91	7.11
9	forest	172	3,685	530.32	548.02	3.65
10	Nick	129	1,888	482.46	500.16	4.20
11	Hoel	61	85	467.86	485.55	7.60
12	Patricia	73	359	410.27	427.96	5.78
13	Westerford	35	0	374.40	392.09	136.68
14	Douggie	35	2	358.85	376.55	12.20
15	Mimas	33	0	351.99	369.69	136.59
16	trunks	73	578	347.43	365.13	5.09
17	Olivia	86	1,073	340.85	358.55	4.43
18	Sih	32	0	340.79	358.48	136.55
19	Hsuin	32	0	340.79	358.48	136.55
20	branches	102	1,861	336.86	354.56	3.89
21	species	97	1,849	311.79	329.49	3.82
22	Pavlicek	26	0	273.57	291.27	136.25
23	forests	56	415	269.16	286.85	5.19
24	Chestnut	53	349	265.17	282.87	5.36
25	Mulberry	34	52	248.15	265.85	7.46
26	hundred	170	9,521	245.53	263.23	2.27
27	Dorothy	60	902	212.00	229.70	4.17
28	Appich	20	0	206.36	224.05	135.87
29	trunk	73	1,947	186.40	204.09	3.34
30	Ray	81	2,607	182.13	199.83	3.07
31	Fir	33	147	181.57	199.27	5.92
32	wants	122	6,480	181.41	199.11	2.34
33	comes	141	9,034	171.42	189.12	2.07

34	seeds	47	684	165.02	182.71	4.21
35	scroll	35	246	164.96	182.66	5.26
36	branch	57	1,327	155.43	173.13	3.53
37	sempervirens	15	0	150.34	168.04	135.46
38	loggers	25	78	148.78	166.48	6.43
39	Redwood	26	97	147.41	165.10	6.18
40	needs	89	4,120	147.29	164.99	2.54
41	knows	129	8,640	146.74	164.44	2.01
42	Brinkman	15	1	142.87	160.57	11.98
43	bark	47	887	142.80	160.50	3.84
44	sits	93	4,844	136.98	154.68	2.37
45	Firs	21	57	127.11	144.81	6.64
46	sees	94	5,334	125.93	143.62	2.25
47	tells	77	3,541	125.88	143.58	2.55
48	reads	52	1,424	125.26	142.96	3.30
49	mastery	23	100	122.17	139.87	5.96
50	learners	17	20	121.85	139.54	7.84
51	Pine	52	1,498	120.63	138.33	3.23
52	Maple	35	496	120.07	137.76	4.25
53	wood	81	4,128	119.85	137.54	2.40
54	starts	86	4,679	119.39	137.08	2.31
55	grows	39	747	114.44	132.13	3.82
56	leaves	92	5,584	113.28	130.98	2.15
57	keeps	62	2,586	107.92	125.61	2.69
58	Carmen	31	421	106.74	124.43	4.31
59	remembers	42	1,033	105.76	123.46	3.46
60	thinks	83	4,883	104.46	122.15	2.20
61	Aspens	16	28	104.07	121.77	7.27
62	Amelia	30	412	102.11	119.81	4.30

test of statistical significance, it indicates the degree to which findings are not random but reflective of the data sample. Log likelihood values of 3.83, 6.64, and 10.83 correspond to p-values of .05, .01, and .001 (McEnery & Xiao, 2006). However, the use of log likelihood as a singular metric for assessing keyness is problematic, even "unreliable and misleading" (Gabrielatos, 2018), as p-values are greatly influenced by the frequency of items and the size of corpora.

Though statistical tests such as log likelihood have been critiqued, they remain a useful technique for the corpus linguist's toolkit. While log likelihood was an output of the Wordsmith keyword analysis performed in this illustration, it serves only marginal usefulness in this instance. As the node corpus was approximately 200,000 words and the reference corpus was nearly 50 million, the frequency differences for hundreds of lexical items were quite large. Indeed, even with the p-value set at 0.001, the operation resulted in greater than 500 potential key items.

A log likelihood measure can be effectively paired with an effect size measure such as log ratio. Such coupling of complementary measures allows "the items returned from an automated frequency comparison to be ranked according to the size of the frequency difference" (Gabrielatos, 2018, p. 238). As Andrew Hardie explains, a statistical significance measure such as log likelihood "tells us how much evidence we have for a difference between two corpora" but it does not reveal "how big/how important a given difference is" (Hardie, 2014, para. 3). Thus, coupling a significance measure and an effect size measure is not simply a matter of reducing a keyword list to a manageable amount, but rather, it is a fundamental aspect of the analysis. In a study of immigration discourse, Fitzsimmons-Doolan (2019) produces an initial list of possible key items using Wordsmith Tools applying a p-value of 0.005 and a log ratio threshold of 1.5. Once generated, the list of candidates was sorted by the log ratio measure to narrow the list of items for further analysis of items which both were statistically significant and had the highest effect size number. This is a sound methodological approach for identifying key items, but this specific method was not adopted in the current illustration for it too greatly privileged character names over other lexical items; it is not surprising that a comparison of one work of fiction to other literary work would yield such a character-focused list. That said, the addition of the BIC metric discussed in the following paragraph allowed the keyness list to capture a broader range of lexical items.

Coupling Log L and Log R is an effective approach for identifying key features, but Gabrielatos (2018) argues for the adoption of Bayes Factor (BIC) for it incorporates the log-likelihood measure while also accounting for the size of the corpora. The BIC measure proved insightful and appropriate for the current study as it identified a greater number of non-character lexical items. Though character names from *The Overstory* such as Mimi, Neelay, Adam, and Douglas remain in the keyness list when this method is applied, there is greater coverage and inclusion of lexical items from other word classes. The final list of key items for the present study includes the sixty-two words ranked by BIC score included in Table 6; the table reports both the log likelihood and log ratio scores. The cutoff for inclusion was a BIC score of 100, an admittedly arbitrary threshold but one which limited the data to a manageable level for the present chapter. To clarify, the process followed these steps: 1) generation of potential key items through an automated procedure with a p-value of 0.001, 2) a narrowing of the list to items with log ratio greater than 2.0, and 3) ranking the key items according to their BIC score with a threshold set at 100.

4.6 Keywords in *The Overstory*

It is useful to first provide some general observations on the list of keywords. First, it is unsurprising that many of the lexical items populating the list are the names of human characters. In fact of the sixty-two total items, twenty-four (approximately 40 percent) of the items are character names. As keyness analysis identifies the greatest differences in frequencies of items in one corpus when compared to a second corpus, it is expected that the unique character names of *The Overstory* such as Neelay, Adam, and Nick would appear prominently on the list. Of greater interest are the names *Maidenhair* and *Mimas*. The first is a name taken by a lead female character as her sensitivity and awareness of the natural world increases while the second, *Mimas,* is the name of the giant redwood tree center to much of the novel's plot. These names challenge an imagined boundary between human and natural worlds, speak to the interconnectedness of human and nonhuman worlds, and contribute to the discursive production of trees as animate and agentive.

A second observation is the presence of twenty-one items referencing nature broadly and trees specifically. It is worth noting that *branch, branches,* and *leaves* have both a clear reference to a part of a tree and a second use as a verb. Though some of the instances in *The Overstory* are for the verbal use, the words appear on the list for they are key to *The Overstory* due to the increased use in relation to trees and forests. In the references to nature, the items are both general (*tree, trees, forest, forests*) and specific (*chestnut, mulberry, fir, redwood*). And finally, the balance of the list are thirteen verbs and several common nouns.

4.6.1 Animation and Agency of Trees

For any reader of *The Overstory,* the appearance of numerous lexical items on the keyness list which refer to trees generally as well as specific tree species is unsurprising. As is typical in fiction, the reader learns much of the family histories and lives of the central characters. However, in *The Overstory,* similarly detailed accounts are provided for trees in addition to humans, as they function in this text as central characters rather than narrative adornment. Trees are not passive scenery intended to provide a colorful backdrop for the foregrounded actions of human characters. Indeed, as Richard Powers comments in a 2018 interview, "This book is about taking the nonhuman world seriously. It is about realizing that we are not alone on this earth. And the rest of creation is not there simply to be a resource to us" (The Waterstones Interview). The narrative reflects this notion as it pairs the drama and unfolding events of the human characters with similarly rich and poignant narrative arcs of trees.

The comments from Powers regarding trees as agentive characters in the narrative raise relevant ecolinguistic questions. Indeed, in Halliday's seminal contribution to ecolinguistics (1991), he laments patterns of language which produce "a world made entirely of things" (p. 189) and observes that the grammar of English grants agency to entities along a continuum from most to least likely to initiate actions and events and various mental and verbal processes. Humans occupy the pole representing the most agentive with a typically inanimate nature placed at the opposite. As he writes, "the grammar does not present inanimate objects as doers" (p. 194). Of relevance for the present analysis is Halliday's elaboration that due to this feature of grammar, English users "have problems" with expressions such as "What's the forest doing?" As a dissonance is produced, Halliday speculates that the interlocutor is more likely to imagine and subsequently respond "Why is it there? Remove it!" than other options depicting an agentive forest through utterances such as, "it's holding water in store, it's cleaning the atmosphere, it's stopping flooding, it's stabilizing the soil, harbouring life forms and so on" (p. 194). Thus, as Halliday asserts, "language makes it hard for us to take seriously the notion of an inanimate nature as an agentive process" (p. 194). The question thus arises: in what roles do trees and forests function in Powers' text? Though the keyness analysis identifies *tree/s* and *forest/s* as salient, further analysis is necessary to more fully reveal the discursive production of trees and nature in the novel.

As Table 6 displays, the lexical item *tree* occurs 412 times, and with a BIC score greater than 1,000, it is the third most key word in the novel. To explore the depiction and characterization of *tree/s*, concordance and collocation analysis was performed. The most frequent verb appearing in a 3L-3R collocation window is the copula *is*. On the opening page of the novel, the very first of the 412 instances of *tree* occurs in the sentence: "The tree is saying things, in words before words." Though Powers only needs approximately fifty words before extending trees the agency to speak to and influence others, in the 1 billion word Corpus of Contemporary American English which spans nine registers of language use from fiction, academia, and speaking and numerous additional sub-registers, there is not one example which mirrors the same *tree is saying* phrasing.[2] It seems quite extraordinary—perhaps even surprising—that in 1 billion words of contemporary language use from 1990 to 2019 there is not one instance where a tree is discursively depicted in a similar manner. From this first instance on the opening page of the novel, the discursive production of *trees* and *forests* diverges from prevailing modern discourse.

The agency and animacy of the aforementioned sample persists throughout the novel in *tree + verb* patterns such as *tree + bulks, gives, changes, spreads, yields, contains, becomes, needs, oozes, arrives, chokes, saves, drops, makes, gets, looks, runs, becomes embarrassed, drugs a person, pounds, waves, listens, travels, buds, pips, feels, produces, flutters, bares, launches, learns, falls, materializes, billows,* and *rises*. While some of these verbs are collocates of *tree* in prevailing language use, there are many others which are typically not ascribed and licensed to trees. For instance, while a language user may be primed to utter phrases pairing *tree* with certain items (e.g., *tree + needs, drops, produces*), many other verbs such as *listens* (no instances in COCA), *arrives* (three instances in COCA, all related to decorating Christmas trees), *chokes* (no instances in COCA), *feels* (three instances in COCA but each conveys the sensation of a human feeling a tree) are paired with *tree*. Such frequent patterning construes *trees* as sensing and feeling in a manner typically reserved for humans and, to a lesser extent, nonhuman animals. It is not one *tree + verb* patterns that activates the agentive and animate force of trees, but rather the frequent appearance of *tree* with a diverse range of dynamic verbs. Holistically, the full balance of *tree + verb* functions to characterize *trees* as sentient, feeling, and agentive in a manner not typically observed in other domains of language use.

Similar patterning occurs with the plural form *trees* throughout the text as well (see Table 7) with patterns such as *trees + can, grow, save, want, sense, spread, talk, make, feed,* and more. The previous claims of the discursive production of *tree* are reflected in similar patterns with its plural form. Interestingly, several of the instances of trees quite closely advance these claims and highlight Hallidayan statements on animacy and agency. In these patterns, trees are animated as social beings embedded in complex communities.

Though the social lives of trees may be increasingly recognized by the scientific communities (see *The Hidden Life of Trees: What They Feel, How They*

Table 7 Verbal patterns with trees

trees feed and heal each other, trees feed their young, trees sense the presence of other nearby life, trees can sense an invasion, trees want something from her, trees used to talk to people, trees talk to each other, trees were talking to each other, trees send messages, trees send out alarms, trees send each other chemical warnings

Communicate—Discoveries from a Secret World [Wohlleben, 2015]), novels such as *The Overstory* animate them in a manner that perhaps resonates more deeply and more broadly. Such a discourse that produces a perception of trees as feeling, communicative, and social diverges from a dominant conceptualization which Powers' text challenges and which one lead human character in the book explicitly critiques:

> No one sees trees. We see fruit, we see nuts, we see wood, we see shade. We see ornaments or pretty fall foliage. Obstacles blocking the road or wrecking the ski slope. Dark, threatening places that must be cleared. We see branches about to crush our roof. We see a cash crop. But trees—trees are invisible.

Of additional interest are instances in which *tree* is present in agentive roles in patterns with a form of the verb *be*. In some of these patterns, *tree* is followed by the linking verb and a subject complement (see Table 8). These subject complements (e.g., *a passage, a wondrous thing, an infinite hotel, its own distant epic*) poetically convey and discursively construct the intrinsic value of trees. These patterns instantiate trees as worthy of reverence both across its full lifespan and beyond into their afterlife. These declarative patterns depict trees as passages, wondrous, ever present, epic, and complex. Such a discourse positively subverts language use that construes trees and forest as passive and inanimate resources made visible only for the ways in which they serve human by instead presenting trees as unequivocally beautiful and inherently valuable.

In a related pattern, the *be* verb serves as an auxiliary in a *be + progressive* verb pattern. For instance, samples 8 and 10 in Table 8 construe trees as breathing and speaking—not common representations in prevailing discourse—and thus able to affect human action while also being affected by action. Such instances further animate these central characters to the novel.

The nouns *forest* and *forest* similarly reflect how trees are discursively produced as animate and agentive in the novel as do many of the specific tree species the novel includes. Indeed, the reader learns a great deal about a wide range of tree species throughout the novel. From the chestnut tree standing in

Table 8 Concordance lines of tree

1. ... bed for his sister and throws it on the fire. A **tree** is a passage between earth and sky.
2. He finds the words in a book: A **tree** is a passage between earth and sky. He messes up
3. Above the ground, the **tree** is only a few hundred years old. But below, in
4. ... the Appich kids fight over whose **tree** is the most beautiful. They fight again when ...
5. She remembers the Buddha's words: A **tree** is a wondrous thing that shelters, feeds, and ...
6. The breakfast **tree** is budding too early. The snow is going to kill ...
7. "A dead **tree** is an infinite hotel." She tells him about the ...
8. ... no one intervenes. "Dad, stop! That cloth. The **tree** is choking. Its roots can't breathe."
9. "The losses we're incurring. Huge fines." "This **tree** is worth it." The next day ...
10. The **tree** is saying things, in words before words.
11. ... eye up close to the last ring. "The third **tree** is all around you: Now ..."
12. ... the **tree** is done with its century of unfolding, old chestnut words of extinct ...
13. "... that because you already know which **tree** is whose." Adam will preach the point to
14. Each new **tree** is its own distinct epic, changing the story of what is possible.
15. 'It's sometimes hard to say whether a **tree** is a single thing or whether it's a million."

the Hoel family's front yard for generations or the mulberry outside the Ma's breakfast window, trees are central characters intimately interconnected to their human counterparts throughout the novel. Yes, the frequent mention of trees would be noticed by likely any reader of the text—in other words, a reader of the text is not surprised by the numerous tree-related lexical items on the keyword list. However, it is the manner in which trees are made animate and agentive which may evade our notice as reader. It is these discursive patterns that bring trees to life for the reader and cultivate a greater awareness and appreciation of trees for their ecological importance.

4.7 Conclusion and Further Research

In the essay *The Trouble with Wilderness* (1996), William Cronon writes that our relationships with wilderness and the natural world constrain our ability to think and act in more ecologically responsible ways. He argues that we narrowly and harmfully imagine experiences with nature to be "limited to the remote corners of the planet" and to "pristine landscapes we ourselves do not inhabit" (1996, p. 24). In Cronon's view, the tree in our garden is "no less worthy of our wonder and respect than the tree in an ancient forest that has never known an ax or saw" (p. 24). Cronon challenges readers to shatter a false dichotomy that presents the trees in our yards, in our city parks, and in our neighborhoods as somehow "artificial" and "unnatural" while the trees beyond the horizon are imagined as "pristine and wild." The message of a complex, wondrous natural world to which we must awaken is shared by both Cronon and Powers. While Cronon's message is delivered concisely and explicitly in the form of an academic journal article, Powers' thesis is curated more covertly in the discursive patterns that present trees and forests as animate, agentive, complex, social, and deeply interconnected with their human relatives. Cronon presents a cogent and precise critique and challenge to notions of environmentalism in North America, but Powers moves his reader on a deeper emotional level to experience and be joyful in the presence of trees and the natural world. Set in an immediate and identifiable present, *The Overstory* cultivates a consciousness of interconnectivity between humans, trees, and the natural world that is beneficial for the achievement of more sustainable ways of being.

The corpus-assisted ecolinguistic approach detailed and briefly illustrated opens multiple avenues for an expanded ecolinguistics research agenda. Researchers in this space could explore discourses across the numerous genres of environmental writing employing a range of corpus analytic techniques. For example, though an introductory keyness analysis of lexical items was conducted here, a keyness analysis of semantic meanings and part of speech tags could affirm and/or extend the current analysis. Briefly, the meaning "plants" ranks as the second most key semantic annotation in a keyness analysis of semantic meaning in the text. The current analysis focused primarily on *tree* and *trees* but this evidence possibly indicates that many other plants are discursively made animate and agentive within the text. Thus, a semantic analysis may provide further evidence than offered in the brief analysis of the chapter.

Additionally, corpus-assisted ecolinguistic analyses in this domain could explore the other genres of environmental writing reviewed in the chapter. Such work could analyze changes in environmental writing diachronically or compare discursive depictions of nonhuman animals and the natural world. Research could also identify discourses underpinning the alternative futures frequently presented in climate crisis and speculative fiction, highlight beneficial discourses in these texts, and critique the discursive features judged as problematic. Perhaps most importantly, such analyses could expose superficially positive discourses that actually perpetuate attitudes, beliefs, and dispositions toward the environment that are unsustainable—such narratives may be critiqued for simply exporting the same social and economic constructs that have produced the present crisis into a new time period and fictional world. In one such project, Poole and Spangler (2020) expose problematic discourse practices within a popular digital simulation game, which on first appearance seems rather eco-friendly, and argue that the game construct perpetuates beliefs and attitudes regarding human dominion over the natural world.

Corpus-assisted ecolinguistics of literary texts opens a compelling research space and enables researchers to investigate both the overt and more covert stories which shape attitudes, perceptions, and actions toward the environment. As the earlier quotation noted, stories can change minds, and thus, it is necessary for ecolinguists to further understand how such stories can contribute to the creation of ecologically sustainable civilization.

5

Roving Beasts and Bolting Bovines: Wordplay in the Reporting of Animal Escapes

5.1 Introduction

It seems undeniably true that in the modern world humans have become far removed from the origins of their food and that the overwhelming majority of people will never actually have contact with the animals they consume beyond selecting a neatly plastic-wrapped chicken breast, porkchop, or steak from their local supermarket. This growing disconnect between humans and animals means "people's attitudes towards animal issues are consequently increasingly prone to manipulation through language" (Heuberger, 2003, p. 103). When humans have little experience with an issue, in this case the animal farming industry and animal welfare, media representations become a powerful site in the manufacturing of public perception (Freeman, 2016; Gitlin, 2003). As our interactions with nonhuman animals beyond our common animal companions continue to decrease, our perceptions and understandings of "the existence, interests, attributes, and treatment of animals relies less on empirical knowledge than it does on our existing beliefs and myths, built largely from children's stories and our exposure to farmed animals through the media" (Freeman, 2016, p. 169).

The food industry is quite cognizant of the role of language in media, advertising, corporate messaging, and elsewhere in shaping people's perceptions of and attitudes toward food and their industry's practices. In fact, it is not uncommon for the industry to pursue legal action or support lobbying efforts designed to shape language use in society. For example, the US dairy industry has attempted to limit and even disallow the use of the term *milk* for increasingly popular plant-derived milk substitutes such as almond milk, oat milk, soy milk, etc. Recently, the matter was even litigated in US Federal courts in the case of *Painter v. Blue Diamond* (2018). The case concerned whether Blue Diamond, a US-based food company, could label its almond milk product as "milk" or whether they should be required to instead state "imitation milk" on the label. Ultimately, the court rejected the appeal and Blue Diamond was permitted to continue using the term on its labels and in its advertisements (Axworthy, 2019). Similar litigation concerning plant-based meat substitutes is progressing, and farming industry groups have actively lobbied to make it illegal to use terms such as *meat* or *sausage* that are produced with plant-based ingredients (Popper, 2019). Both of these cases reflect the industry's recognition of the power of language for shaping the attitudes and beliefs and ultimately the purchasing and consumption habits of the general public.

Ecolinguistics has often critiqued language practices which shape attitudes and perpetuate ideologies that contribute to animal suffering and ecological degradation. Similarly, analysts have challenged practices which function to distance humans from the reality of animal exploitation and suffering, reinforce human–animal separation, commodify animals into economic outputs, and/or metaphorically represent animals as machines. This chapter continues this research agenda with its corpus-assisted study of wordplay in the reporting of animal escapes. In doing so, this chapter highlights a destructive discursive practice that trivializes animal welfare. Though a modicum of empathy and compassion would seemingly lead many to recognize the tragedy of these animal escape events that are interrogated in this illustration, popular news reporting makes light of the events through wordplays and framings that serve to produce a comedic and entertaining effect. The whimsical and humorous tone of the reporting minimizes, obscures, and ultimately erases these animals' suffering by realizing an incongruence between the reality of the event and the language selected in the accounts. For Martin (1993, p. 238), "A congruent relationship is one which the relationship between semantic and grammatical categories is natural: people, places, and things are realized nominally, actions are realized verbally"; therefore, "unnatural relationships are possible" as nominalizations realize actions in the form of nouns. The incongruence often present in the representations of nonhuman animals functions then to downplay and obscure the suffering of nonhuman animals entrapped in the factory farming industry while likewise distancing human consumers from the reality of their meat consumption practices.

The methodology illustrated in the present chapter is rather distinct from its companion illustrations elsewhere in the text for the node corpus is admittedly hardly a corpus at all. In fact, it is a rather small collection of texts reporting on the escapes of animals, primarily cows, from their impending deaths at slaughterhouses, though one article focuses on penguins fleeing a zoo in Denmark. Such a data-limited approach may seem counter intuitive and even antithetical to the corpus linguistic enterprise for at the heart of corpus linguistics is an affinity for large collections of language data through which various investigations of authentic language use may be pursued. Indeed, CADS partially emerged as a response to critiques of critical, qualitative approaches to discourse analysis for subjectively cherry-picking confirming texts to support *a priori* positions of the researcher. Perhaps some may critique this chapter for similarly narrow text selection practices; however, this chapter aims to illustrate how corpus analytic techniques can be implemented effectively in situations where the primary text/s under analysis is/are limited in size. A large corpus is generally preferred, but there are indeed instances where small, specialized corpora are appropriate for the research question under investigation. Online comments to newspaper articles, interviews of particular stakeholders on various issues, statements from corporations, speeches from climate crisis activists, and social media feeds from certain individuals or organizations are salient discursive spaces of ecolinguistic interest which may not be represented by copious data but which nevertheless may be fruitfully analyzed with CADS techniques.

In this analysis, the theoretical frameworks of lexical priming (Hoey, 2005) and framing (Lakoff, 2010) as well as corpus-assisted discourse analytic strategies from humor studies are implemented for the study of a small, specialized corpus. The subsequent discussion reviews research exploring representations of animals in a range of sites and then details how lexical priming and framing may be applied for corpus-assisted analysis of language use patterns in cases where a small corpus is under investigation. The approach illustrated in the present chapter offers a way forward for analysts seeking to enhance their analysis of important yet infrequent texts. Thus, this illustration interrogates representations of nonhuman animals in media, but it also illustrates a theory-driven, corpus-assisted approach for the analysis of small corpora of ecological relevance.

5.2 Representations of Nonhuman Animals

Retrospectives of the field of ecolinguistics uniformly identify Einar Haugen's *The Ecology of Language* (1972/2001) and Michael Halliday's *New Ways of Meaning: The Challenge to Applied Linguistics* (1990/2001) as foundational pillars in the field's development. While Haugen's work opened a domain of research not generally present in this text, Halliday's contribution is attributed with opening the critical discourse analytic strand of ecolinguistics from which this text emerges. Though Halliday's influence is undeniable, an earlier article, *Grammaticalizing Ecology: The Politics of Baby Seals and Kangaroos* (Martin, 1986), that investigated the function of grammatical metaphor and nominalization in texts from the Canadian Wildlife Federation (CWF) and the Australian Conservation Fund (ACF) should not be overlooked for it quite compellingly demonstrated how a linguistic feature can function in ecological discourse to represent animals in a problematic and destructive manner.

In the analysis, Martin analyzed grammatical metaphor in two texts: a CWF text discussing the killing of seals and one from ACF doing much the same but in regard to kangaroos. The analysis, grounded in systemic functional grammar, first displayed how the CWF text depicts seals as a resource to be managed through frequent framings primed by lexical items such as *harvest*, *take*, *hunt*, *limit*, *quota*, and *control*. Contrastingly, the Australian advocacy group portrays kangaroos as victims through rather oppositional lexical items than those deployed by the CWF text. Additionally, Martin argued how the use of nominalizations within the texts are incongruent with reality, as the linguistic feature transforms the processes and actions encoded in verbs into things and objects presented in nominals. He argues that nominals such as *slaughtering operation*, *killing methods*, and *killing techniques* erase the affected animal, "thereby immobilizing the most unsavory part of the seal hunt" (p. 43). As Martin asserted, this nominalization process influences the level of abstraction within the texts and produces a disconnect between the reality of the event and the grammatical structure which represents it. In other words, nominalizations function to obscure reality and provide distance between reader and event.

Following Martin, the sites in which ecolinguistic analyses of animal representation (and erasure) have been conducted have indeed been diverse. While the depictions of animals in texts such as those employed in Martin's study seem obvious locations for such work, one may not anticipate destructive, anthropomorphic language practices to be so readily observable in English-language dictionaries, encyclopedia, publication manuals, or style guides. Yet, these sites have traces of "destructive discourses [that] represent animals in ways that promote inhumane treatment" (Stibbe, 2012, p. 3). For example, Gilquin and Jacobs (2006) analyze the use of the relative pronoun "who" with animals in dictionaries, encyclopedias, grammar texts, publication manuals, and style guides with an additional focus on the stated policies of the pronoun's use in the resources. They note that five of the nine dictionaries reviewed stipulated that "who" is not to be used for animals, eight of thirteen grammar texts instruct readers that "who" similarly should not be used in these contexts, and nine newspapers and news services advise that the relative pronoun should be limited to situations where the animal's sex is known or the animal has a name.

In a similar study, Hueberger observed "a striking tendency to emphasize anthropocentric features within the definitions" of numerous species in English-language dictionaries (2003, p. 95). In the analysis, he displayed how dictionaries define animals primarily by their perceived usefulness to humans. In numerous entries in the dictionaries, animals are not defined in an objective and scientific manner but rather for subjective, anthropocentric qualities such as taste and edibility. Evidence of such tendencies is pervasive with countless animals presented not by their "phenotypical characteristics" but for the benefit that humans extract from them (p. 97). On such anthropomorphic language practices, Hueberger writes that the prevailing modern view imagines animals to be "renewable resources for nutrition, clothing, experimentation, and labour" and that anthropocentric language practices perpetuate "pain, suffering, and deprivation" (p. 94).

Representations of animals as produced in common idioms, metaphors, and euphemisms have also been critiqued to display the pervasiveness of speciesism—a bias against members of other animal species—in English-language use. For Smith-Harris (2004), the prevalence of cruel and violent idioms, metaphors, and euphemisms "indicate that there is a societal permissiveness to implied cruelty towards nonhuman animals" (p. 12). While she comments that language is not immediately culpable for violence and abuse of animals, language functions as "an important tool in the social construction of permissive societal attitudes towards such treatment of animals; allowing humans to accept the normalness of having control over other animals, including cruelty and the ability to inflict violence" (p. 12). Many of these phrases, e.g., "there's more than one way to skin a cat," "kill two birds with one stone," "beat a dead horse," and "like a chicken with its head cut off," describe, trivialize, and essentially condone the violent treatment of animals. Stibbe (2012) provides an extensive list of idioms that incorporate notions of animal cruelty and observes that "the closer the relation of dominance of a particular species by humans, the more negative the stereotypes contained in the idioms" (p. 24). Stibbe further critiques the common discursive practice in which the individuality of animals is erased through the use of noncount rather than count nouns, thereby perpetuating an ideology that views individual animals as "just a replaceable representative of a category" (p. 24).

Several studies have explored representations of animals in popular media. Jepson (2008) investigated the terms used to refer to the killing of nonhuman animals through a comparison to related terms employed in the cases of the killing of humans. At the heart of the study is an attempt to answer how humans frame the killing of animals in a manner that feels "less objectionable" and that functions to mitigate feelings of remorse and discomfort (p. 129). In the study, Jepson compares the use of terms used in the context of the killing of animals (*euthanize, put to sleep, destroy,* and *slaughter*) with common terms used for killing of humans (*euthanize, execute, murder, slaughter*). In the context of human killing, the terms are rather specific and "carry large amounts of information about various aspects of the context for the killing" (p. 136) while contrastingly, the terms for animal killing are largely interchangeable, "carrying little information about the agent, the reason for the killing, the patient, or the speaker's attitudes" (p. 137). To explore one term in particular, *euthanize* in cases of animals occurs in contexts of research purposes, overpopulation, perceptions of danger, and disease prevention yet it has a highly specific and constrained meaning when used with humans. And while much information is related about the human experience, very little, if any, is present for animals. Similar verbal patterns were noted in Argentina's Pet Responsibility Act (Forte, 2015) as verbal phrases such as "practicing euthanasia" created ambiguity of agent, patient, and the act itself.

In a study briefly discussed in Chapter 2, Goatly (2002) analyzed depictions of animals on the BBC World Radio Service. In the article, he asserted that grammar functions on a subconscious level and therefore is more likely to "convey latent ideology"—a claim to which other studies in this space implicitly align (p. 5). In the study, he analyzed the concordance lines of various categories of animals (insects, birds, land animals, aquatic animals) and other lexical items from nature (water, land and landscape, weather, disease), classifying the role of each in the concordance lines (e.g., actor in transitive clause, actor in an intransitive, affected, prepositional complement, premodifier). He concluded that on the BBC there are "frames of consistency" as to how nature is represented while noting that the BBC consistently presents nature as acted upon rather than actor (p. 20). Nature is typically only presented as having agency when viewed as a threat to human life, e.g., disease, earthquakes. With echoes of Whorfianism, Goatly argues that language "predisposes us to perceive, think, and act in certain ways, and makes it more difficult to perceive and think in alternative ways" (p. 2). Thus, the consistency of these discursive representations effects cognition and how individuals perceive and think about nature and animals.

Perhaps the most comprehensive of analyses of media is Freeman's analysis of greater than 100 news articles from major US news outlets such as the *New York Times*, finding that the majority of articles reproduce speciesism through their objectification of farmed animals. Consistently, the articles failed to engage with the ethics of the factory farming system, erased the farmed animals' individual identities, and commonly referred to animals as commodities. For example, nonhuman animals were not referred to as cow, pig, bird, etc. but rather as their "end purpose" as pork, poultry, veal calves, amongst others. Additionally, the commodification is reinforced in frequent treatment of the monetary value to be lost due to epidemics such as Mad Cow disease. Anecdotally, similar practice was prevalent in US media during the COVID-19 pandemic. For example, in a statement published in several major US newspapers from Tyson Foods, a major US food corporation and self-proclaimed "protein-based food company," the company states, "Millions of animals—chickens, pigs, and cattle—will be depopulated because of the closure of our processing facilities," "millions of pounds of meat will disappear from the supply chain," and farmers "will not have anywhere to sell their livestock to be processed." The economic commodification of these animals and their deaths euphemized and thereby obscured in lexical items *depopulated* and *processed* is immediately clear.

A Freeman-like analysis of the discursive treatment of animals in popular media was also the topic of Khazaal and Almiron's study (2016) comparing the discursive treatment of animals in articles from the US-based *New York Times* and the Spain-based news outlet *El Pais*. The authors contend that both publications conceal the "cruel reality" or animal conditions (p. 1). They critique the practices of the *New York Times* as particularly deceptive, projecting an "ethical façade" while camouflaging pervasive speciesism (p. 9). These linguistic practices of the two publications reinforce and perpetuate "nonhuman oppression by perpetuating speciesism" (p. 14). In alignment with other research, they critiqued devices that served to commodify nonhumans while likewise obscuring animal suffering and erasing individuality. Beyond their critiques, they also identify "hopeful signs" and the possibility of "a more responsible journalism" (p. 15) by calling upon journalists to engage with animal well-being in a manner that is not tethered to human interests while also challenging journalists to refrain from presenting the farming industry in such "happy, promotional pieces" (p. 15).

Actual textual products of the animal farming industry have also been explored. In one such study, Glenn (2004) highlighted the frequency with which farmed animals are euphemized as objects and commodities through labels such as *inventory* and by referencing animals as *beef* instead of *cows*. Stibbe (2012) captures the range of studies in this space and their general findings in the opening pages to *Animals Erased*:

> Animal industry discourses use the pronoun *it* to refer to animals, use expressions that represent animals as machines, use the passive to hide the agent of killing, and use a range of other features that combine together to model a world where animals are constructed as objects.
>
> (p. 5)

Stibbe then proceeds to document instances of these practices in farming industry texts. In one cluster of examples, he demonstrates a destructive discourse that frames animals as resources. He notes such samples as "bird damage" for the substitution of damage for injury—products get damaged, beings are injured—metonymies such as broilers, breeders, and beef that name animals for cooking method, function, and flesh which serve to deprive the animals of agency and by doing so make their oppression seem natural and normal. And again, in pork industry discourse, pigs are represented for their function as nursery pig, grower pig, feeder pig, etc. Additionally, the metaphor "pig as machine" is frequent and salient: "boars remain structurally sound," "boar power," "pigs suppress eating and increase water intake," "sow breakdown." In these samples, pigs are metaphorically reconceptualized as machines and inanimate objects. Stibbe contends as animals "are represented as objects or machines, and their health and lives are defined narrowly in terms of profitability, then this both justifies and provides a blueprint for a system of farming that is both inhumane and environmentally destructive" (p. 46).

These studies provide keen insights into the varying depictions of animals in a range of texts and discourse spaces. Though this chapter's illustration diverges in some regards, this study also observes and critiques language use which serves to minimize animal suffering and diffuse the emotional weight of such suffering for consumers. The following section provides a brief overview of the two theoretical frameworks that are integrated and applied in this study.

5.3 Lexical Priming and Framing

In debates of corpus linguistics as theory or method, the proponents of corpus linguistics as a theory-driven endeavor are supported by the theory of lexical priming (Hoey, 2005). Priming is a "psycholinguistic phenomenon whereby speakers have been observed to understand a given word more quickly if it is presented immediately after a semantically related word, rather than an unrelated word" (McEnery & Hardie, 2012, p. 145). Lexical priming, thus, becomes a way for understanding how individuals both acquire and use language. Priming creates efficiency in processing for language users as the presence of one lexical item activates, i.e., primes, in the mind of the individual the increased probability of subsequent lexical items and grammatical features. In essence, the presence of one lexical item narrows a user's number of possible selections from the language system. Rather than selecting each word in succession from a full system of language, the presence of one word can be viewed as easing the selection process. As Hoey originally forwarded, collocational patterns, thus, are due to the fact that all words are attached their own complex of primings, and thus, collocation—discussed in detail in Chapter 3—can thus be viewed as textual evidence of priming and corpora then may be imagined as "the repository of and evidence for writers' and speakers' acquired language primings" (Partington, 6).

The framework of lexical priming has been applied in humor studies for it provides insight into the comedic effect of various forms of wordplay. As noted by Skalicky (2018), when a language user deviates from conventional language primings, the "incongruity" of the divergent pattern may produce a humorous effect (p. 584). In essence, listeners and readers, based on their lifetimes of language experience, are primed to anticipate certain linguistic patterns. When the conventionalized pattern is not produced, the unexpectedness of the transgression generates a dissonance which, in certain contexts, results in a comedic effect. This incongruity between a listener/reader's expectation and the actual speaker/writer's language output has been offered as an explanation for how humor is produced and understood (Skalicky, 2018). Goatly suggests that the "unexpectedness essential to jokes" can be understood through the "overriding of primings of collocations, semantic set associations, grammatical functions, textual semantic association and grammatical category association" (2017, p. 52). Though incongruity and unpredictability may be produced through various means, the transgression or "the canceling" (Goatly, 2017) of conventionalized primings, as operationalized in corpus-assisted studies of humor, can explain the humorous effect of jokes, puns, and other forms of wordplay.

Lexical priming, as it has been developed within corpus linguistics, shares characteristics with framing (Lakoff, 2010) developed within cognitive sciences and applied within ecolinguistics (Stibbe, 2015). As noted, priming is not restricted to lexical items but extends to grammatical structures commonly used in contexts with a word as well as the semantic associations and evaluations invoked. A lexical item primes more than simply the subsequent words in the utterance—the priming also activates information about semantic associations and textual contexts. In this sense, priming can be understood similarly to framing (Lakoff, 2010). For Lakoff, humans "think in terms of typically unconscious structures"; in other words, humans apply frames of "semantic roles, relations between roles, and relations to other frames" (p. 71). For example, if an utterance begins, "The doctor...," the listener activates frames of hospitals, doctors, nurses, medicines, etc. Thus, frames, activated by the use of a particular "trigger words" (Stibbe, 2015, p. 47), prime a reader/listener to structure and conceptualize one domain of experience through the frame of another domain. Stibbe (2015) investigates the varied framings of "development" and displays how frames such as "sustainable development" have been appropriated by powerful nations to legitimize and maximize continued economic growth.

This chapter focuses upon wordplay within the reporting of animal escape events and is informed by lexical priming and framing. Puns are a clear form of wordplay which, when produced and integrated effectively into language use, often produce a humorous and/or entertaining effect. However, the frames activated by certain lexical choices may not seem to immediately share such a function, yet this analysis demonstrates how the deployment of certain lexical features within these articles functions as a form of wordplay through their deliberate framing of these events through frames imported from other domains of experience. In total, these frames contribute to the humorous and entertaining characteristic of these articles by imposing one domain of experience upon a second target domain. When these features cluster together, they function to trivialize the suffering of nonhuman animals as their experiences are manufactured into comedy and entertainment.

5.4 Method and Corpus

This case study aims to demonstrate how various linguistic features present in the reporting of animal escapes function to minimize the suffering of the nonhuman animal protagonists in these accounts. The analysis critiques media treatment of nonhuman animals and illustrates yet another discursive space in which the suffering of animals is minimized and/or erased to seemingly diffuse the discomfort readers may experience. The analysis is primarily grounded in the theory of Lexical Priming as previously applied in humor studies and is also informed by frames and framing (Lakoff, 2010).

In a manner reflective of Goatly (2017) and Skalicky (2018), this analysis compiles a small corpus of texts in which salient features are identified and subsequently compared to their frequency, function, and contexts of use in large reference corpora: the 1.0 billion word Corpus of Contemporary American English (COCA) and the greater than 12 billion word News on the Web (NOW) Corpus. The use of reference corpora makes possible both quantitative and qualitative comparative analyses to demonstrate how certain features in the texts transgress conventional language patterns while other features activate frames from other domains. Thus, this illustration reveals how subverting common lexical primings and/or activating frames from other discursive spaces creates the humorous and entertaining tone of these accounts.

As briefly mentioned previously, the approach for this illustration diverges from others presented elsewhere in this text. This study is informed by corpus-assisted humor studies which similarly employ rather small corpora due to constraints on the collection of humorous language. For instance, Bucaria (2004) created a corpus of 135 newspaper headlines to explore lexical and syntactic ambiguity as a source of humor. However, Skalicky (2018) studied only three headlines from the satirical outlet *The Onion* while Goatly analyzed fewer than ten jokes. In other chapters, the analysis is advanced through the creation of somewhat large, specialized corpora: nearly 1 million words for the geographical text analysis and several hundred thousand words for the corpus-assisted eco-stylistic analysis of *The Overstory*. There is also the diachronic analysis of *wilderness* in the nearly one half billion-word COHA. However, the creation of a large corpus for this chapter's illustration is not possible. Animal escapes are not particularly common, and when they do occur, they do so without broad media treatment; the escapes discussed in this chapter attracted attention because they occurred in large metropolitan areas.

The corpus for this analysis is rather small—it is approximately 5,000 words. Indeed, a larger corpus is preferable—this is not disputed—but there are instances where the creation of a large corpus may not be possible. For instance, one may wish to analyze the social media posts or press releases from a particular corporation or in reference to a particular event or hashtag to critique practices of greenwashing. It is unlikely such texts when compiled would yield a sizable corpus. Similarly, Greta Thunberg's 2019 speech to the United Nations Climate Summit could be explored for beneficial discursive practices. Though fewer than 500 words in length, it is perhaps one of the more salient and influential texts of the climate crisis movement. It could be similarly valuable to explore the texts of climate crisis activists from indigenous communities such as Autumn Peltier, Thomas Lopez, Zeena Abdulkarim, or Militza Flaco. Certainly, qualitative critical discourse analytic approaches can be productively applied in these cases, but CADS techniques can supplement and add value to the analyses of such texts. This chapter aims to illustrate the value CADS may be implemented in such data-limited situations. However, this is not intended as an argument for the use of small corpora broadly, but rather an affirmation that in certain contexts and for particular research questions, the analysis of a small corpus with CADS measures can yield valuable insights.

Goatly (2017) and Skalicky (2018) are particularly relevant to the approach and design of the present study. In the former, Goatly operationalizes lexical priming in the analysis of the "incongruity, unpredictability, and ambiguity" (p. 52) present in the humor of only eight jokes. To assess these qualities, Goatly used the CoBuild Bank of English to illustrate how linguistic patterns of the jokes override conventionalized patterns as demonstrated in the collocational data of the reference corpus. In the latter, Skalicky explored only three phrases embedded within three headlines—each of which produces humor through the unexpectedness of its use. For example, the analysis displays the most frequent collocates for the phrase *death toll* to demonstrate how the conventional primings and associations of the phrase are transgressed in the headline, thus producing the satirical, humorous effect. In other words, the phrase when used in the headline does not align with its frequent uses in the multi-million word COCA. Thus, the "violation of primings" provides the reader/listener a signal to reach a satirical and humorous interpretation (p. 600).

The primary texts are sourced from a range of publication outlets from national US publications such as *USA Today* and the *New York Times*, local outlets such as *The New York Daily News* and the New York affiliate of the National Broadcasting Company (NBC), and online magazines such as *Zenger* and *Atlas Obscura* (see Table 9). The article from *Vegan Life* is also included for though it includes some of the destructive practices critiqued, it also produces a beneficial discourse that more accurately represents the nonhuman animals in these events and engages with animal welfare and rights—this counter discourse present in the *Vegan Life* article will be discussed. Finally, it should be noted that the articles were not sourced through a systematic process. In fact, several of the articles were collected for use in a classroom activity designed to enhance students' critical language awareness; additional articles were added over time. The eight articles comprising the corpus are listed in Table 9.

Table 9 Corpus of nonhuman animal escape articles

1. Bowerman, S. Group of penguins attempt escape at Denmark zoo. (November 17, 2015). *USA Today*.
2. Burrows, T. (January, 22, 2016). On the moove! Astonishing moment a runaway cow canters through the streets of New York. *Mail Online*.
3. Giamo, C. (July 22, 2015). Emily the cow ran away from the slaughterhouse and became a star. *Atlas Obscura*.
4. Sandoval, E. & Tracy, T. (February 21, 2017). Bull that escaped slaughterhouse dies after being tranquilized in Queens backyard. *The New York Daily News*.
5. Rogue bull at center of wild Queens chase dies hours after capture. (February 21, 2017). *NBC of New York*.
6. Stack, L. (March 19, 2019). Slaughter-bound calf escapes on expressway, earning new name and life of leisure. *New York Times*.
7. Crafty cow hides out in the woods after escaping slaughter. (March 3, 2020). *Vegan Life*.
8. King, J. (January 13, 2021). Moo-ving on: Cow escapes slaughterhouse, gets gift of life. *Zenger*.

5.5 Findings and Discussion

5.5.1 Puns

The first feature to be critiqued for contributing to the entertainment quality of these accounts is the pun. An often-cited definition for this type of wordplay describes puns as the "bisociation of a single phonetic form with two meanings—two strings of thought tied together by an acoustic knot" (Koestler, 1964, p. 65, as cited in Partington, 2006). In Partington's *Linguistics of Laughter* (2006), he uses the following example to demonstrate an exact pun—a pun that draws upon homonymy or homophony to produce the bisociative quality.

"Do you believe in clubs for young people?"
"Only when kindness fails."

In this sample, the pun is produced by the varied meanings of the homonym *club*. As Partington describes, the preferred reading of *clubs* as associations for young people must be reinterpreted to the secondary meaning of *heavy instrument used as a weapon* by the response. Though puns may produce a comedic effect, humor is not always manifested. However, the wordplay does at minimum elicit the attentional focus of the listener/reader, and in the instances subsequently discussed, likely distracting readers from the tragedy at the heart of these events.

Several puns are present in the articles, but those appearing in the headlines seem a logical place to begin the discussion. In two articles' headlines, the wordplay "mooving" is used; the additional letter -*o*- in the spelling enables the onomatopoeia of the vocalization of a cow while also capturing the meaning of movement of the escaped animal. There are approximately forty instances of this particular pun in the NOW Corpus with the most recent sample "Mooving in: Kansas family welcomes calf as one of their own." Many of the instances of the "mooving" pun occur in contexts discussing cows, though most are largely mundane, perhaps even heartwarming, rather than tragic as is the case with the events reported here. In the COCA, "mooving" is less common and several of the fewer than ten instances seem misspellings or errors in the data rather than plays on words. However, these cow-related puns are attested on *National Geographic Kids* and the *Big Brother* reality show, reflecting the playful nature of the pun and its use in entertainment contexts. These puns immediately present in headlines initiate the comical effect of the articles. While the *move/mooving* pun occurs twice in the headlines, it also reappears multiple times in the main texts.

Beyond the headlines, puns appear often in these articles and are perhaps the most salient feature contributing to the playful tone and entertaining quality of the texts. In the opening paragraph of the *New York Daily News* text, the article states that the escaped bull "died after getting into a beef with cops who shot him up." The pun at the heart of the passage plays with the idiomatic meaning of *get in a beef* as having an argument or conflict coupled with the additional framing of cow for its end product for human consumption. In the COCA, the idiom *[get] in a beef*[1] is present only seventeen times and is largely constrained to popular US television crime dramas such as *Law & Order*, *CSI:Miami*, and *Hawaii Five-O*. In all of these instances in the COCA, the idiom appears in contexts where a witness explains how two individuals had an argument prior to a murder or other serious crime. The pun creates its light-hearted, comedic effect through its manipulation of meanings connecting cow, beef, and argument. The pun also frames the event as criminal, thus simultaneously representing the cow as subject of comedy but also as criminal and perhaps deserving of punishment. Indeed, the reporting becomes somewhat farcical and cartoonish with the pun mitigating any potential emotional impact the bull's death may have on the reader.

Similar creative puns are present in the following sentences: "The roving beast steaked its claim to the Queens neighborhood" and "Police shouted at neighbors to steer clear." In the former, the idiom "stake a claim" is manipulated to create the pun "steak a claim." A search of COCA reveals approximately half of the 1,100 instances of *stake* as a verb appear in variations of this phrase, e.g., *stake a claim, staked his claim, stake their claim*. Thus, the pun draws upon a somewhat commonly used idiomatic phrase meaning to claim and establish ownership rights. The wordplay here facilitates a humorous and entertaining reading by employing its homophone *steak* in reference to the end product of the slaughtered animal. Indeed, this pun is rather novel as there is not one instance of it in the one-billion word COCA or the greater than 12 billion word NOW corpus. Thus, the pun subverts primed expectations, thereby drawing reader's attention to the cleverness of the wordplay rather than the suffering of the animal. In the latter, the homonym *steer* and its meanings of to avoid or keep away in addition to male cow produce the comedic relief as the interplay activates the more common usage but also delivers the secondary meaning. These uses of *stake/steak* and *steer* for the puns exploit the homonymy of these lexical items to form exact puns—the use of only one sound sequence in the bisociative use of a word creates an exact pun. These subtle, creative wordplays construe a serious event as entertainment and comedy, creating a sort of cartoon-like playfulness to the event that draws the attention of the reader to the comedic puns rather than the tragic nature of the event.

5.5.2 Reference

The manner in which the nonhuman animals are mentioned and modified in the articles contributes to the distancing of reader from event. In one article, the headline reads "Crafty cow hides out …" while a second offers "Rogue bull at center of wild chase …." The alliteration of "crafty cow" produces a playful tone, but when coupled with "hides out," the pattern activates a frame of an escaped human prisoner or criminal. In the COCA, the most common collocates with *[hide] out* are the nouns *place, somewhere, sight, woods, garage, cave, basement*, and *compound*, and review of the concordance lines reveals a frequent contextual association of a person evading capture from law enforcement. Also collocating with instances of the phrasal verb *[hide] out* are lexical items *cops, fugitive, gangsters, thieves,* and *killers*. Thus, the phrasal verb draws upon a meaning typically used in contexts of crimes and criminals to frame the animal as criminal—such a framing would seemingly lessen the emotional impact of the animal's death. In other words, the escaped animal is not depicted and perceived as an innocent and harmless sentient being fleeing its own death but rather as guilty, even dangerous, and deserving of a justifiable punishment.

The pairing "rogue bull" is again not a common one. As previously argued, these discursive framings of cows as criminals contribute to the entertaining quality of these articles. In this instance, the adjective *rogue* typically collocates with nominals such as *nation, regime, agent, cop, terrorist, spy, pirate,* and *thief*—thus, the framing produced by the pairing positions the animal as not conforming to certain social and legal constructs or expectations. In a sense, the animal has become an outlaw operating beyond the expectations of law-abiding society. The headline continues with *wild chase* to further strengthen the crime and criminal frame applied to the nonhuman animal. This pairing of *rogue bull* with *wild chase* construes the cow with a negative semantic prosody as frequent collocates of *chase* in COCA and NOW are *police, cop, suspect,* and *criminal*. These pairings depict the escaped animals as clever and cunning, erratic and dangerous, and criminals and escaped prisoners. Once this framing is sedimented, the discomfort and objection of the reader that could likely be prompted by the animals' deaths is likely lessened. Rather than engaging with the accounts from a position of compassion or from a concern of animal welfare, the articles take the form of farce and comedy to be consumed as entertainment rather than news.

Similar sorts of *crafty cow* and *rogue bull* referential pairings are present throughout these articles. In the *New York Daily News* alone, the cow is referred to as *raging bull, black bovine,* and *bolting bovine*. The first pairing, *raging bull,* primes the entertainment feel of the article as it references a popular US film of the 1980s and its main character—a troubled, aging professional boxer. In fact, two articles explicitly connect the events to movies: the *New York Times* describes the event as "like the movie *Chicken Run*" while *USA Today* similarly describes an event as "similar to a scene from the movie *Penguins of Madagascar*." The latter two references employ the wordplay device of alliteration—the repetition of the initial sound or letter in adjacent word—perhaps most associated with literature and poetry.

An additional reference to the escaped cow as *roving beast* is clearly negative in its semantic association. The adjective *roving* primes strongly the nouns *eye, band, gang,* and *pack*. Inspection of concordance lines of these terms, e.g., *roving eye, roving band/gang/pack*, reveals the consistently negative contexts in which these pairs occur. For *roving eye*, the context is most typically in reference to the gaze of an unfaithful, adulterous male. In the other common collocates of *roving*, a concordance line analysis reveals frequent associations of *danger, drugs,* and *crime*. For example, the lexical item *gang* most commonly appears with *drug/s, violence, rape, crime,* and *prison*, amongst other similarly negative pairings. *Beast* produces a similar negative loading as the nominal co-occurs with adjectives *wild, savage,* and *strange*. Thus, the pairing *roving beast* primes a network of meanings that are rather negatively loaded. It seems reasonable to conclude that these features minimize the emotional impact of the animals' ultimate outcomes. In other words, as the animal is represented as a *roving beast*, it only seems rational that the animal would be killed. The framings enabled by the premodifying adjective and the subsequent referent are frequent and functional in the texts. Other references to the escaped cow include *mischievous bovine* and *fugitive cow*, but perhaps the most creative is the phrase *Holstein Houdini*, a playful alliteration framing the cow as a magician.

5.5.3 Framing

Repeatedly throughout the texts allusions to the criminal justice system are manifested through lexical choices most frequently used within and associated with legal settings. Most notably, and as previously mentioned, the animals in the texts are discursively framed as criminals; one article even begins with the exclamation "Jailbreak!" in reporting of a group of penguins attempting to escape a zoo in Denmark. Interestingly, the allusions to the criminal justice system partially recognize and affirm the reality of the situations from which these animals are so desperately fleeing. Yet, this realization to the conditions of their existence remains only a rhetorical ploy and not a journalistic focus. The following table lists the lexical items and phrases that contribute to the animal-as-criminal framing in the various articles.

The words and phrases present in the articles and listed in Table 10 construe these nonhuman animals as criminals by activating contexts and meanings commonly present in legal contexts. Though numerous items contribute to this framing, several items are of particular interest for they typically appear quite narrowly in contexts of crime. For example, the items *at large*, *on the loose*, and *on the lam* consistently collocate with terms that prime meanings from the legal system. Additionally, though *at large* has one meaning of *in general/generally* as reflected in the common pairings *society/public/world + at large*, the idiomatic phrasing in these instances is used in instances where a criminal that has escaped has eluded capture by police. When looking specifically at the phrase "remains at large," the bundle overwhelmingly occurs in contexts where an individual accused of a crime has evaded apprehension. Such individuals include *attackers*, *murderers*, and *killers*—these are the nominals often preceding the phrase. Often occurring in these slots are the actual proper nouns of humans accused of murder, assaults, and other serious crimes. The idiomatic phrase *on the lam* in the COCA seems uniformly constrained to contexts of criminals and gangsters. In sample after sample in the COCA, the idiom appears in concordance lines where a criminal figure is trying to escape capture. The collocations in the COCA for the phrase reflect this criminal context; common phrasings include *fugitive + on the lam, criminals + on the lam, convicts + on the lam, thieves + on the lam*.

Another item on the list is the verb *apprehend*. In the COCA, there are nearly 3,000 instances of variants of [apprehend] with approximately 800 occurring in passive constructions where something or someone was apprehended. In the NOW Corpus, the verb occurs nearly 70,000 times and again largely in contexts of crime and criminals—several of the top collocates in NOW are *police, suspects*, and *criminals*. In the COCA, the first of its noun collocates is *border*, referring to the place of apprehension (e.g., at the border) or to whom completed the action (e.g., the Border Patrol). Other groups responsible for the action are also frequent on the list: *police, authorities, officers, agents, security, officials*. Relatedly, the person or persons apprehended (*suspect, suspects, criminals, killer, terrorists*) collocate with the verb:

The activation of meanings from crime and legal settings is also reflected in the phrase *into custody* and *fugitive*. In the NOW Corpus, the phrase associates consistently with lexical items reflective of law enforcement contexts. For example, the top collocates with the phrase *into custody* are *police, incident, man, suspect, officers, authorities, charges*, and so on. In the list of 100 noun collocates, the items seem uniformly related to such criminal justice settings. Indeed, the textual context of the many concordance lines of *into custody* is easily repaired into a sort of exemplar structure using the previously listed common collocates: *A suspect/man was taken into custody by police/officers/ authorities*. The framing is similarly furthered by the use of *fugitive*. As evident by its common collocates provided in the table, it loads a similar complex of meanings from law enforcement settings.

These words and phrases displayed in the table cluster to construe these events of animal escapes in a manner quite similar to human beings accused and/or convicted of crimes who are now evading capture by law enforcement

Table 10 Framings

Activating word or phrase	Frequency	Common collocates in the Corpus of Contemporary American English
escape/escapes/escaped/ escaping	37	nouns: prison, notice, attempt, prisoner adjectives: unscathed, unable, desperate, unharmed verbs: try, manage, attempt, flee

police	17	nouns: officer, department, chief, force adjectives: local, military, secret, chief verbs: arrest, report, state, investigate
give chase/wild chase	12	nouns: car, dream, dog, police adjectives: high-speed, elusive, foul, fleeing verbs: flee, storm, romps, instigate
into custody	9	nouns: child, police, battle, case, suspect adjectives: protective, joint, full, federal verbs: take, release, remain, fight
footage	5	nouns: video, camera, file, security, surveillance verbs: show, shoot, watch, release
fled	4	nouns: country, scene, refugees, homes, violence, suspect adjectives: neighboring, Nazi, nearby, empty-handed, frightened, abusive, terrified verbs: leaving, escape, abandoned, escaped adverbs: shortly, reportedly, abroad, allegedly
Fugitive	4	nouns: slave, justice, law, act adjectives: wanted, federal, dangerous, violent verbs: harbor, hide, capture, arrest
on the loose	4	nouns: killer, serial killer, murderer, rapist, shooter, maniac, gunman, killers, monster, psycho, suspect, madman, fugitive, predator
apprehended	2	nouns: police, border, suspect, criminals adjectives: illegal, responsible, dangerous, suspected, violent verbs: charged, attempting, detain, arrested
at large	2	nouns: society, public, world, community, suspects, killer, suspect, shooter verbs: remains, remain, remained
on the lam	1	nouns: years, life, fugitive, months verbs: went, remained, spent

officers. This discursive treatment conflates cows fleeing slaughter with humans convicted of crimes. This framing erases the conditions from which these cows are fleeing and provides justification for the common outcome of these events—the death of the animal.

5.5.4 An Alternative Discourse

The article from *Vegan Life* presents an alternative representation of nonhuman animals and a more objective treatment of the conditions experienced by animals entrapped in the factory farming industry. First, it is the one article that depicts an animal as having and demonstrating the capacity for perception and feeling through the use of the lexical item *sentient*. While the balance of articles playfully and problematically treats the animals as dangerous criminals, *Vegan Life* reporting recognizes cows as sensing, feeling, knowing beings. In the COCA, *sentient* commonly collocates with terms such as *intelligent*, *capable*, *conscious*, and most importantly, *suffering*. Of the many semantic framings previously critiqued, here lies one of the few beneficial and worthy of promotion. If a cow is recognized as sentient, then one may then connect nonhuman animals within this system as sensitive to and aware of the suffering which they experience. This discourse, thus, represents nonhuman animals as agentive and as having a complex of feelings and emotions, thereby opening space for a discourse of animal rights. And as the closing line of the article forwards, by recognizing and valuing nonhuman animals as sentient, we are increasingly likely to reduce consumption and help "break the system that exploits them." Thus, framing as sentient is meaningful and potentially impactful.

This quality of sentience extended to this animal is reflected elsewhere in the article. For example, one sentence of the article states, "He no longer has to fear slaughter or harm from humans." This sentence represents a cow as an emotional being able to experience fear, uses a personal pronoun rather an impersonal *it* often used elsewhere (approximately half of all instances of *it* in the articles are in reference to an animal), and syntactically positions the cow as having the capacity to sense and feel fear. The author writes that animals "want to live" and that they "deserve the right to life." There are no similar affirmations found elsewhere in these articles, and in the top 100 collocates of "right to life," there is not one item on the list that attaches right to life with animals. This representation of animals as sentient with the right to life beyond their conditions of abuse in the factory farming system counters the discursive framing elsewhere in the articles. Though limited, these positive practices are worthy of promotion.

5.6 Conclusion and Further Research

The corpus-assisted analysis of the present chapter displays how wordplay of various sorts operates within these articles to trivialize escape events and thus minimize the suffering of animals. The wordplays and framings in the reporting manifest a playful, entertaining, often comedic tone that produces an incongruence between the harsh reality of these events and the language used to report them. The articles, with the exception of *Vegan Life*, failed to engage with the ethics of the factory farming system. These articles and the playful language they employ function to frame these events in a manner that makes the treatment of these animals less objectionable and less emotionally impactful while also reflecting and perpetuating the permissive societal attitudes toward animal cruelty and suffering. As concern for animal welfare is obscured in favor of entertainment, readers are released to accept the treatment as natural and normal. This illustration demonstrates yet another in a list of discursive spaces where anthropocentrism and speciesism are normalized and perpetuated.

In his critique of farming practices, Stibbe writes that "the mass confinement and slaughter of animals in intensive farms depend on the implicit consent of the population" (2001, p. 145). This consent is manufactured and maintained through language use of the sort present in these articles that obscures and erases animal suffering in order to diffuse an emotional response and forestall any ethical reckoning on the part of the general public. There are spaces in the articles where consent is challenged. Not surprisingly, one of these instances occurs in *The Vegan Life* article when it states, "The adventurous cow inspired many around him, including the woman who first saw him in her backyard in New Britain—upon realising Finn's desire to live, she made the *ethical connection*, and has since transitioned to a meat-free diet." In another case, the animal's plight motivated protests with individuals commenting that "It's amazing how brave these animals are" and "everyone should know all those animals want their freedom." In another case, a rescuer comments, "As soon as she had a name she had a face and a personality, and people were rallying behind her." And in that same case, when the cow later died, a local town erected a sculpture of her to honor her. Even in the articles most dense with wordplay, evidence of compassion were present: "I felt bad for him. He was in distress." The "ethical connection" and its consequence are likely why these accounts receive little attention and why animal industry practices are a fervently managed secret.

From a methodological perspective, one may question whether a corpus approach is appropriate and well-suited for such cases where the corpus is small and the number of texts is few. For the present context, the paucity of texts, and hence size of the corpus, is perhaps problematic in a corpus analytic sense. Some may contend, therefore, that corpus analysis has little to offer in such cases where texts are few. This illustration, however, displays otherwise, as the theoretical frameworks of lexical priming and framing coupled with basic corpus techniques demonstrate how language use in a small collection of texts can be investigated. As noted previously, there are sites of ecolinguistic interest that may not yield large data but are nonetheless salient. Comparative corpus techniques of the sort applied here enable the researcher to demonstrate the peculiarity of a particular text in a rather concrete way. Rather than being constrained by our intuitions that a text feels divergent in some meaningful way, the use of contrastive CADS methods allows one to demonstrate quantitatively how features in a certain text deviate from conventional language patterns and then provide qualitative interpretations of why such divergence is meaningful.

In this study, divergence from conventional primings was generally operationalized in a manner that facilitated a critique of these articles and their language use. However, it is important to note that divergence may similarly be present in ways that may be viewed as beneficial and in alignment with one's own ecosophy. In this way, CADS techniques may similarly be implemented to highlight emergent positive discourse practices that contribute to more ecological ways of being. Such beneficial language practice may not yet prevail in general language use, but corpus analysis can be applied in these spaces to highlight emergent discourses that promote ecological sustainability, animal welfare, etc. Thus, CADS can help reveal and challenge discursive practices that perpetuate ecological harm and nonhuman animal suffering, but it may also be applied to identify and promote emergent, beneficial discourses that may at present be both minimalized and marginalized.

6

Geographical Text Analysis for Corpus-Assisted Ecolinguistics

6.0 Introduction

The iconic Blue Marble image taken in 1972 by the crew of Apollo 17 had profound impact on how humanity imagined its place in the cosmos. The captivating image of Earth in orbit, floating in time and space, "vulnerable and isolated," in a manner humans had never before seen enabled humans to imagine and visualize the planet as a unified, complex, interconnected ecological system (Attenborough, 2020). As David Attenborough asserts, the image of our "blue sphere in the blackness" awakened a consciousness that there was indeed "an edge to our existence" and that humanity is "ultimately bound by and reliant upon the finite natural world about us" (2020). Such a profound and pervasive reconfiguring of how humanity views place may not ever be matched, though one recent technology is revealing similarly transformative images.

In recent years, we have gained access to a new imaging technique that is reshaping how we understand the Anthropocene and the undeniable and far-reaching impact of the human species on the planet. As the Anthropocene is intended to convey, human impact on the planet defines the present geological era; however, the once narrow timespan of this period has significantly expanded due to the technological advances in imaging. The technology, light detection and ranging, more commonly known by its acronym of LIDAR, employs laser imagery to detect structures long hidden by dense rain forest vegetation or covered by desert sands. Recent projects employing LIDAR have enabled archaeological discoveries of ancient structures, greatly informing what we know about past civilizations and their influence on the places we have long inhabited and transformed for our needs. One realization of such discoveries is that human influence on the planet is much more extensive and dates far beyond what we previously conceived. Of course, this chapter is not pursuing an ecolinguistic application of LIDAR, but it is prompted by the zeitgeist of place spreading across the humanities motivated by a desire to more deeply explore human understandings of and relationships to places. More specifically, this corpus-assisted ecolinguistic exploration investigates the discursive representations of place and how such framings reflect and perpetuate a complex of culturally-situated and ever-evolving beliefs and attitudes about the physical world.

While the aforementioned LIDAR technology is revolutionizing archaeology of the Anthropocene (Blakemore, 2019, National Geographic), the renewed interest in place across the humanities is partially prompted by the proliferation of Geographical Information Systems (GIS). GIS has sparked a "spatial turn" within the humanities as it makes possible new inquiries into "the influence of geographical space on human behavior and cultural development" (Bodenhamer, Corrigan & Harris, 2010). This emergent paradigm, often referred to as Spatial Humanities, has the power "to create a step-change" in the humanities with its power to make "applied contributions to knowledge" (Gregory et al., 2015, p. 1).

Language and discourse studies is also following this spatial trajectory. One example of a particularly powerful application of geo-spatial technologies and methods for understanding language use is Guo, Kasakoff, and Grieve's (2016) analysis of regional linguistic variation in the United States through the analysis of 924 million geo-tagged tweets consisting of nearly 8 billion words. As they assert, the analysis of geo-tagged data makes possible a level of "spatial and temporal continuity" and "up-to-date dynamics" never previously achieved in language studies. Subsequent discussion will provide additional examples of GIS-informed research across the humanities and social sciences, but the Guo et al. (2016) study usefully highlights the somewhat untapped potential of GIS for the analysis of language and discourse.

For ecolinguistics, the analysis of the discursive production of place is not altogether new. Indeed, in the previously mentioned *The Ecolinguistics Reader*, Carbaugh (2001) explored representations of place and how such depictions indexed views toward a controversial local project. This chapter similarly aims to illustrate the functional and rhetorical salience of place references in language use, how semantic meanings attached to places influence perception and action, and how writers situate and anchor their texts in places. For this illustration, the chapter synthesizes the affordances of GIS and corpus-assisted ecolinguistics in its analysis of places and their discursive (re)production in discourses pertaining to two controversial projects (Rosemont Copper Mine and Pebble Gold Mine), the conservation of the United States' largest estuary in Chesapeake Bay, and the protection of perhaps North America's most iconic natural place—the Grand Canyon of Arizona.

6.1 GIS and Geographical Text Analysis

GIS, rendered most simply, is a process of assigning latitude and longitude coordinates to data points, i.e., places, for their subsequent mapping and visualization. In the past, sophisticated GIS platforms such as ArcGIS and ESRI seemed the restricted purview of specialists alone due to the significant learning curves to be overcome by novice users. However, the emergence of accessible and intuitive platforms such as Carto, Mango Maps, and others makes utilizing the power of GIS achievable to a broader range of users. Such accessibility of GIS platforms and the seeming ubiquity of GIS applications in our daily lives contribute to the increased interest in place in the social sciences and humanities. Though this interest is expanding, the following review narrows to investigations that specifically employ large collections of text as opposed to more common GIS data sources such as census reports, mortality data, economic reports, etc. Thus, the following surveys a collection of noteworthy projects which integrate GIS and CADS for the analysis of principled collections of language use rather than the historically more common GIS analyses of vector-based geographical data. Such a geographical text analysis procedure ultimately enables researchers to answer what places are referenced in a corpus, and through additional procedures, what semantic themes frequently collocate with those named places and what places are tethered to shared themes (Smail, Gregory, & Taylor, 2019). First, some shared qualities of GIS and CADS are discussed.

There are qualities present in GIS and CADS that contribute to a potential synergy between the two approaches. One of these qualities is their shared affinity for large data sources. Within CADS, the researcher aims to reveal salient linguistic patterns within often massive collections of annotated textual data, while somewhat similarly, GIS practitioners seek to produce visualizations of geo-referenced data present within countless rows of spreadsheet data. As CADS explores language patterns such as collocation and colligation to make statements about language and discourse in a range of settings, GIS similarly seeks to "discover relationships that make a complex world more immediately understandable by visually detecting spatial patterns that remain hidden in texts and tables" (Bodenhamer, Corrigan, & Harris, 2010, p. vii). As Gregory and Hardie (2011) assert, GIS practitioners are more likely to plot census data than locations present in collections of texts while conversely CADS research has generally paid little attention to the spatial elements within texts, thereby creating an opportunity for a useful synergy between the two approaches (Gregory & Hardie, 2011). Thus, for this place-based case study, a synthesis of GIS and corpus-assisted ecolinguistics enables analyses which join the affordances of each approach in an attempt to "discover the meaning of text and reveal implications and significance of places" (Yuan, 2010, p. 116). As Yuan suggests, an integration of GIS and CADS techniques could enable corpora to "tell stories" of the geographic influences present within texts (Yuan, 2010, p. 111). It is such storytelling that this chapter aims to achieve.

One research space already seeking to tell such stories is Historical GIS. As evident in the name of the field of study, Historical GIS explores questions of historical relevance and importance through the application of GIS to inform data analysis. Gregory and Hardie (2011) are early proponents of an integrated GIS–CADS approach through an approach which they term *Visual GISting*. Indeed, they assert their study to be "the first time that techniques to demonstrate and quantify the geographical distributions within texts have been developed" (p. 304). In their analysis of a section of the Lancaster Newsbooks Corpus, they map not only the place name mentions but also the common semantic themes collocating with those places. For example, they visually map place names associated with the semantic themes of money and war. In doing so, they demonstrate the synergy of corpus linguistics and GIS for exploring textual data in order to produce semantic visualizations as a means to reveal novel insights about places and their discursive representations. Admittedly, the methodological procedures applied in the case study to follow are reflective of the procedures developed in their work.

Geographical text analysis (GTA) of the sort pursued by Gregory and Hardie continues to develop. One study pursuing a text-based approach in this space integrates corpus linguistic and natural language processing techniques with GIS for the study of greater than 200,000 pages and more than 5 million words of Registrar General's Reports from the 1840s to 1880s in England and Wales with targeted focus on textual references to cholera and other diseases in the period (Flores et al., 2015). In the approach, place name references were mapped to better understand how various places were affected by the disease in this period. Such an analysis "made it possible to identify in an automated way the most relevant episodes in the history of cholera" as depicted in the reports (p. 317). As the authors note, their study demonstrated "the potential that linguistic and spatial techniques have for analyzing large volumes of texts" while also opening "new exciting possibilities" for studies not only in history but across a range of domains with interests in places and their discursive depictions (p. 317). Importantly, their approach can be applied to any corpus to unveil what places are being mentioned, how those places are represented, and how those representations evolve diachronically.

Employing similar CADS-GIS methods, studies of literary texts have also pursued inquiries regarding place and its importance in texts and world-building. Noteworthy projects in literary mapping include offerings such as Representations of Race and Ethnicity in American Fiction from the Stanford Literary Lab, Mapping the Lakes from Lancaster University, and the Digital Literary Atlas of Ireland amongst others. Though each of these projects is exemplary, the research focused on the depictions of the Lake District of England has likely been the most extensive and varied due to the creation of the 1.5 million word Corpus of Lake District Writing. In one study emerging from the Mapping the Lakes project, Donaldson, Gregory, and Taylor (2017) perform a geographical text analysis procedure to examine the use of the words *beautiful, picturesque, sublime,* and *majestic* in writings about the English Lake District. In the analysis of travel writing and literature on the region from the eighteenth and nineteenth centuries, it was observed that *beautiful* and *picturesque* were associated with different parts of the Lake District than were the terms *sublime* and *majestic.* In the corpus, *beautiful* and *picturesque* were tethered semantically to places at lower elevations while *sublime* and *majestic* appeared more commonly with locations of greater elevation. In a related project, and employing the same Corpus of Lake District Writing, language use regarding constructs of tranquility and silence was generally presented with a positive semantic sentiment and certain places were frequently associated with qualities of tranquility and silence (Chesnokova et al., 2019). Such findings demonstrate how geographic text analysis can provide insights into the manner in which natural spaces are discursively depicted in language use.

These studies inform the present work for they illustrate how a geographical text analysis approach drawing upon GIS and CADS can produce insights into the discursive production of place. Importantly, these studies do not only map the geographical locations mentioned within texts. Rather, these studies move beyond first level mapping of place names to additionally explore and highlight the semantic meanings connected with locations and the rhetorical functions such associations manifest. By doing so, these studies tell revealing stories of place and their discursive depiction which would likely be inaccessible to other approaches.

6.2 Studies of Place in Ecolinguistics

Studies in discourse analysis broadly and ecolinguistics specifically have explored the production of place in discourses of ecological relevance. In one previously mentioned contribution, Carbaugh (2001) discusses the "dueling depictions"

(p. 125) of nature present in the debate surrounding a development project in eastern Massachusetts that aimed to build ski facilities and condominiums near Mt. Greylock, the tallest peak in Massachusetts. The variation in geographical referencing reflected and produced various motives for acting in relation to the environment and revealed several practices that Carbaugh claimed index differing stances toward the proposal. Carbaugh writes, "When one makes a reference to this land, in some communicative context, a selection is made from a set of terms" with selections such as "the mountain" attaching an ecological aesthetic while "the project" highlights meanings of economic value and interest (p. 139). For Carbaugh, "communicating about natural space is a way of anchoring messages in physical space, but in so doing, more than a physical space is involved" as "the communicative process of depicting nature carries with it a potent complex of socio-cultural messages" (p. 139).

In a similar investigation, the tour presentations of official national park guides are contrasted with the presentations of Native American Blackfoot guides leading tourist groups through Glacier National Park in Montana, USA (Carbaugh & Rudnick, 2006). In the tours, the analysts observed that references to either "the park" or "the reservation" indexed the positionality and stance of the storyteller and functioned to situate the audience in the space in rather divergent ways. Cascading from these initial discursive choices, the Blackfoot guides produced a rich and elaborate discourse steeped in ancestral history, settler contact, and the many challenges and hardships faced by their people. These guides forwarded a grounded and situated history with references to historical, spiritual, and sacred events that occurred at particular places in the area. In contrast, the official park guides presented a discourse of discovery and development as features are referenced from a settler point of view and with little mention of the region's history prior to the park's establishment. Provocatively, the authors assert that "to name a place, or to refer to a place, is to make a move in a cultural political game" (p. 182) and that "how one refers to a place produces a particular view of the place" (p. 183). Their detailed ethnographic work enables readers to *see* places more deeply and recognize the importance place naming practices serve within discourse.

Investigations of place, their naming, and the values and positions indexed by such invocations have been productively explored from a critical discourse analysis perspective as well. For example, Kidner (2016) analyzes the discourse surrounding the Athabasca Tar/Oil Sands, an area in northeastern Alberta, Canada known for large deposits of crude oil and bitumen. The study demonstrated how selection of either "Athabasca Tar Sands" or "Athabasca

Oil Sands" reflects divergent stances toward the deeply polarizing issue. In the work, Kidner notes the use of *oil sands* perpetuates prevailing frames that promote development. For the speakers in the study, *tar sands* seemed to indicate opposition and environmentalism while *oil sands* reflected support for industry and the development. Interestingly, some speakers chose to alternate terms, but those who did so were uniformly against the tar/oil sands development, suggesting that the alternation was a rhetorical strategy of negotiation. Consistently, government and industry speakers used *tar sands* while environmentalists, researchers, and the general public at times alternated. As this study additionally demonstrates, naming of place can function to index opposing perspectives of the debate.

An additional ecolinguistic study highlighting the importance of place analyzes the presence and function of "location circumstantials" within oppositional texts from the Japanese Whaling Research Institute and Greenpeace (Haig, 2001, p. 254). The ideologically oppositional texts respond to a specific event, a confrontation between a Japanese whaling ship and a Greenpeace ship seeking to disrupt a whale hunt. In the texts from the two clear adversaries, each group is keenly interested in "pinning down their accounts of what happened in time and space" (p. 215) through the deployment of various deictic markers. The situated quality of the discourse reflects the importance and function of place in environmental communication. Though the present illustration does not attend to deictic markers, the potential for further research regarding deixis in environmental discourse is later discussed.

To my knowledge, the only corpus-assisted investigation of place applying an ecolinguistic framework are my own earlier studies exploring the discourse regarding the proposed construction of a copper mine in southern Arizona—this is the same Rosemont Mine that is part of the illustration of this chapter (Poole, 2016a, 2017b). In those projects, a specialized corpus of press releases from a multinational mining corporation was analyzed along with a corpus of blog posts from an environmental group from the region. The studies displayed the divergent depictions of place in these oppositional discourses with the mining corporation referencing places in semantic clusters of money and resources within messages that painted the proposed mine as an inevitable and foregone conclusion even though years after that original research the mine has yet to gain full approval to proceed. As the mining discourse named global financial centers and only referenced the mountain site in relation to the minerals that could be extracted and the economic value that could be rendered, the environmental group instead grounded their message with frequent mentions of geographical features unique to the local ecology and numerous references to local places embedded within a discourse of ecological stewardship and one which asserted the intrinsic value of natural spaces. When mapped using the Carto platform, the resulting visuals displayed the divergence in textual mentioning of place names in the two corpora and the differing semantic fields collocating with place names central to the discourse.

The illustration to follow expands upon these place-based investigations and elaborates the earlier integration of CADS, GIS, and ecolinguistics. This chapter asserts that these ecolinguistic studies of place and their importance within environmental discourse can be extended and enhanced by merging GIS and CL techniques. Informed by the geographical text analysis methodology of Gregory and Hardie (2011), this chapter illustrates a corpus-assisted ecolinguistic analysis integrated with and enhanced by GIS to enable spatial representations of places within environmental communication. Drawing from previously discussed place-based work yet extending through the integration of corpus-aided ecolinguistics and GIS, this chapter investigates place names, their discursive function within these texts, and the manner in which places are discursively framed and depicted. This illustration displays the salience of place name mentions within environmental discourse while highlighting the potential of the approach within the expanding corpus-assisted ecolinguistics research space.

6.3 Illustrating Geographical Text Analysis and Corpus-Assisted Ecolinguistics

This case study analyzes blogs written and published by four environmental groups. Two of the groups, Rosemont Mine Truth (RMT) and Save Bristol Bay (SBB), are local activist groups specifically opposing major mining proposals (Rosemont Mine and Pebble Mine) in their states of Arizona and Alaska. Rosemont Mine and Pebble Mine share a number of characteristics. First, both mines, if constructed as proposed by the mining corporations seeking approval, would be absolutely massive open-pit mines. For Rosemont, it would become the third largest open pit mine in the United States while Pebble would be the nation's largest. These massive projects and their undeniable potential ecological impacts have stirred considerable public opposition in local communities and across their states. In Arizona, activists stress the irreversible impacts such a project would have on a vibrant local tourist industry supported by numerous recreational activities such as the finest bird-watching in the United States. Further, in Arizona, where water is of constant concern, activists argue that local water resources for the city of Tucson and other small towns in Pima County would be adversely impacted by the demand the proposed mining operation would place on water in the region. And finally, but perhaps most importantly, the mine is planned for development on the ancestral homeland of the Tohono O'dham people who quite legitimately worry that the proposed mine would devastate their homeland. As of late 2020, construction of the site has begun on an area secured from private landowners, but the mine has yet to be approved for the adjoining public lands, though the approval seems to be forthcoming.

The proposed Pebble Mine of Bristol Bay, Alaska pits similar foes with similar arguments as present with Rosemont. The heart of the matter concerns the potential impact to Bristol Bay, an important body of water home to one of "the world's most productive wild salmon strongholds that supports a $1.5 billion commercial and sport fishery" (savebristolbay.org). As noted on the SBB website, "Bristol Bay continues to produce the world's largest sockeye salmon fishery and one of the most prolific king salmon runs left on earth." Additionally, the Bristol Bay region is home to approximately thirty indigenous groups whose culture and way of life would be impacted by such a massive mine project. Local, and even national, opposition has been robust with resistance to the mine uniting traditional partisan foes. In 2020, approval seemed imminent, but the public release of an undercover video showing mining executives discussing their scheme angered many and embroiled key proponents in controversy. As of late 2020, the proposal has not yet been approved, and a project that once seemed to be approaching approval does not seem certain any longer.

The remaining two groups diverge from the first two as they focus not on specific projects but more with general advocacy for the conservation of two iconic places in North America: the Chesapeake Bay and the Grand Canyon. These groups, The Chesapeake Bay Foundation (CBF) and The Grand Canyon Trust (GCT), were selected due to their targeted advocacy efforts in relation to specific geographical locations rather than broader environmental advocacy efforts of well-known groups such as The Sierra Club and Conservation International. These selected groups are not engaged directly with advocacy efforts to address the climate crisis, species loss, pollution, or other general environmental matters. Instead, the efforts of these groups are aimed at the protection and preservation of specific places of immense ecological and cultural value. Other iconic sites exist in North America, but these are noteworthy as they represent the largest canyon and the largest estuary in the United States.

Other locations and groups which advocate for various places and causes were considered for inclusion in the analysis; yet, for various reasons, these four were ultimately selected for this case study. For this study, only groups which maintained an active presence through regular blog posts were possible selections. Some groups not included either do not have an active blog presence (opting instead for brief press releases or social media postings) or post only sparingly. For example, one group which was considered, The Everglades Foundation, produced only 40,000 words between the period of 2012 and 2020.

6.3.1 Corpora and Semantic Tagging

The full corpus for the present study includes 1,437 blog posts consisting of 797,480 words (see Table 11). The posts were collected from 2010 to 2020; variation with publication frequency amongst the groups is present due to the varying timelines of the projects they oppose or nature of their advocacy. Each blog produces texts broadly designed to engage and educate primarily local but also national readers. The blogs function as a public relations-type outlet for the advocacy groups, e.g., Rosemont Mine Truth blog is produced by the Save the Santa Ritas Organization while the Save the Bay blog is maintained by the Chesapeake Bay Foundation. The sites publish frequently regarding the deleterious impacts of the mining developments, relevant legal actions pertaining to the approval proceedings, and other events or information relevant to their missions. For example, the RMT blog aims to persuade local residents and Arizonans to challenge the proposed copper mine. Similarly, Save Bristol Bay (SBB) seeks to push public opinion toward opposition of the project in favor of

Table 11 The Environmental Organizations Corpus

Organization	Site	Time Period	# of Texts	Tokens
Grand Canyon Trust	grandcanyontrust.org/	10/02/2012–10/07/2020	526	304,836
Save the Bay	https://www.cbf.org/blogs/save-the-bay/	01/03/2017–10/09/2020	559	282,551
Rosemont Mine Truth	rosemontminetruth.com/	09/30/2010–04/19/2019	224	132,192
Save Bristol Bay	savebristolbay.org/	01/06/2015–09/23/2020	128	77,901
			1,437	797,480

preservation of Bristol Bay and its rich ecology. The corpora are exhaustive as all blog posts over the lifespan of these organizations are included.

As the corpora are of varying sizes, the frequency data, when necessary and appropriate, are normed. Norming is a recommended method for comparing frequencies across differently sized corpora. Typically, norming is performed at per 10K, 100K, or 1 million words with selection of a norming rate based primarily on the various sizes of the corpora. In the present case, downscaling (norming to a lower rate, e.g., per 10K words) is problematic for it constrains the number of geo-referenced features available for subsequent mapping. Conversely, upscaling to 1 million is not advisable for it makes significant assumptions that the geo-referenced items will continue to be employed at the same rate. Thus, it was determined that a norming rate of frequency per 191,369 would be applied. This figure is the mean of the largest corpus (The Grand Canyon Trust) and the smallest corpus (Save Bristol Bay). The use of this rate mitigates concerns of downscaling and upscaling, though one could offer critiques of this figure as well. To some extent, selection of a norming rate is arbitrary, yet the approach to norm at the mean of the smallest and largest corpus seems sensible in this case.

For the mapping of place names, the corpora were tagged using the CLAWS parts-of-speech tagger embedded in the WMatrix online platform (Rayson, 2009). As geo-referenced place names are proper nouns, the items tagged NP1/Proper Noun were extracted. Non-place names, primarily the names of individuals, were manually removed. The lists were further reviewed to confirm accuracy. This process was time consuming for it involved confirming numerous items. For example, Chaco, New Mexico, was retained but Chaco footwear removed; the place Monticello was initially marked as being located in Virginia but the one mentioned is in Utah; Santa Cruz refers not to the city in California but to the river in Arizona. Place names which occurred greater than five times cumulatively across the four corpora were included in the analysis; it was not required that the place name reference occurred in all four corpora— only that it appeared greater than five times in total. The resulting list of place names meeting this frequency threshold was then geo-referenced with latitude and longitude coordinates using a gazetteer, normed at the aforementioned rate, and spatially mapped using the Carto online mapping software. Briefly, Carto is an interactive GIS platform with numerous visualization options. Users are able to zoom in and out as desired and can click on various geo-referenced points to gain additional information, namely location name and frequency in this case though additional glossing could be added. In this chapter, screen captures of the various maps produced by the platform are included, but the

Table 12 Semantic tag frequencies with place names

Place Name	Latitude	Longitude	Freq	A1	A1.1.1	A1.1.2	A1.2	A1.3	A1.4	A1.5
Arizona	34.39534	-111.763	322	0	41	8	0	0	0	0

maps can be published and hosted by creators so that users may interact with the visualizations.

For the analysis involving the mapping of semantic meaning, the corpora were annotated with semantic tags using the USAS semantic analysis framework (Rayson, 2008; Wilson & Rayson, 1993) again through W-Matrix (Rayson, 2009). The USAS tagger applies semantic meaning tags to all lexical items in a corpus through the application of a framework of twenty-one discourse fields. For example, the tag B is assigned to words referring to the body and the individual while the tag I is assigned to words related to money, industry, and commerce. Other tags are assigned to words referencing emotion, education, time, life and living things, etc. Each of the twenty-one major discourse fields is then subdivided into more specific categories. For example, the semantic field I for money is extended through additional annotations such as I.1.1+ for money: affluence while I.1.1− refers to words referencing money: debt. Following semantic tagging, spreadsheets were generated that listed the place names mentioned in each of the corpora aligned with the frequencies of their semantic tag collocates. The semantic tags which frequently co-occurred with place name mentions were mapped using the Carto platform once more. To illustrate, Table 12 displays a snapshot of the data and how the data were organized with each row listing the place, its geographical coordinates, frequency of occurrence, followed by a column for each of the approximately 225 semantic category labels. When the spreadsheet is loaded into a GIS platform, one can then produce multi-layered maps based on the frequencies of any selected semantic tag.

6.4 Mapping Places

Before proceeding, it seems beneficial to revisit briefly the core rationale motivating this endeavor. As previously stated, the integration of GIS and CADS within an ecolinguistic framework seeks to highlight the spatial component embedded within texts. Such spatial representation thus aims to "tell stories" (Yuan, 2010, p. 111) of the geographic influences present within a corpus or corpora—this project seeks to uncover and interpret such stories through an ecolinguistic framework. Additionally, the foundation of which this case study rests is adherence to the quotation previously referenced: "to name a place, or to refer to a place, is to make a move in a cultural political game" and that "how one refers to a place produces a particular view of the place" (Carbaugh & Rudnick, 2006, pp. 182–3). This case study similarly argues that the referencing of place names within these corpora is neither arbitrary nor random but that each mention serves functional and rhetorical value within this discourse space.

The first maps presented in Plates 2 and 3 display the place names mentioned in the four respective corpora with several patterns, or stories, revealed by the visualizations. The first story reflected in the map is the clustering of place name references in close proximity to each of the central locations: the Grand Canyon, the Chesapeake Bay, Rosemont Mine in the Santa Rita Mountains, and Pebble Mine of Bristol Bay. There is a clear tendency of each blog to situate and ground their communications and advocacy firmly within their local contexts. The density of these place name mentions reflects the importance of these developments on local communities and regions. The Grand Canyon Trust names numerous locations across the southwestern United States from Moab, Utah to Phoenix, Arizona and Las Vegas, Nevada to Gallup, New Mexico while the blog of the Chesapeake Bay Foundation mentions places from the collection of states surrounding the Chesapeake but also others of the region which do not. Such clustering indicates attempts to engage local communities and cultivate local stakeholders to support conservation efforts. To a large extent, the success of these groups' advocacy efforts is based upon their ability to activate local communities in opposition in cases of the mines and support in cases of preservation. Place name referencing reflects such attempts to engage both the communities in immediate geographical proximity as well as those throughout the region. While this clustering of place names in the periphery or the central locations is not unsurprising, it is nonetheless revealing, as the clustering displays the rooted quality of the discourse and an underlying rhetorical imperative to cultivate consciousness and awareness in local populations toward actions in their area. Similarly revealing is the story told by place name mentions that lie far beyond the geographical region of these four locations.

A second observation made possible through the spatial visualization are both the referencing of places names beyond the US context in which these locations are situated and the variation in non-U.S. places mentioned in these four corpora. In the smallest of the corpora, the Save Bristol Bay blog advocating against Pebble Mine of Bristol Bay, Alaska, it invokes only one non-US location,

China, in the approximately 80,000-word corpus of posts. In contrast, Rosemont Mine Truth, though the third largest of the corpora, frequently mentions a range of non-US places. As displayed in Plate 4, RMT invokes Vancouver, Canada (126); Constancia, Peru (84); Manitoba, Canada (64), Guatemala (58); Toronto, Canada (48); Mount Polley, Canada (46); Flin Flon Mine, Canada (45); British Columbia, Canada (35); Mexico (33); China (16); Korea (9); Buenavista Mine, Mexico (9); El Estor, Guatemala (9); Sardinia, Italy; Las Bambas Mine, Peru; Brazil (6); Ontario, Canada (6); London, UK (4); Asia (3); Europe (3); Australia (1); Polley Lake, Canada (1); and finally, Quesnel Lake, Canada (1). Upon visual inspection of the maps, the place naming practice of RMT appears to exceed the remaining groups as well. For example, GCT invokes numerous non-US locations but at a much lower frequency. To illustrate, the highest frequency location present in the GCT corpus is Canada but at only at a normalized rate of ten; contrastingly, RMT had many places named at a higher frequency. GCT does, however, mention non-US places not shared by the others (Estonia [8]; Japan [6]; Paris, France [93]) while also sharing several locations with RMT (China [5]; Asia [5]; Australia [4]; Europe [3]; Korea [1]). And finally, Save the Bay maps few non-US place name mentions with the first such non-US location barely ranking in the top 50 frequent place names within its texts—its first non-US place mention is Manila, the Philippines (5) with few others to follow: Japan (3), Mexico (3), Europe (2), China (1), Brazil (1), China (1).

This initial visual inspection of the place names as represented on the map is insightful as the spatial representation of place name mentions enabled a discovery that may have remained occluded within the rows and columns of a spreadsheet for many of these locations do not occur at a frequency which would make them immediately noticeable through other techniques. It is likely that the clustering noted previously was not particularly surprising as one would expect locations in the shadows of these central places to be frequently invoked. However, an answer to why certain places beyond this immediate geographical proximity would be named is not so readily available. The following explores this question in an attempt to display how the naming of these places performs an important rhetorical function within the discourse. To illustrate this assertion, the following further examines place name mentions in RMT blog posts along with discussion of their function within these communications.

As noted, RMT invokes a greater number of non-US locations than the other three groups. Closer inspection of these naming practices reveals several patterns in the names invoked. First, several of these locations are beyond the US cite-specific locations where the mining corporation proposing the Rosemont

Mine has operated other qualitatively similar mines whether it be similar size, mineral target, or extracting process. These include the Constancia Mine of Peru (one of the largest copper mines in the world), the Flin Flon Mine of Manitoba, Canada, the Buenavista Mine of northwestern Mexico, and the El Estor Mine of Guatemala. When these mines and the communities for which they are named are asserted, the rhetorical prosody is almost uniformly negative with these mines often referenced for the ecological degradation which they have caused. Thus, the naming of these mine sites serves as a not so subtle warning to the residents of the communities surrounding RMT of the consequences likely to follow if the project advances. One example is the frequent invocation of Mount Polley, Polley Lake, and Quesnel Lake. These locations were deeply affected by the Mount Polley Mine Disaster and its release of 24 million cubic tons of mine waste into the local waterways—the company's negligence has been widely attacked. Mount Polley regularly occurs in textual contexts which cite this event through frequent collocations with *collapse, disaster, failure, breach,* and *release* accompanied with statements impressing the severity of the disaster, e.g., *billions of gallons of wastewater, billions of liters of mine tailings, 10 million cubic metres.* Rhetorically, this impresses upon the readership the likelihood of a similar disaster to their community if the mine proceeds.

In the list of frequent place names invoked in RMT are two of the largest cities in Canada: Vancouver and Toronto. In approximately 40 percent of the mentions of Vancouver, the city is present in the patterns *Vancouver-based* or *Vancouver B.C.-based* followed by a noun phrase referent referring to the mining corporation pursuing the project. Similarly, the balance of Vancouver references functions to situate the mine owner's non-U.S. location. The authors of the posts could select differently from the language system and thus remove this situated framing, yet the rhetorical effect potentially manifests opposition by the project through its nationalist appeal that presents the mining company as other. While the project was initially pursued by Augusta Resources, a Vancouver-based entity, the mining rights were later sold to Toronto-based Hudbay Mineral Resources with the same discursive framing adopted. Again, the consistent practice to attach *Toronto-based* reflects a discursive othering as the non-Arizona, non-US location of the corporation is repeatedly invoked. A similar hyphenated pattern is present in *London-based, Korea-based,* and *Australia-based.* Clearly, this attached location modifier is not necessary or required—it is a choice from the language system made in lieu of other available options. These selections are not made arbitrarily and are not empty geographical identifiers. In my view, and echoing Carbaugh and Rudnick (2006), these are meaningful moves in the discourse, and each performs important rhetorical functions for the local readers of these texts.

This practice of othering has been present throughout the local discourse surrounding the Rosemont Mine. For example, the cartoon included in Plate 5 was printed in a regional newspaper, the Arizona Daily Star, in January of 2021 and shared across the RMT blog and social media accounts. Though the previous paragraph discussed a rather covert othering of non-US stakeholders, the cartoon more explicitly delivers this same message. The place naming practices within the RMT texts reflect this rhetorical aim to frame non-US parties as exploiting local resources while being less mindful of the ecological consequences local communities and ecosystems will encounter. This rhetorical current flows throughout the discourse of this mine.

Constancia, Peru and El Estor, Guatemala are two additional non-US places frequently produced in the RMT messages. While Vancouver and Toronto emphasize the location of the mining corporations' headquarters, references to Guatemala and Constancia serve to document the company's history of problematic, and rather troubling, activities at other mine sites which they operate. For the former, the references to Guatemala along with the mining company frequently occur in textual contexts which document charges of human rights abuses in which the company is implicated; the accusations include forced relocation of indigenous peoples, gang rapes, and murder. These charges have prompted criminal charges against company officials in Guatemala and Canada. Instances of Constancia occur in contexts where local community protests to the mine are referenced, where statements regarding mine production are framed as false or misleading, and in contexts where revenues have been shown to fall below company projections. The rhetorical effect of these invocations of Guatemala and Peru again functions as warnings to local communities to be impacted by another of the company's mining operations. The message forwarded is that the company's public relations campaign which promises jobs and economic development should not be trusted, as the company is framed negatively and their trustworthiness challenged.

The claims to the rhetorical importance of place naming in the RMT texts are supported by the comparatively low frequency on non-US place names in the other corpora. Similar place name invocations are not as frequently present in the three other comparable corpora, indicating the salience of place naming within RMT advocacy. If place naming were not integral to the meaning-making process of the RMT texts, one would anticipate uniform frequency rates across the four corpora in a manner reflective of the shared frequency of functional items such as pronouns and determiners. It is reasonable to assert that such insight into the functional value of place naming could be revealed through traditional corpus linguistic or discourse analytic techniques. That said, the spatial representation unveils a story that could easily evade observation in the frequency-based metrics common of corpus linguistics and CADS.

6.4.1 Mapping Meaning

The previous section mapped place name mentions across the four corpora followed by qualitative interpretations and discussion of the rhetorical salience of place naming practices. In this section, the maps displayed are not visualizations of the frequency of place name mentions but instead are visualizations of the frequent and contested semantic meanings occurring in a 4L-4R collocational window with place names.

With such a preponderance of data (the tagging framework includes greater than 200 tags), a process to narrow the data to a more manageable amount was required. An initial step in this process generated a list of key semantic tags collocating with place names through a similar keyness analysis process as described in Chapter 4. Several tags occurring prominently on the list were discarded for they seemed generally irrelevant to the semantic framing of the target items; these discarded items were tags such as Z5: grammatical items, Z99: unmatched items, Z1: personal names, and Z8: pronouns. In the remaining tag list, a cluster of categories corresponding to life and living things (L1), living creatures generally (L2), and plants (L3) was present as well as a group of tags pertaining to money, e.g., tags I1: Money generally and I1.3: Money: Price. These respective tag groups were summed into two clusters: 1) Life and 2) Money. Thus, the following series of maps display semantic meanings of life and money operating in the collocational windows of the place names in the corpora. As done previously, an initial analysis of the maps is followed by closer qualitative analysis.

It becomes evident in the semantic tag frequency data that the discursive production of place is complex and multifaceted. One may initially theorize that place name representations will be somewhat cohesive—in other words, it seems reasonable to imagine a restricted semantic framing of places in this particular discourse. From an ecolinguistic orientation, one may hope to find evidence of an underlying beneficial discourse that positively frames these locations in a manner that reflects their intrinsic values to local ecologies. Similarly, an ecolinguist would likely critique the presence of a discursive framing that frequently attaches places to the economic value they make possible in the neoliberal capitalist construct that privileges a monetary valuation as the defining metric of worth. These maps, however, show that such framings are both present and are in competition with each other as the messages both attempt to convey and express the natural beauty and splendor of place while likewise recognizing their economic worth to citizens and communities both near and far.

The global visualization of semantic tags of money (see Plate 6) in contexts of place reveals seemingly similar and frequent framings connecting place name to the money construct, yet variation is again evident amongst the corpora. Again, the RMT texts display greater variation. For the CBF and the GCT, with a few exceptions, their uses of money with place seem largely clustered around the locations for which they advocate. However, RMT appears less likely to attach framings of money to sites within close proximity to the proposed mine and also greater likelihood of attaching meanings of money to places more distant within the US and internationally. RMT mentions international financial centers and national capitals such as Washington DC and London, international markets for copper in South Korea and China, and the international mining projects of the mining corporation. RMT less frequently attaches the money semantic domain to the site it aims to protect while the communications of the CBF reflect a rather frequent framing of money in their advocacy. All but one CBF place mentions in the context of money are to locations within the continental United States while RMT contrastingly invokes numerous overseas locations within this framing. Such divergence may reflect the greater urgency of RMT efforts in challenging the yet to be approved project. While CBF's practice will be explored further in the next paragraph, RMT appears again to project a sort of economic nationalism which aims to appeal to their local communities. The previous discussion on *based* attached to a city is present here as well with instances such as *London-based hedge fund, London-based RK Capital Management, London-based copper hedge fund.* These ascriptions of location are not necessary but do produce an othering/distancing rhetorical effect.

An additional story revealed is the prevalence of semantic tags reflecting meanings of money in the context of the Chesapeake Bay (see Plate 7). Indeed, a log likelihood calculation revealed that the place "Chesapeake Bay" collocated frequently with meanings of money—tag I1 was the third item on the key tag collocates list. A close reading of concordance lines in which Chesapeake Bay occurred with the money tags reflects the tenuous funding situation of the foundation and the various projects it supports. At the core of its purpose is the development and support of initiatives and programs which support conservation efforts; thus, securing donations from the public and lobbying for federal and state funds is central to its mission. The lines presented below highlight this rhetorical exigency. Though unsurprising that such an aim informs the textual production of these texts, the prevalence of references to money does potentially shape public attitudes toward conservation and preservation as places become deeply linked with economic meanings. In a moment where public unity of purpose is needed, conservation efforts become connected to and politicized within discourses of budgets and economic policy. In several samples below, this polarization is reflected through phrases such as "A budget battle …". Additionally, two samples join the item *investment* with Chesapeake Bay. In the Corpus of Contemporary American English, the word *investment* and its ties to financial discourse are clearly evident in common collocates *bank, capital, company, firm, fund, banking*. Though the term is broadened to other contexts, it is undoubtedly most strongly linked to economic meanings. Such tethering of conservation of natural spaces to discourses driven by monetary valuations as sole determiners of value is problematic as a long-term discursive strategy. Though such meanings may produce short-term engagement, a discourse which frames iconic places within such an economic framework denies nature its intrinsic value.

1. proposal would reduce annual *funding* for EPA's **Chesapeake Bay** cleanup project by 93 percent
2. budget that eliminates all *funding* for the **Chesapeake Bay** Program, a critical part of
3. sign our petition urging Congress to keep the **Chesapeake Bay** Program fully *funded*
4. losing significant *investments* from the **Chesapeake Bay** Program couldn't come at a worse time
5. A *Budget* Battle for the Bay: **Chesapeake Bay** Foundation
6. to completely eliminate federal *funding* for the **Chesapeake Bay** Program (CBP)
7. protect *funding* for the critical **Chesapeake Bay** Program. But we can't do it without you
8. Trump wants to eliminate all *funding* for the **Chesapeake Bay** Program, one of the
9. Urge Congress to preserve *funding* for the **Chesapeake Bay** and its rivers and streams!
10. truly is the best long-term *investment* in the **Chesapeake Bay**.

The final map (see Plate 8) spatializes meanings of life and living things in the context of place names. Again, there is clustering in the geographical proximity to the four central locations, reflecting the contested and interwoven semantic framings the places invoke. In this map, the geographical spread of RMT again appears to be greater than its peer advocacy groups. Closer inspection of life tags with these international locations revealed unexpected findings. For instance, it was anticipated that life and living things would largely speak to the biological diversity that must be protected at these places. Indeed, this patterning was present as each group invoked local wildlife deserving protection somewhat frequently. For instance, in RMT texts, there are common references to the few remaining jaguars of the southwestern US roaming southern Arizona and the diversity of birds that lure tourists to the region. However, for references beyond the United States, the connections of life to place were more troubling. The samples most highlighting this framing are highlighted in the discursive attention provided to the El Estor Mine of Guatemala. Tragically, indigenous peoples have been displaced and terrorized, and thus, the attachment of life semantic tags is in the context of lives lost and lives displaced as a result of human rights abuses. Somewhat similarly, references to places in Canada refer to the aforementioned release of toxic metals that poisoned both wildlife and people. Importantly, several of these instances charge the company with *knowingly* poisoning people and covering up the severity.

The visualizations of the maps help assess the variation and salience of place name mentions across the four corpora. Though clusterings around the central locations were present throughout the mappings, divergence in place name mentions and their semantic framing revealed valuable insights to functional importance of place naming in environmental communication. It seemed evident that a contributing factor shaping place naming is the primary rhetorical aim of the blog. For CBF and GCT, their place naming was situated and grounded in close geographical proximity to the canyon and the estuary as they continue to advocate for the protection of these two places. Their messages were legal and political in nature as they often were aimed at securing support for legislation and policy, but most frequently, they aimed to raise financial support to enable conservation efforts. It is unfortunate that these organizations must fight for such iconic places whose federal funding and protections seem unpredictable at best and declining at worst. It is perhaps telling that preservation of these places seems to rely more squarely on local communities than federal agencies. Though little can be offered for Save the Bay due to its small size, RMT is active in stirring local engagement and utilizes all available resources to do so. The naming of places and their discursive framing serves important rhetorical value in the cultivation of their local support against the proposed mine.

6.5 Conclusion and Further Research

This chapter and its illustration of an integration corpus-assisted ecolinguistics and GIS for the visual mapping of place names and their discursive production display potential for further investigation of the representations of place in environmental discourse as well as other discourse domains. Through the spatialization of corpus data, intuitive interpretations of data are made possible and stories perhaps occluded within the rows and columns of a database or within the lists of frequency-based output produced from corpus techniques are revealed. While the visual representations reveal meaningful discursive practices, the illustration also shows the necessity of additional qualitative inspection of the patterns in question to further unveil how place names are purposefully invoked in discourse.

This illustration focused broadly on place name practices in these corpora, but subsequent analysis could also interrogate a narrowed list of places of interest, e.g., the Grand Canyon, Chesapeake Bay. There is also potential to explore changing discursive representations of place diachronically. As discussed in Chapter 3, CADS is uniquely equipped to explore evolving diachronic representations. While Chapter 3 explored changing depictions of *wilderness*, diachronic representations of place names could be similarly investigated. GIS data can be annotated to account for time; thus, time-lapse maps could be produced to show the emergent depictions of certain places diachronically. For example, one could explore changing representations of natural spaces such as the Everglades or the Grand Canyon or even metropolitan areas such as New York City or Washington, DC. Such diachronic investigations would reveal how changing conceptualizations of places reflect broader shifts in ecological consciousness.

This case study produced spatial maps of only two clusters of semantic tags, yet greater than 200 semantic meanings could have been mapped with Carto with simply the click of a mouse on a different data column. It is possible, perhaps even likely, that this case study overlooked other salient mappings that would tell other stories. Importantly too is the limitation of the present case study to only explore place naming within the blog posts from four largely similar organizations. The corpora did enable comparative analysis of place naming practices, but this could be expanded to incorporate texts from other relevant stakeholders. For example, mapping press releases of the multinational mining corporations or the environmental impact statements of governmental agencies such as the Environmental Protection Agency or the Corps of Civil Engineers could also reveal differing discursive framings of place. There are numerous elaborations that could be productively pursued.

The GIS–CADS approach for this elaboration of corpus-assisted ecolinguistics presents a range of opportunities for further investigation of environmental discourse. This study focused specifically on the georeferencing of place names and their semantic collocates. This process was made possible by semantic annotations through the USAS tagger and the CLAWS part of speech tagger. While part of speech taggers such as CLAWS or the Stanford Tagset are likely the most frequently applied annotation schemes along with the USAS tagger, these are not the only tagging frameworks available or conceivable. For example, there are a range of deictic features present in discourse that could similarly and productively be explored. Gregory and Hardie (2011) discuss deixis, the linguistic forms which create distance, proximity, and spatial relations between a speaker, hearer, or object, and note the potential of these features to be reflected in GIS maps, and Haig (2001) notes a high frequency of "location circumstantials" (p. 209) as environmental texts seem concerned with situating events firmly within a specific time and place. The density and nature of deictic markings could reflect both spatial and ideological distance between interest groups and the place at the center of a debate. These deixis features could be tagged, analyzed, and mapped through similar procedures applied here. Present within texts are directional indicators, geographical terms, and place names that could inform our understanding of how places are discursively depicted in environmental communication.

One final research trajectory is reflected in the growing body of research applying GIS techniques to the mapping of messages on social media sites such as Twitter. This work has often focused on mapping political discourses (e.g., Hanna et al., 2011), but it has also been applied to tracking responses to environmental events such as hurricanes (Shelton et al., 2014). And as asserted by the Guo, Kasakoff, and Grieve's study (2016) discussed in the introduction, social media provides a vast geo-referenced data source that could support various research agendas. Such data could be used to further display the importance of place and its discursive production in environmental communication. With corpus-assisted ecolinguistics integrated with GIS affordances, the potential to produce intuitive and insightful visualizations to help discover and disseminate key research findings is great.

7

Conclusion

This book illustrated multiple applications of a corpus-assisted approach to ecolinguistics for the analysis of a range of discourses through which ideologies, attitudes, beliefs, and practices regarding the environment, physical places, and nonhuman animals are reflected and (re)produced. These case studies presented corpus-assisted ecolinguistics in action with each designed to venture into underexplored discourse spaces and/or apply corpus analytic techniques less frequently implemented in ecolinguistics. As noted in the introductory chapter, much corpus-assisted research in ecolinguistics has focused upon the discourse of climate change in the media of various national contexts. This is valuable research offering important insights into the discursive representations of climate change in the media of numerous settings. Such corpus-assisted media studies have made and will continue to make valuable contributions to our understanding of how language use mediates our perceptions and shapes our understandings of the climate crisis while also influencing the actions we choose to take to mitigate its effects. However, while these perceptions and understandings are somewhat explicitly on display in communications specifically regarding the environment, a similar complex of beliefs and attitudes is reflected and perpetuated in numerous discursive spaces which may not be immediately identified as ecologically relevant. Corpus-assisted ecolinguistics can be applied to these spaces beyond greenspeak (Harre et al., 1998) to demonstrate how prevailing perceptions of nature, place, and nonhuman animals permeate throughout English language use.

The first empirical illustration presented in Chapter 3 demonstrated the utility of diachronic corpus analysis for revealing the evolving ways a construct of ecological importance is represented. The approach implemented diachronic collocation analysis supplemented by the statistical measure of the Kendall's Tau correlation coefficient along with the framework of evaluation to explore the changing representations of *wilderness* in US discourse over an approximately 200-year period. Diachronic corpus-assisted ecolinguistics can provide insight into the dynamic manner by which physical places, nonhuman animals, and environmental issues are discursively constructed and how these representations evolve over time. Such diachronic work has the capacity to provide social evidence of changing attitudes, beliefs, and practices and unsettle notions that the present and prevailing complex of perceptions and attitudes regarding human relationships with the physical world and its many inhabitants is somehow natural and normal.

Though diachronic analysis has been pursued in ecolinguistics previously, it is an underexplored space with compelling potential to demonstrate the evolving nature of attitudes, beliefs, and practices popularly viewed as objective renderings of present-day conditions. In the illustration of the changing evaluations of *wilderness*, the varied depictions of *wilderness* as savage, dangerous, and barren to more recent evaluations as true, remote, and pristine may be initially viewed as positive discursive shifts. Indeed, if such evaluations reflect and/or promote an emergent ecological ethic, then such shifting evaluations are beneficial developments. However, as the chapter asserted, the romanticization of a distant and pristine wilderness may function to reify such government-protected spaces alone as worthy of conservation while countless other rivers, lakes, mountains, and more beyond those officially designated boundaries neither receive such positive sentiment nor subsequent protection. Ecolinguistics should remain vigilant to linguistic practices which serve to fragment humans from their environments while also highlighting those linguistic practices which break down false barriers that function to separate humans from the natural world in which they are embedded.

It is my position that diachronic discourse analysis pursued through an ecolinguistic framework is particularly important for highlighting how humans understand and engage with the natural world and environmental concerns. Diachronic studies could apply a similar methodology as applied in this text to explore the evolving manner by which various other ecologically relevant constructs and resources are represented and evaluated. Perhaps present in the evaluative patterns through which such salient eco-keywords—water, air, energy, hurricane, flood, forest, ocean, recycle, sustainable, organic—are constructed and represented, we can further observe the emergence of attitudes and beliefs that are positive or challenge those judged as problematic while highlighting the contested, dynamic qualities of such representations.

The analysis presented in Chapter 3, the previous diachronic studies in ecolinguistics such as Frayne (2019) and Fusari (2018), and the ideas suggested in the previous paragraph are focused on a particular word or set of words deemed relevant to ecological sustainability and wellbeing. In this text, the focus was upon *wilderness* while Fusari (2018) tracked *animal* and Frayne (2019) expanded to numerous species names. Though I have asserted research of this sort to be promising, there is no reason why diachronic studies should be solely lexically oriented. Rather, corpus-assisted ecolinguistics may also explore lexicogrammatical features and colligational patterns and their realizations and functions within discourses of ecological relevance. For example, Halliday (1990/2001) cited four lexicogrammatical features of English as contributing to our present climate crisis (see Chapter 1 for further discussion). Additionally, Goatly (2001) posited that the frequency of ergative verbs may have increased over the past 100 years as "a kind of adaptive response to the insights of modern scientific thinking" (p. 217) and further asserts that the ergative clause type "can construe a reality in which energy is not simply imposed on an inert nature … but in which nature provides its own propensity for spontaneous change" (p. 217). Tracking the emergence of ergativity patterns as well as exploring a range of reciprocal verbs such as *cooperate, coexist, interact, intersect*, and others could be explored to possibly demonstrate an evolving ecological awareness which reflects greater understanding of interconnectivity between humans and ecosystems. One could argue that increases in ergative and reciprocal verbs in certain discursive settings—if this does indeed exist—is a positive discursive shift reflective of humanity's increased understanding of interconnection with the natural world. Here is not the space to explore this question more deeply, but I do hope this brief discussion illustrates the possibility for various research trajectories in this space.

Moving from diachronic study, the illustration in Chapter 4 pursued an integration of corpus stylistics and corpus-assisted ecolinguistics for the analysis of a literary text: *The Overstory* (2018) by Richard Powers. Ecolinguists are quite familiar with the idea of stories as Arran Stibbe's *Ecolinguistics: The stories we live by* has permeated throughout the field since the first edition was published in 2015. As one of the characters from *The Overstory* asserts, "The best arguments won't change a person's mind. Only a story can do that" (Powers, 2018, p. 336). As this quotation from Powers' novel reflects, there is great power in stories to transform how people perceive and act—this stance is shared by ecolinguistics. Humans are quite challenged to imagine alternative futures that move beyond current political, economic, and social systems whose confluence has manifested our present ecological crisis—"It's easier to imagine the end of the world than the end of capitalism" (Fisher, 2009, p. 1). However, within the stories present in climate crisis and speculative fiction, authors construct imagined worlds that may prompt readers to reflect upon the "trajectory of the present" (Schneider-Mayerson & Bellamy, 2020, p. 3). Such narratives of possible futures and imagined worlds may inspire new ways of thinking and being in the present.

Powers' novel exemplifies this potential for inspiring new ways of thinking and being, as the novel challenges the reader to reimagine and reconfigure their feelings and beliefs toward trees and forests. Typically represented as passive and inanimate, trees in *The Overstory* become agentive, social beings foregrounded as characters rather than background scenery to situate the actions of humans. Corpus-assisted eco-stylistics may be implemented to identify and highlight such discursive practices in the manner illustrated in Chapter 4. Indeed, other literary texts in these genres may similarly be praised for imagining worlds and using language that realizes and encodes alternative ways of thinking and being in relation to nature. Contrastingly, there are possibly, even likely, other texts in these genres that although they may construct captivating alternative futures for their audiences produce discourses that reflect and reproduce the same complex of ideologies and systems which have produced our present ecological crisis. In these cases, these practices should be challenged and critiqued—corpus-assisted ecolinguistics is well suited for such an exercise.

While Chapter 4 applied its corpus-assisted eco-stylistic approach to a popular novel, a similar analytic approach may be implemented for the study of stories and narratives elsewhere. For example, corpus-assisted ecolinguistics could pursue analyses of the language of digital games, the worlds present in their game spaces, and the stories underpinning game play. Though this may seem divergent, the influence of digital gaming should not be overlooked by researchers interested in the power of narratives for influencing identities and behaviors. Digital gaming is tremendously popular around the world and its cultural influence at least approaches that of movies, music, and television if it does not already exceed (Chatfield, 2010). Bogost writes that we must "critique the representations of our world" (2007, p. vii) presented in digital games as games have the power to 'disrupt and change fundamental attitudes and beliefs about the world" (2007, p. ix). Implementing an ecolinguistic framework, Poole and Spangler (2020) critiqued the popular simulation game *Animal Crossing: New Leaf* and demonstrated how unecological practices are embedded within an ostensibly eco-friendly game; for example, players are encouraged to recycle in order to earn points simply so that they may then purchase and consume more goods. As the virtual worlds of digital games become more immersive and complex, the stories they tell, or retell, are worthy sites of investigation for ecolinguistics.

In the penultimate illustration, yet another site which erases the lived experiences of nonhuman animals, minimizes their suffering, and represents them as commodities is critiqued. The chapter interrogated the reporting of animal escapes and displayed how wordplays that transgress conventionalized lexical primings function to trivialize these escape events through their playful even comedic tone. Along with wordplays of various sorts, the animals are referenced and discursively framed as criminals and thus threats to these communities. With this animal-as-criminal framing sedimented, the potential emotional impact to be felt by readers is mitigated as the language use legitimizes and normalizes the oppressive conditions of the animals and provides justification for the actions taken against them. That said, traces of a positive discourse were evident in the *Vegan News* article and its use of the term *sentient* for animals and its engagement with the animal farming industry and animal rights. Such positive practices seem uncommon in media, and thus, activists and ecolinguistics should continue to expose language use that perpetuates the suffering of nonhuman animals.

This illustration of Chapter 5 shows how an exploration of a small, specialized corpus with CADS techniques can yield valuable insights. Some may critique the approach for its use of a rather selective and specialized corpus. Indeed, at times, I have critiqued corpus-assisted research in ecolinguistics that employs small corpora for too often, in my opinion, these studies underutilized the affordances of CADS in their explorations of texts. However, there are undoubtedly ecologically relevant texts which though they may not make possible the compilation of a large corpus, they are indeed salient and worthy of inspection. While other more qualitative discourse analytic approaches can be applied in these cases, CADS techniques, particularly comparative analysis using large general corpora, can supplement such work by providing quantitative insights into the degree to which the patterns either converge or diverge with prevailing language use. Additionally, comparative analysis can illuminate the framings and semantic prosodies construed in popular language use, and by doing so, report data to support claims of how the patterns in the text/corpus under investigation are either problematic/negative or beneficial/positive. In such studies, Lexical Priming (Hoey, 2005) and Framing (Lakoff, 2010; Stibbe, 2015, 2021) can provide the theoretical support to help researchers make sense of the language use of such short texts and provide grounding for forwarding statements about language use in these spaces.

In the final case study, an integrated GIS, CADS, and ecolinguistics approach for the study of place was presented. The work of Donal Carbaugh (2001) established the foundation for ecolinguistic analyses of place and his work remains a powerful display of the importance of place referencing in language use. As displayed in the literature review of the chapter, the application of GIS has increased in recent years to answer a diversity of research questions across the humanities to such a degree that the emergent paradigm earned its own title: the Spatial Humanities. For ecolinguistics, the attention to place made possible through a GIS–CADS integration presents two primary affordances. First, it facilitates a continued and elaborated interest of ecolinguistics in the discursive representation of place and the interconnections of place and language. Secondly, the visualizations produced in such work enable an intuitive means to disseminate findings and ultimately to tell stories to a broader audience in both a compelling and accessible manner. Though the methodology presented in the chapter has room for refinement, the approach illustrated has numerous applications within a corpus-assisted ecolinguistic research enterprise.

Beyond the case studies, I would like to comment more broadly on additional paths corpus-assisted ecolinguistics could pursue. First, these chapters and their respective case studies were presented as distinct approaches for the elaboration of corpus-assisted ecolinguistics, yet opportunities for synthesis across approaches do exist. For example, a synthesis of corpus-assisted eco-stylistics with GIS is readily possible to map how authors reference and represent places in their work. As evident in the literature review of Chapter 5, this work is underway in various projects at universities internationally; however, it has not been pursued within an ecolinguistic framework. There is also the possibility to explore depictions of place as imagined in climate crisis and speculative fiction. Likewise, the frameworks of evaluation, framing, and lexical priming could be applied for a range of projects. Thus, researchers should be guided by the unique parameters of their own corpora and research questions, and thus, they should integrate and adapt as required for their particular projects.

Additionally, these case studies primarily focused on divergence and difference—the reality is most CADS work focuses on difference rather than similarity. Baker (2006) attributes this search for variation to the "corpus linguist's love of comparison" and asserts that our focus on divergence and the "obsession with difference" may result in overlooking the ways in which texts and corpora are similar (p. 182). This concern for a too narrow focus on difference in CADS was revisited more recently by Taylor (2018). In her work, Taylor asserts that "looking both ways," in other words, accounting for both similarity and difference, should become "standard practice and methodological principle" within CADS (p. 23). Such practice would inform analysis and also open research spaces for analysts to pursue. While the studies in this text generally emerge from an attention to divergence, each could be elaborated through search for similarity as well. For example, the keyness analysis of Chapter 4 focused upon those lexical items in *The Overstory* which diverged in use from the reference corpus of fiction texts. However, it is conceivable that similarities of salience likewise were present and deserving of discussion. Additionally, diachronic studies can highlight how certain representations have converged over time. For example, one could explore how media representations of climate crisis discourse have increasingly aligned in their representation of climate change rather than its general explorations to date on how such depictions have differed. Or studies could demonstrate how corporate discourses on the environment appropriated the language of sustainability in recent history while doing little to meaningfully incorporate more ecologically responsible practices.

Corpus-assisted ecolinguistics should also pursue analyses of corpora comprised of texts in other national contexts and of non-English languages. The reader likely noticed that the analyses of the present text were largely of corpora consisting of language use from the United States. This should not necessarily be viewed as a shortcoming, for if considering my positionality as a researcher in the United States, it seems only valid that my case studies would investigate contexts of which I am experienced and knowledgeable. Though corpus linguistics and CADS are perhaps popularly imagined as a largely quantitative endeavors, such a characterization is incomplete as CADS couples quantitative methods of analysis with qualitative interpretations. Corpus techniques indeed facilitate the identification of patterns of language use, but those patterns must still be contextualized and interpreted by the researcher. Such interpretations will undoubtedly be richer and more nuanced if the researcher has knowledge of the cultural, social, and political contexts from which the texts emerge. Though this text explores language use in corpora comprised of texts from a US context, the approach pursued and methods applied can be extended to other national contexts and languages other than English.

In addition to corpora from outside of the United States, there is also need and opportunity to create and analyze spoken corpora. The *People, Products, Pests, and Pets: The Discursive Representation of Animals* project advanced through the collaboration of Kings College London and Lancaster University presents a model for how such work may be structured and the insights such analysis may yield (see Sealey & Pak, 2018). In the project, researchers collected transcripts from interviews of producers of texts as well as transcripts from focus groups in which participants discuss texts concerning animals. Such corpora are laborious and time-consuming to construct, but as Cook and Ancarno (2019) display, they can offer keen insights into the discursive construction of eco-relevant issues. It is much easier to compile corpora of readily-available written texts, yet the analysis of spoken corpora has much to offer.

Finally, it is worthwhile to identify the EcoLexicon English Corpus (León-Araúz et al., 2018) and the research opportunities it makes possible. Comprising greater than 23 million words from contemporary environmental texts from various national contexts, it is an excellent resource for the study of modern environmental communication—in fact, it is the first corpus of environmental texts of its kind. This specialized corpus of environmental discourse includes texts and genres of environmental relevance unavailable in general corpora such as the COCA and BNC. For example, while the COCA does include a subcorpus of academic texts from 10 academic disciplines (e.g., Education, History, Business, etc.), the EcoLexicon includes texts from all domains of environmental studies (e.g., Environmental Law, Meteorology, Ecology, etc.). In addition, it includes various genres such as journal articles, books, and websites and from different sources: researchers, business, and government. This corpus presents numerous investigative possibilities for corpus-minded ecolinguists to pursue.

To researchers in CADS who are perhaps new to ecolinguistics, I hope this text has piqued your interest in ecolinguistics and demonstrated how you may apply your expertise in corpus approaches to projects of ecological relevance. I hope you will seek opportunities in your research to apply an ecolinguistic lens to the discourses which you study. Wherever you have focused your analytic interests, perhaps you can bring your knowledge of CADS to ecolinguistics and contribute to the further development of ecolinguistics and its mission. This may take place in the analysis of classroom discourse in language learning classrooms, corpus studies of language learning materials and resources, investigations of academic and science writing, studies of immigration discourse, and myriad other discourse domains in which you are experts and in which the application of an ecolinguistic lens could prove insightful.

Conversely, to ecolinguists perhaps unfamiliar with a corpus approach for discourse analysis, it is my hope the illustrations and their application of a range of corpus analytic techniques provide the necessary primer for you to integrate corpus techniques into your ecolinguistics research program. These analytic techniques present numerous affordances for the analysis of discourse, but researchers should be mindful of the myriad choices that must be carefully made throughout the research process. This book has hopefully illuminated some of these choices in corpus-assisted research and introduced those unfamiliar with corpus techniques to the fundamentals of such a data-driven approach to discourse analysis. Some may be wary of corpus linguistics and perceive the approach as having too great a learning curve or requiring technological skills they may not possess. In recent years, however, the number of publicly available corpora has greatly increased and their interfaces have become more user-friendly and intuitive. Further, corpus tools such as AntConc, WMatrix, LancsBox, Wordsmith Tools, and others provide useful tutorials and supportive communities. These developments have eased the hurdles to implementing a corpus approach for discourse analysis. This is not to say a corpus approach is simple, for it comes with its own challenges, and anyone seeking to implement corpus analysis techniques in their work would be wise to further review texts in the field such as *Using Corpora for Discourse Analysis* (Baker, 2006), *Corpus Approaches to Discourse* (Taylor & Marchi, 2018), or *Corpora and Discourse Studies* (Baker & McEnery, 2015).

If I may be so indulgent, I would like to close with some personal comments on ecolinguistics and the transformative influence it has had on me. In 2013, I stumbled upon the article which I have referenced so frequently in this text: M.A.K. Halliday's *New Ways of Meaning: The Challenge for Applied Linguists* (1990/2001). A serendipitous discovery, it reconfigured my ways of speaking and thinking of the environment. That influential article and this field continue to shape my existence well beyond my research and academic pursuits. So often now I reflect upon whether my language use helps me cultivate and promote greater ecological awareness for myself but also for those around me. The field and my work have challenged me to see the hypocrisies of my existence: how can I write that but do this? I now ask that question with less frequency as my actions increasingly align with my personal ecosophy. Indeed, the continued reflective work required to shape and put into action a guiding ecosophy has contributed to me becoming a better steward of the physical world and all of its inhabitants.

Perhaps in my account lies some hope for an alternative future in what feels a rather bleak present. Transformation and growth are possible, and our work must carry on even in these volatile days. Though hope feels elusive and even quite foolish at times, we must persist. As Eric Holthaus writes in the closing of *The Future Earth*, achieving a just and sustainable world is not possible "if we don't believe it's possible" (2020, p. 194). Perhaps I am naïve to believe ecolinguistics can contribute to the sort of radical, transformational change required to avert the cascading effects of climate crisis. Yet, for Holthaus, the path to change is clear: "billions of people just showing up in their own lives, energetic and ready to struggle together" (p. 194). This book is me showing up. I hope you will join me.

Notes

Chapter 2

1 For a detailed discussion of how such a large, thematically focused corpus is constructed, see Sealey and Pak's 2018 article titled, "First Catch Your Corpus: Methodological Challenges in Constructing and Thematic Corpus" in *Corpora*.

Chapter 3

1 In 2021, updates to the COHA added data from 2010 to 2019 and removed data from 1810 to 1819. This data analysis was conducted with data collected prior to these updates.

Chapter 4

1 The Corpus of Contemporary American English was updated in April 2020, and it now includes 120–130 million words of fiction. The data used in this illustration were downloaded prior to the update, and thus, the reference corpus is smaller than would now be possible.
2 In the one instance where the pattern *tree is saying* appears in the corpus, the word *tree* is a person's name.

Chapter 5

1 The bracket [] signals that all forms of the word *get* (get, gets, getting, got, gotten) were queried in the search and included in the results. Brackets are used in this manner throughout this chapter.

Bibliography

Alexander, R. (1999). Ecological commitment in business: A computer-corpus-based critical discourse analysis. *Language and ideology: Selected papers from the 6th International Pragmatics Conference, 1*(14–24), 14–24.

Alexander, R. (2002). Everyone is talking about "Sustainable Development". Can they all mean the same thing? Computer discourse analysis of ecological texts. In A. Fill, H. Penz, & W. Trampe (Eds.), *Colourful green ideas: Papers from the conference "30 years of language and ecology"* (pp. 239–54). Peter Lang.

Alexander, R. J. (2008). Parallels and paradoxes in the englishized "construction" of contemporary globalizing environmental discourse. In M. Doring, H. Penz, & W. Trampe (Eds.), *Language, signs, and nature: Ecolinguistic dimensions of environmental discourse. Essays in honour of Alwin Fill* (pp. 29–45). Stauffenburg.

Alexander, R. J. (2009). *Framing discourse on the environment: A critical discourse approach*. Routledge.

Alexander, R. (2013). Shaping and misrepresenting public perceptions of ecological catastrophes: The BP Gulf oil spill. *Critical Approaches to Discourse Analysis across Disciplines, 7*(1), 1–18.

Alexander, R., & Stibbe, A. (2014). From the analysis of ecological discourse to the ecological analysis of discourse. *Language Sciences, 41*, 104–10.

American Psychological Association. (2020). *Publication manual of the American Psychological Association* (7th ed).

Ana, O. S. (1999). "Like an animal I was treated": Anti-immigrant metaphor in US public discourse. *Discourse & Society, 10*(2), 191–224.

Anthony, L. (2020). AntConc (Version 3.5.9) [Computer Software]. Waseda University. https://www.laurenceanthony.net/software

Atkinson, D. (1999). *Science writing in sociohistorical context*. Lawrence Erlbaum.

Attenbourough, D. (2020, October 4). *David Attenborough: A life on our planet* [film]. Attitude Films.

Augoustinos, M., Crabb, S., & Shepherd, R. (2010). Genetically modified food in the news: Media representations of the GM debate in the UK. *Public Understanding of Science, 19*(1), 98–114.

Aull, L., & Lancaster, Z. (2014). Linguistic markers of stance in early and advanced academic writing: A corpus-based comparison. *Written Communication, 31*(2), 151–83.

Axworthy, N. (2019, January 7). *Federal court rules that almond milk is milk*. VegNews. https://vegnews.com/2019/1/federal-court-rules-that-almond-milk-is-milk

Baker, P. (2006). *Using corpora in discourse analysis*. Continuum.
Baker, P. (2010). Representations of Islam in British broadsheet and tabloid newspapers 1999–2005. *Language and Politics*, 9(2), 310–38.
Baker, P. (2011). Times may change, but we will always have money: Diachronic variation in recent British English. *Journal of English Linguistics*, 39(1), 63–88.
Baker, P., Gabrielatos, C., & Khosravnik, M., et al. (2008). A useful methodological synergy? Combining critical discourse analysis and corpus linguistics to examine discourses of refugees and asylum seekers in the UK press. *Discourse and Society*, 19(3), 273–306.
Baker, P., Gabrielatos, C., & McEnery, T. (2013). Sketching Muslims: A corpus-driven analysis of representation around the word "Muslim" in the British press, 1998–2009. *Applied Linguistics*, 34(3), 255–78.
Baker, P., & McEnery, T. (2015). *Corpora and discourse studies: Integrating discourse and corpora*. Palgrave Macmillan.
Bang, J. C., & Døør, J. (1993). Ecolinguistics: A framework. In R. Alexander, J. C. Bang, & J. Døør (Eds.), *Papers for the symposium "Ecolinguistics: Problems, theories and methods"* (pp. 31–60). AILA.
Bang, J. C., & Trampe, W. (2014) Aspects of an ecological theory of language. *Language Sciences*, 41, 83–92.
Basso, K. (1996). *Wisdom sits in places: Language and landscape among the Western Apache*. University of New Mexico Press.
Bednarek, M., & Caple, H. (2010). Playing with environmental stories in the news—good or bad practice? *Discourse & Communication*, 4(1), 5–31.
Bevitori, C. (2011). "Jumping on the green bandwagon": The discursive construction of GREEN across "old" and "new" media genres at the intersection between corpora and discourse. In *Proceedings of the Corpus Linguistics Conference 2011-Discourse and Corpus Linguistics* (pp. 1–19). https://www.birmingham.ac.uk/research/activity/corpus/publications/conference-archives/2011-birmingham.aspx
Bevitori, C. (2015). Discursive constructions of the environment in American presidential speeches 1960–2013. In P. Baker & T. McEnery (Eds.), *Corpora and discourse studies: Integrating discourse and corpora* (pp. 110–33). Palgrave Macmillan.
Biber, D. (2006). Stance in spoken and written university registers. *Journal of English for Academic Purposes*, 5(2), 97–116.
Biber, D., Conrad, S., & Reppen, R. (1998). *Corpus linguistics: Investigating language structure and use*. Cambridge University Press.
Biber, D., & Finegan, E. (1989). Styles of stance in English: Lexical and grammatical marking of evidentiality and affect. *Interdisciplinary Journal for the Study of Discourse*, 9(1), 93–124.
Biber, D., Johansson, S., Leech, G., Conrad, S., & Finegan, E. (2000). *Longman grammar of spoken and written English*. Longman.

Blakemore, E. (2019, July 29). Lasers are driving a revolution in archaeology. *National Geographic.* https://www.nationalgeographic.com/culture/article/lasers-lidar-driving-revolution-archaeology

Blinder, S., & Allen, W. L. (2016). Constructing immigrants: Portrayals of migrant groups in British national newspapers, 2010–2012. *International Migration Review, 50*(1), 3–40.

Bodenheimer, D., Corrigan, J., & Harris, T. (2010). *The spatial humanities: GIS and the future of humanities scholarship.* Indiana University Press.

Bogost, I. (2007). *Persuasive games.* MIT Press.

Bonnefille, S. M. (2008). When green rhetoric and cognitive linguistics meet: President G. W. Bush's environmental discourse in his State of the Union Addresses (2001–2008). *Metaphorik.De, 15,* 27–61.

Boussalis, C., & Coan, T. G. (2016). Text-mining the signals of climate change doubt. *Global Environmental Change, 36,* 89–100.

Boussalis, C., Coan, T. G., & Poberezhskaya, M. (2016). Measuring and modeling Russian newspaper coverage of climate change. *Global Environmental Change, 41,* 99–110.

Brezina, V. (2018). *Statistics in corpus linguistics: A practical guide.* Cambridge University Press.

Bringhurst, R. (2008). *The tree of meaning: Language, mind, and ecology.* Counterpoint.

Brown, M. (2008). *Managing nature-business as usual: Patterns of wording and patterns of meaning in corporate environmental discourse* [dissertation]. University of Oslo.

Bucaria, C. (2004). Lexical and syntactic ambiguity as a source of humor: The case of newspaper headlines. *Humor, 17*(3), 279–309.

Bunting, M. (2007, July 29). We need an attentiveness to nature to understand our own humanity. *The Guardian.* https://www.theguardian.com/commentisfree/2007/jul/30/comment.bookscomment

Carbaugh, D. (2001). "The mountain" and "the project": Dueling depictions of a natural environment. In A. Fill & P. Mühlhäusler (Eds.), *The ecolinguistics reader: Language, ecology and environment* (pp. 124–42). Continuum.

Carbaugh, D., & Rudnick, L. (2006). Which place, what story? Cultural discourses at the border of the Blackfeet Reservation and Glacier National Park. *Great Plains Quarterly, 26*(3), 167–84.

Carrington, D. (2011, November 22). Hacked climate science emails: Climategate. *The Guardian.* https://www.theguardian.com/environment/2010/jul/07/climate-emails-question-answer

Carson, R. (1962). *Silent spring.* Houghton Mifflin.

Carvalho, A. (2005). Representing the politics of the greenhouse effect: Discursive strategies in the British media. *Critical Discourse Studies, 2*(1), 1–29.

Castello, E., & Gesuato, S. (2019). Pope Francis's Laudato Si: A corpus study of environmental and religious discourse. *Lingue e Linguaggi, 29,* 121–45.

Charles, M. (2006). The construction of stance in reporting clauses: A cross-disciplinary study of theses. *Applied Linguistics, 27*(3), 492–518.

Chatfield, T. (2010). *Fun inc.: Why gaming will dominate the twenty-first century*. Pegasus.

Chesnokova, O., Taylor, J. E., Gregory, I. N., & Purves, R. S. (2019). Hearing the silence: Finding the middle ground in the spatial humanities? Extracting and comparing perceived silence and tranquility in the English Lake District. *International Journal of Geographical Information Science, 33*(12), 2430–54.

Collins, L., & Nerlich, B. (2015). Examining user comments for deliberative democracy: A corpus-driven analysis of the climate change debate online. *Environmental Communication, 9*(2), 189–207.

Conoscenti, M. (2011). *The reframer: An analysis of Barack Obama's political discourse (2004–2010)*. Bulzoni.

Cook, D. (2020). *The new wilderness*. HarperCollins.

Cook, G. (2015). "A pig is a person" or "you can love a fox and hunt it": Innovation and tradition in the discursive representation of animals. *Discourse & Society, 26*(5), 587–607.

Cook, G., & Ancarno, C. (2019). 'I do still love the taste': Taste as a reason for eating nonhuman animals. *Interdisciplinary Studies in Literature and Environmental, 28*(1), 88–112.

do Couto, H. H. (2014). Ecological approaches in linguistics: A historical overview. *Language Sciences, 41*, 122–8.

do Couto, H. H. (2017). Ecosystemic linguistics. In A. Fill & H. Penz (Eds.), *The Routledge handbook of ecolinguistics* (pp. 149–61). Routledge.

Cronon, W. (1996). The trouble with wilderness: Or, getting back to the wrong nature. *Environmental History, 1*(1), 7–28.

Culpeper, J. (2002). Computers, language and characterisation: An analysis of six characters in Romeo and Juliet. In *Conversation in Life and in Literature: Papers from the ASLA Symposium, 15* (pp. 11–30). Universitestryckeriet.

Culpeper, J. (2009). Keyness: Words, parts-of-speech and semantic categories in the character-talk of Shakespeare's Romeo and Juliet. *International Journal of Corpus Linguistics, 14*(1), 29–59.

Davies, M. (2004). *British national corpus*. https://www.english-corpora.org/bnc/

Davies, M. (2008–). *The corpus of contemporary American English*. http://corpus.byu.edu/coca/.

Davies, Mark. (2010–). *The corpus of historical American English*. http://corpus.byu.edu/coha/

Davies, M. (2012–). *The strathy corpus of Canadian English*. https://www.english-corpora.org/can/

Davis, J. E. (2017). *The Gulf: The making of an American Sea*. Liveright.

Demott, R. (1992). Introduction. In J. Steinbeck (Author), *The grapes of wrath* (pp. IX–LVIII). Penguin.

Donaldson, C., Gregory, I., & Taylor, J. (2017). Locating the beautiful, picturesque, sublime and majestic: Spatially analysing the application of aesthetic terminology in descriptions of the English Lake District. *Journal of Historical Geography, 56*, 43–60.

Duguid, A. (2010). Newspaper discourse informalisation: A diachronic comparison from keywords. *Corpora, 5*(2), 109–38.

Durán-Muñoz, I. (2019). Adjectives and their keyness: A corpus-based analysis of tourism discourse in English. *Corpora, 14*(3), 351–78.

Eggins, S. (2004). *Introduction to systemic functional linguistics* (2nd ed.). Continuum.

Fairclough, N. (1989). *Language and power*. Routledge.

Fairclough, N. (1992). *Discourse and social change*. Polity Press.

Fairclough, N., & Wodak, R. (1997). Critical discourse analysis. In T. Van Dijk (Ed.), *Discourse studies: A multidisciplinary introduction* (pp. 258–84). Sage.

Fill, A., & Mühlhäusler, P. (2001). Introduction. In A. Fill & P. Mühlhäusler (Eds.), *The ecolinguistics reader: Language, ecology, and environment* (pp. 1–9). Continuum.

Firth, J. R. (1968). *Selected papers of J.R. Firth 1952–1959*. Longmans.

Fisher, M. (2009). *Capitalist realism: Is there no alternative?* O Books.

Fischer-Starke, B. (2010). *Corpus linguistics in literary analysis: Jane Austen and her contemporaries*. Continuum.

Fitzsimmons-Doolan, S. (2019). Taxpaying, importing, enforcing: Emerging discourse patterns in online newspaper comments about U.S. immigrant education. *Journal of Corpora and Discourse Studies, 2*, 94–116.

Flores, P., Baron, A., Gregory, I., Hardie, A., & Rayson, P. (YEAR). Automatically analyzing large texts in a GIS environment: The registrar general's reports and cholera in the 19th century. *Transactions in GIS, 19*(2), 296–320.

Fløttum, K., & Dahl, T. (2012). Different contexts, different "stories"? A linguistic comparison of two development reports on climate change. *Language & Communication, 32*(1), 14–23.

Fløttum, K., Gjesdal, A. M., Gjerstad, Ø, Koteyko, N., & Salway, A. (2014). Representations of the future in English language blogs on climate change. *Global Environmental Change, 29*, 213–22.

Fortanet, I. (2008). Evaluative language in peer review referee reports. *Journal of English for Academic Purposes, 7*(1), 27–37.

Forte, D. L. (2015). Nonhuman animal legislation and speciesist discourse. Argentina's Pet Responsibility Act: Anti-cruelty law or death row pardon? *Language & Ecology*, 1–19.

Frayne, C. (2019). An historical analysis of species references in American English. *Corpora, 14*(3), 327–49.

Freeman, C. (2009). This little piggy went to press. The American news media's construction of animals in agriculture. *The Communication Review, 12*(1), 78–103.

Freeman, C. (2016). This little piggy went to press: The American new media's construction of animals in agriculture. In N. Almiron, M. Cole, & C. Freeman (Eds.), *Critical animal and media studies: Communication for nonhuman animal advocacy* (pp. 169–84). Routledge.

Fries, C. (1925). The periphrastic future with shall and will in modern English. *Publications of the Modern Language Association of America, 40*(4), 963–1024.

Fusari, S. (2018). Changing representations of animals in Canadian English (1920s–2010s). *Language & Ecology*, 1–32.

Gabrielatos, C. (2018). Keyness analysis. In C. Taylor & A. Marchi (Eds.), *Corpus approaches to discourse: A critical review* (225–58). Routledge.

Gabrielatos, C., McEnery, T., Diggle, P. J., & Baker, P. (2012). The peaks and troughs of corpus-based contextual analysis. *International Journal of Corpus Linguistics, 17*(2), 151–75.

Gee, J. P. (2011). *An introduction to discourse analysis: Theory and method*. Routledge.

Geophysical Fluid Dynamics Laboratory (2021). Global warming and hurricanes: An overview of current research results. https://www.gfdl.noaa.gov/global-warming-and-hurricanes/

Gerbig, A. (1997). *Lexical and grammatical variation in a corpus: A computer-assisted study of discourse on the environment*. Peter Lang.

Gerbig, A. (2003). Book Review of The ecolinguistics reader: Language, ecology and environment. *Current Issues in Language Planning, 4*(1), 91–3.

Giamo, C. (2016, March 30). Why writers fight style guides over animal pronouns? *Atlas Obscura*. https://www.atlasobscura.com/articles/why-writers-fight-style-guides-over-animal-pronouns

Gilbert, I. (2019). An ecolinguistic analysis of pro-dairy discourse on Instagram. Paper presented at the 4th International Conference on Ecolinguistics, Odense, Denmark.

Gilquin, G., & Jacobs, G. M. (2006). Elephants who marry mice are very unusual: The use of the relative pronoun Who with nonhuman animals. *Society & Animals, 14*(1), 79–105.

Gitlin, T. (2003). *The whole world is watching: Mass media in the making and unmaking of the new left*. University of California Press.

Glenn, C. B. (2004). Constructing consumables and consent: A critical analysis of factory farm industry discourse. *Journal of Communication Inquiry, 28*(1), 63–81.

Goatly, A. (2001). Green grammar and grammatical metaphor, or language and myth of power, or metaphors we die by. In A. Fill and P. Mühlhäusler (Eds.), *The ecolinguistics reader: Language, ecology, and environment* (pp. 203–25). Continuum.

Goatly, A. (2002). The representation of nature on the BBC World Service. *Text, 22*(1), 1–27.

Goatly, A. (2004). Nature and Grammar. In C. Coffin, A. Hewings, & K. O'Halloran (Eds.), *Applying English grammar: Functional and corpus approaches* (pp. 197–215). Hodder Arnold.

Goatly, A. (2017). Lexical priming in humorous discourse. *The European Journal of Humour Research, 5*(1), 52–68.

Goodman, J., & Giles, C. (2020, August 29). Amazon fires: Are they worse this year than before? *BBC News*. https://www.bbc.com/news/world-latin-america-53893161

Grant, W. J., & Walsh, E. (2015). Social evidence of a changing climate: Google Ngram data points to early climate change impact on human society. *Weather, 70*(7), 195–7.

Gray, B., & Biber, D. (2012). Current conceptions of stance. In K. Hyland & C.S. Guinda (Eds.), *Stance in written academic genres* (pp. 15–33). Palgrave Macmillan.

Greer, J., & Bruno, K. (1996). *Greenwash: The reality behind corporate environmentalism*. Third World Network.

Gregory, I. N., & Hardie, A. (2011). Visual GISting: Bringing together corpus linguistics and geographical information systems. *Literary and Linguistic Computing, 26*(3), 297–314.

Gregory, I. N., Donaldson, C., Murrieta-Flores, P., & Rayson, P. (2015). Geoparsing, GIS and textual analysis: Current developments in spatial humanities research. *International Journal of Humanities and Arts Computing, 9*(1), 1–14.

Gries, S. T., & Hilpert, M. (2010). Modeling diachronic change in the third person singular: A multifactorial, verb-and author-specific exploratory approach. *English Language and Linguistics, 14*(3), 293–320.

Grundmann, R., & Krishnamurthy, R. (2010). The discourse of climate change: A corpus-based approach. *Critical Approaches to Discourse Analysis across Disciplines, 4*(2), 125–46.

Grundmann, R., & Scott, M. (2012). Disputed climate science in the media: Do countries matter? *Public Understanding of Science, 23*(2), 220–35.

Gupta, A. F. (2006). Foxes, hounds, and horses: Who or which? *Society & Animals, 14*(1), 107–28.

Haig, E. (2001). A study of the application of critical discourse analysis to ecolinguistics and the teaching of eco-literacy. *Studies in Language and Culture, 22*(2), 205–26.

Halliday, M. A. K. (1990/2001). New ways of meaning: The challenge to applied linguistics. In A. Fill & P. Mühlhäusler (Eds.), *The ecolinguistics reader: Language, ecology and environment* (pp. 175–202). Continuum. (Reprinted from "New ways of meaning: The challenge to applied linguistics," 1990, *Journal of Applied Linguistics*, 6, 7–36.)

Halliday, M. A., & Hasan, R. (1985). *Language, context, and text: Aspects of language in a social-semiotic perspective*. Deakin University.

Hanna, A., Sayre, B., Bode, L., Yang, J., & Shah, D. (2011). Mapping the political twitterverse: Candidates and their followers in the midterms. *Proceedings of the International AAAI Conference on Web and Social Media, 5*(1), 1–4.

Hardie, A. (2014, April 28). Log ratio—An informal introduction. Center for Corpus Approaches to Social Sciences. http://cass.lancs.ac.uk/log-ratio-an-informal-introduction/

Hardt-Mautner, G. (1995). *"Only connect": Critical discourse analysis and corpus linguistics*. UCREL.

Harré, R., Brockmeir, M., & Mühlhäusler, P. (1998). *Greenspeak: A study of environmental discourse*. Sage.

Haugen, E. (1972/2001). The ecology of language. In A. Fill & P. Mühlhäusler (Eds.), *The ecolinguistics reader: Language, ecology and environment* (pp. 57–66). Continuum. (Reprinted from *The ecology of language: Essays by Einar Haugen*, pp. 325–329, by E. Haugen, 1972, Stanford University Press.)

Hewings, M. (2004). An "important contribution" or "tiresome reading": A study of evaluation in peer reviews of journal article submissions. *Journal of Applied Linguistics, 1*(3), 247–74.

Hilpert, M., & Gries, S. T. (2009). Assessing frequency changes in multistage diachronic corpora: Applications for historical corpus linguistics and the study of language acquisition. *Literary and Linguistic Computing, 24*(4), 385–401.

Hoey, M. (2005). *Lexical priming: A new theory of words and language*. Routledge.

Hoffman, S. (2002). In (hot) pursuit of data: Complex prepositions in late modern English. In P. Peters, P. Collins, & A. Smith (Eds.), *New frontiers of corpus research* (pp. 127–46). Rodopi.

Holthaus, E. (2020). *The future earth*. HarperOne.

Huang, G., & Zhao, R. (2021). Harmonious discourse analysis: Approaching people's problems in a Chinese context. *Language Sciences, 85*, 1–18.

Huang, Y., Guo, D., Kasakoff, A., & Grieve, J. (2016). Understanding US regional linguistic variation with Twitter data analysis. *Computers, Environment and Urban systems, 59*, 244–55.

Hueberger, R. (2003). Anthropocentrism in monolingual English dictionaries: An ecolinguistic approach to the lexicographic treatment of faunal terminology. *AAA: Arbeiten aus Anglistik und Amerikanistik, 28*(1), 93–105.

Hyland, K. (1996). Writing without conviction? Hedging in science research articles. *Applied Linguistics, 17*(4), 433–54.

Hyland, K. (1998). *Hedging in scientific research articles*. John Benjamins.

Hyland, K. (2005). *Metadiscourse*. Continuum.

Hyland, K. (2010). Constructing proximity: Relating to readers in popular and professional science. *Journal of English for Academic Purposes, 9*, 116–27.

Hyland, K., & Jiang, F. (2016). Change of attitude?: A diachronic study of stance. *Written Communication, 33*(3), 251–74.

Hyon, S. (2011). Evaluation in tenure and promotion letters: Constructing faculty as communicators, stars, and workers. *Applied Linguistics, 32*(4), 389–407.

Incelli, E. (2013). Shaping reality through metaphorical patterns in legislative texts on immigration: A corpus-assisted approach. In G. Tessuto & C. Williams (Eds.), *Language in the negotiation of justice: Contexts, issues and applications* (pp. 235–58). Taylor and Francis.

International Ecolinguistics Association (IEA). http://ecolinguistics-association.org/

Jacobs, G. M., Jayavelu, S., & Greliche, N. (n.d.). Variation in the use of terms related to vegetarianism. *Academia*. Accessed April 2021. https://www.academia.edu/33204380/Variation_in_the_Use_of_Terms_Related_to_Vegetarianism

Jaworska, S. (2013). The quest for the "local" and "authentic": Corpus-based explorations into the discursive constructions of tourist destinations in British and German commercial travel advertising *Tourismuskommunikation. Im Spannungsfeld von Sprach- und Kulturkontakt*, 75–100.

Jaworska, S., & Krishnamurthy, R. (2012). On the "F" word: A corpus-based analysis of media representations of feminism in British and German press discourse. *Discourse & Society, 23*(2), 401–31.

Jepson, J. (2008). A linguistic analysis of discourse on the killing of nonhuman animals. *Society and Animals, 16*, 127–48.

Johansson, C. (2002). Pied piping and stranding from a diachronic perspective. In P. Peters, P. Collins, & A. Cohen (Eds.), *New frontiers of corpus research: Papers from the twenty first international conference on English language research on computerized corpora Sydney 2000* (pp. 147–62). Brill.

Khazaal, N., & Almiron, N. (2016). "An angry cow is not a good eating experience": How US and Spanish media are shifting from crude to camouflaged speciesism in concealing nonhuman perspectives. *Journalism Studies, 17*(3), 374–91.

Kidner, K. (2016). Neutral ground and naming: The implications of Tar Sands and Oil Sands for environmental debates in Alberta. *Critical Approaches to Discourse Analysis across Disciplines, 8*(2), 1–18.

Kingsland, S. (1991). Defining ecology as a science. In L. Real & J. Brown (Eds.), *Foundations of ecology: Classic papers with commentaries* (pp. 1–13). University of Chicago Press.

Koestler, A. (1964). *The act of creation*. Hutchinson.

Koteyko, N. (2010). Mining the internet for linguistic and social data: An analysis of "carbon compounds" in web feeds. *Discourse & Society, 21*(6), 655–74.

Koteyko, N., Jaspal, R., & Nerlich, B. (2013). Climate change and "climategate" in online reader comments: A mixed methods study. *The Geographical Journal, 179*(1), 74–86.

Kutter, A., & Kantner, C. (2012). Corpus-based content analysis: A method for investigating news coverage on war and intervention. *International Relations Online Working Paper, 1*, 4–35.

Lakoff, G. (2010). Why it matters how we frame the environment. *Environmental Communication, 4*(1), 70–81.

Lakoff, G., & Johnson, M. (1980). *Metaphors we live by*. The University of Chicago Press.

Leech, G. (2002). Recent grammatical change in English: Data, description, theory. In K. Aijmer & B. Altenberg (Eds.), *Proceedings of the 2002 ICAME conference* (pp. 61–81). Rodopi.

León-Araúz, P., San Martin, A., & Reimerink, A. (2018). The EcoLexicon English Corpus as an open corpus in Sketch Engine. *Proceedings of the 18th EURALEX International Congress*, 893–901.

LeVassuer, T. (2015). Defining "ecolinguistics?": Challenging emic issues in an evolving environmental discipline. *Journal of Environmental Studies and Sciences, 5*, 21–8.

Lindenmayer, D., & Taylor, C. (2020). New spatial analyses of Australian wildfires highlight the need for new fire, resource, and conservation policies. *Proceedings of the National Academy of Sciences of the United States of America, 117*(22), 12481–5.

Lischinsky, A. (2011). The discursive construction of a responsible corporate self. In A. E. Sjölander, & J. Gunnarsson Payne (Eds.), *Tracking discourses: Politics, identity and social change* (pp. 257–85). Nordic Academic Press.

Lischinsky, A. (2015). What is the environment doing in my report? Analyzing the environment-as-stakeholder thesis through corpus linguistics. *Environmental Communication, 9*(4), 539–59.

Lischinsky, A., & Sjölander, A. E. (2014). Talking green in the public sphere: Press releases, corporate voices and the environment. *Nordicom Review, 35*, 125–39.

Liu, M., & Li, C. (2017). Competing discursive constructions of China's smog in Chinese and Anglo-American English-language newspapers: A corpus-assisted discourse study. *Discourse & Communication, 11*(4), 1–18.

Long, H. (2020, January 23). Treasury secretary Mnuchin says climate activist Greta Thunberg should go study economics. *The Washington Post.* https://www.washingtonpost.com/business/2020/01/23/us-treasury-secretary-mnuchin-says-climate-activist-greta-thunberg-should-go-study-economics/

Luzón, M. J. (2012). "Your argument is wrong": A contribution to the study of evaluation in academic weblogs. *Text & Talk, 32*(2), 145–65.

Macfarlane, R. (2013). Environment: New words on the wild. *Nature, 498*, 166–7.

Maci, S. M. (2012a). "Click here, book now!" Discursive strategies of tourism on the web. *Textus: English Studies in Italy, 1*, 137–56.

Maci, S. M. (2012b). Tourism as a specialised discourse: The case of normative guidelines in the European Union. *Token: A Journal of English Linguistics, 1*, 37–58.

Maci, S. M. (2012c). Fast-track publications: The genre of medical research letters. In M. Gotti (Ed.), *Academic identity traits* (pp. 243–62). Peter Lang.

Maci, S. M. (2012d). The genre of medical conference posters. In M. Gotti (Ed.), *Academic identity traits* (pp. 283–301). Peter Lang.

Macintosh, R. P. (1985). *The background of ecology: Concept and theory.* Cambridge University Press.

Mahlberg, M. (2007). Lexical items in discourse. Identifying local textual functions of sustainable development. In M. Hoey, M. Mahlberg, M. Stubbs, & W. Teubert (Eds.), *Text, discourse & corpora: Theory and analysis* (pp. 191–218). Continuum.

Mahlberg, M. (2013). *Corpus stylistics and Dicken's fiction.* Routledge.

Mahlberg, M., Stockwell, P., de Joode, J., Smith, C., & O'Donnell, M. B. (2016). CLiC Dickens: Novel uses of concordances for the integration of corpus stylistics and cognitive poetics. *Corpora, 11*(3), 433–63.

Mair, C. (2002). Three changing patterns of verb complementation in late modern English: A real-time study based on matching text corpora. *English Language and Linguistics, 6*(1).

Marchi, A. (2010). "The moral in the story": A diachronic investigation of lexicalised morality in the UK press. *Corpora*, 5(2), 161–89.

Martin, J. R. (1986). Grammaticalizing ecology. The politics of baby seals and kangaroos. In T. Threadgold, E. Grosz, G. Kress, & M. Halliday (Eds.), *Semiotics, ideology, language* (pp. 235–67). Sydney Association for Studies in Society and Culture.

Martin, J. R. (1993). Life as a noun: Arresting the universe in science and humanities. In M. A. K. Halliday & J. R. Martin (Eds.), *Writing science: Literacy and discursive power* (pp. 221–67). Routledge.

Martin, J. R. (2000). Beyond exchange: Appraisal systems in English. In. S. Hunston & G. Thompson (Eds.), *Evaluation in text: Authorial stance and the construction of discourse* (pp. 142–75). Oxford University Press.

McEnery, T., & Hardie, A. (2012). *Corpus linguistics: Method, theory and practice*. Cambridge University Press.

McEnery, T., Xiao, R., & Tono, Y. (2006). *Corpus-based language studies: An advanced resource book*. Taylor & Francis.

McIntyre, D., & Walker, B. (2019). *Corpus stylistics: Theory and practice*. Edinburgh University Press.

Milizia, D. (2009). Migration of n-grams and concgrams in political speeches. In *Forms of Migrations—Migration of Forms: Atti del XXIII Convegno Nazionale AIA* (pp. 496–514). Progedit.

Milizia, D. (2010). Keywords and phrases in political speeches. In M. Bondi & M. Scott (Eds.), *Keyness in Text* (pp. 127–45). John Benjamins.

Milizia, D. (2012). *Phraseology in political discourse: A corpus linguistics approach in the classroom*. LED.

Millar, N. (2009). Modal verbs in TIME: Frequency changes 1923–2006. *International Journal of Corpus Linguistics*, 14(2), 191–220.

Morley, J., & Taylor, C. (2012). Us and them: How immigrants are constructed in British and Italian newspapers. In P. Bayley & G. Williams (Eds.), *European identity: What the media say*. Oxford University Press.

Mühlhäusler, P. (2003). *Language of environment, environment of language: A course in ecolinguistics*. Battlebridge.

Murray, R., & Heumann, J.K. (2016). *Monstrous nature: Environment and horror on the big screen*. University of Nebraska Press.

Murrieta-Flores, P., Baron, A., Gregory, I., Hardie, A., & Rayson, P. (2015). Automatically analyzing large texts in a GIS environment: The registrar general's reports and cholera in the 19th century. *Transactions in GIS*, 19(2), 296–320.

Naess, A. (1975). The shallow and the long range, deep ecology movement. In A. Drengson & Y. Inoue (Eds.), *The deep ecology movement: An introductory anthology* (pp. 3–10). North Atlantic Books.

Nartey, M., & Mwinlaaru, I. N. (2019). Towards a decade of synergizing corpus linguistics and critical discourse analysis: A meta-analysis. *Corpora*, 14(2), 1–26.

Nash, J., and Mühlhäusler, P. (2014). Linking language and the environment: The case of Norf'k and Norfolk Island. *Language Sciences, 41*, 23–33.

Nerlich, B., Forsyth, R., & Clarke, D. (2012). Climate in the news: How differences in media discourse between the US and UK reflect national priorities. *Environmental Communication, 6*(1), 44–63.

Nerlich, B., & Koteyko, N. (2009). Compounds, creativity and complexity in climate change communication: The case of "carbon indulgences." *Global Environmental Change, 19*, 345–53.

Nerlich, B., Koteyko, N., & Brown, B. (2010). Theory and language of climate change communication. *WIREs Climate Change, 1*(1), 97–110.

Ooi, V. B. Y. (2017). A corpus-based linguistic profiling of marine humanities discourse. *Journal of Global and Area Studies, 1*(2), 85–109.

Partington, A. (2003). Corpora and discourse strategies in action: From footing to fooling. In B. Lewandowska-Tomaszczyk (Ed.), *PALC 2001: Practical applications in language corpora* (pp. 179–92). Peter Lang.

Partington, A. (2006). *The linguistics of laughter: A corpus-assisted study of laughter-talk*. Routledge.

Partington, A. (2010). Modern diachronic corpus-assisted discourse studies (MD-CADS) on UK newspapers: An overview of the project. *Corpora, 5*(2), 83–108.

Partington, A. (2012). The changing discourses on antisemitism in the UK press from 1993 to 2009. *Journal of Language and Politics, 11*(1), 51–76.

Partington, A., & Morley, J. (2004). At the heart of ideology: Word and cluster/bundle frequency in political debate. In B. Lewandowska-Tomaszczyk (Ed.), *PALC 2003: Practical applications in language corpora* (pp. 179–92). Peter Lang.

Patel, K. (2018, December 5). Six trends to know about fire season in the western U.S. *NASA Global Climate Change*. https://climate.nasa.gov/blog/2830/six-trends-to-know-about-fire-season-in-the-western-us/

Piao, S., Bianchi, F., Dayrell, C., D'Egidio, A., & Rayson, P. (2015). Development of the multilingual semantic annotation system. *Proceedings of the 2015 conference of the North American chapter of the Association for Computational Linguistics - Human Language Technologies* (pp. 1268–74). Association for Computational Linguistics.

Plappert, G. (2017). Candidate knowledge? Exploring epistemic claims in scientific writing: A corpus-driven approach. *Corpora, 12*(3), 424–57.

Plec, E., & Pettenger, M. (2012). Greenwashing consumption: The didactic framing of ExxonMobil's energy solutions. *Environmental Communication, 6*(4), 459–76.

Poole, R. (2016a). A corpus-aided ecological discourse analysis of the Rosemont Copper Mine debate of Arizona, USA. *Discourse & Communication, 10*(6), 576–95.

Poole, R. (2016b). Good times, bad times: A keyword analysis of letters to shareholders of two Fortune 500 banking institutions. *International Journal of Business Communication, 53*(1), 55–73.

Poole, R. (2017a). "New opportunities" and "strong performance": Evaluative adjectives in letters to shareholders and potential for pedagogically-downsized specialized corpora. *English for Specific Purposes, 47*, 40–51.

Poole, R. (2017b). Ecolinguistics, GIS, and corpus linguistics for the analysis of the Rosemont Copper Mine debate. *Environmental Communication, 12*(4), 525–40.

Poole, R., Gnann, A., & Hahn-Powell, G. (2019). Epistemic stance and the construction of knowledge in science writing: A diachronic corpus study. *Journal of English for Academic Purposes, 42*(19), 1–12. doi:https://doi.org/10.1016/j.jeap.2019.100784.

Poole, R., & Spangler, S. (2020). "Eco this and recycle that": An ecolinguistic analysis of a popular digital simulation game. *Critical Discourse Studies, 17*(3), 344–57.

Popper, N. (2019, February 19). You call that meat? Not so fast, cattle ranchers say. *New York Times*. https://www.nytimes.com/2019/02/09/technology/meat-veggie-burgers-lab-produced.html

Potts, A. (2015). Filtering the flood: Semantic tagging as a method of identifying salient discourse topics in a large corpus of Hurricane Katrina reportage. In P. Baker & T. McEnery (Eds.), *Corpora and discourse studies: Integrating discourse and corpora* (pp. 285–304). Palgrave Macmillan.

Potts, A., Bednarek, M., & Caple, H. (2015). How can computer-based methods help researchers to investigate news values in large datasets? A corpus linguistic study of the construction of newsworthiness in the reporting on Hurricane Katrina. *Discourse & Communication, 9*(2), 149–72.

Powers, R. (2018). *The overstory*. W. W. Norton & Company.

Prentice, S., Rayson, P., & Taylor, P. J. (2012). The language of Islamic extremism: Towards an automated identification of beliefs, motivations and justifications. *International Journal of Corpus Linguistics, 17*(2), 259–86.

Rayson, P. (2008). From key words to key semantic domains. *International Journal of Corpus Linguistics, 13*(4), 519–49.

Rayson, P. (2009). *Wmatrix: A web-based corpus processing environment*. Lancaster University. http://ucrel.lancs.ac.uk/wmatrix/.

Rothman, J. (2015, January 14). The weird Thoreau. *The New Yorker*. https://www.newyorker.com/culture/cultural-comment/weird-thoreau-jeff-vandermeer-southern-reach

Rume, T., & Islam, S. M. D. (2020). Environmental effects of COVID-19 pandemic and potential strategies of sustainability. *Heliyon, 6*(9), 1–8. doi: https://doi.org/10.1016/j.heliyon.2020.e04965.

Rust, S. A., & Soles, C. (2014). Ecohorror special cluster: "Living in fear, living in dread, pretty soon we'll all be dead". *Interdisciplinary Studies in Literature and Environment, 21*(3), 509–12.

Sapir, E. (1912/2001). Language and environment. In A. Fill & P. Mühlhäusler (Eds.), *The ecolinguistics reader: Language, ecology, and environment* (pp. 13–23). Continuum. (Reprinted from "Language and environment," 1912, *American Anthropologist, 14*(2), 226–42.)

Schmidt, A., Ivanova, A., & Schäfer, M. S. (2013). Media attention for climate change around the world: A comparative analysis of newspaper coverage in 27 countries. *Global Environmental Change, 23*(5), 1233–48.

Schneider-Mayerson, M., & Bellamy, B. R. (2020). *An ecotopian lexicon*. University of Minnesota Press.

Scott, M., & Tribble, C. (2006). *Textual patterns: Key words and corpus analysis in language education*. John Benjamins Publishing.

Sealey, A. (2018). Animals, animacy and anthropocentrism. *International Journal of Language and Culture, 5*(2), 224–47.

Sealey, A., & Oakley, L. (2013). Anthropomorphic grammar? Some linguistic patterns in the wildlife documentary series Life. *Text & Talk, 33*(3), 399–420.

Sealey, A., & Pak, C. (2018). First catch your corpus: Methodological challenges in constructing a thematic corpus. *Corpora, 13*(2), 229–54.

Seneviratne, S., Nichols, N., & Easterling, D., et al. (2012). *Changes in climate extremes and their impacts on the natural physical environment*. International Panel on Climate Change.

Shelton, T., Poorthuis, A., Graham, M., & Zook, M. (2014). Mapping the data shadows of Hurricane Sandy: Uncovering the sociospatial dimensions of "big data". *Geoforum, 52*, 167–79.

Shi, Y., & Lei, L. (2020). The evolution of LGBT labelling words: Tracking 150 years of the interaction of semantics with social and cultural changes. *English Today, 36*(4), 33–9.

Sinclair, J. (2004). *Trust the text: Language, corpus and discourse*. Routledge.

Sinclair, J., & Coulthard, M. (1975). *Towards an analysis of discourse: The English used by teachers and pupils*. Oxford University Press.

Singer, P. (1990). *Animal liberation*. New York Review.

Skalicky, S. (2018). Lexical priming in humorous satirical newspaper headlines. *Humor, 31*(4), 583–602.

Smail, R., Gregory, I., & Taylor, J. (2019). Qualitative geographies in digital texts: Representing historical spatial identities in the Lake District. *International Journal of Humanities and Arts Computing, 13*, 28–38.

Smith, N. (2001). Ever moving on? The progressive in recent British English. In *New frontiers of corpus research: Papers from the 21st international conference on English language research* (pp. 317–30). Brill.

Smith-Harris, T. (2004). There's not enough room to swing a cat: And there's no sense flogging a dead horse: Language usage and Human perceptions of other animals. *ReVision, 27*(12+), 12–16.

Staples, S., & Biber, D. (2014). The expression of stance in nurse-patient interactions: An ESP perspective. In M. Gotti, & D. S. Giannoni (Eds.), *Corpus analysis for descriptive and pedagogical purposes: ESP perspectives* (pp. 123–42). Peter Lang.

Steffensen, S. V., & Fill, A. (2014). Ecolinguistics: The state of the art and future horizons. *Language Sciences, 41*, 6–25.

Stibbe, A. (2001). Language, power and the social construction of animals. *Society & Animals*, *9*(2), 145–61.

Stibbe, A. (2003). As charming as a pig: The discursive construction of the relationship between pigs and humans. *Society & Animals*, *11*(4), 375–92.

Stibbe, A. (2012). *Animals erased: Discourse, ecology, and reconnection with the natural world*. Wesleyan University Press.

Stibbe, A. (2014). An ecolinguistic approach to critical discourse studies. *Critical Discourse Studies*, *11*(1), 117–28.

Stibbe, A. (2015). *Ecolinguistics: Language, ecology and the stories we live by* (1st ed.). Routledge.

Stibbe, A. (2018). Critical discourse analysis and ecology. In J. Flowerdew & J. Richardson (Eds.), *The Routledge handbook of critical discourse analysis* (pp. 497–509). Routledge.

Stibbe, A. (2021). *Ecolinguistics: Language, ecology and the stories we live by* (2nd ed.). Routledge.

Stubbs, M. (1994). Grammar, text, and ideology: Computer-assisted methods in the linguistics of representation. *Applied Linguistics*, *15*(2), 201–23.

Subtirelu, N. C. (2013). "English ... it's part of our blood": Ideologies of language and nation in United States Congressional discourse. *Journal of Sociolinguistics*, *17*(1), 37–65.

Suldovsky, B. (2017). The information deficit model and climate change communication. *Oxford Research Encyclopedia of Climate Science*, 1–29. doi: https://doi.org/10.1093/acrefore/9780190228620.013.301.

Swan, M. (2011). Grammar. In J. Simpson (Ed.), *The Routledge handbook of applied linguistics* (pp. 577–90). Routledge.

Tabbert, U. (2013). *Crime through a Corpus: The linguistic construction of offenders, victims and crimes in the German and UK press*. [dissertation] University of Huddersfield.

Taylor, C. (2018). Similarity. In C. Taylor & A. Marchi (Eds.), *Corpus approaches to discourse: A critical review* (pp. 19–37). Routledge.

Taylor, C., & Marchi, A. (2018). *Corpus approaches to discourse: A critical review*. Routledge.

Thompson, G., & Hunston, S. (2000). Evaluation: An introduction. In S. Hunston & G. Thompson (Eds.), *Evaluation in text: Authorial stance and the construction of discourse* (pp. 1–26). Oxford University Press.

Tognini-Bonelli, E. (2004). Working with corpora: Issues and insights. In C. Coffin, A. Hewings, & K. O'Halloran (Eds.), *Applying English Grammar* (pp. 11–24). The Open University.

Trexler, A. (2015). *Anthropocene fictions: The novel in a time of climate change*. University of Virginia Press.

van Dijk, T. (1990). Social cognition and discourse. In H. Giles & W. P. Robinson (Eds.), *Handbook of language and social psychology* (pp. 163–83). Wiley.

Vincent, B., & Clarke, J. (2017). The language of A Clockwork Orange: A corpus stylistic approach to Nadsat. *Language and Literature, 26*(3), 247–64.

Voegelin, C. F., Voegelin, F. M., & Shutz Jr, N. W. (1967). The language situation in Arizona as part of the southwest culture area. In D. Hymes & W. Bittle (Eds.), *Studies in southwestern ethnolinguistics: Meaning and history in the languages of the American Southwest* (pp. 403–51). Mouton.

Wang, D. (2013). Applying corpus linguistics in discourse analysis. *Studies in Literature and Language, 6*(2), 35–9.

Widdowson, H. G. (2000). On the limitations of linguistics applied. *Applied Linguistics, 21*(1), 3–25.

Widdowson, H. G. (2004). *Text, context, pretext: Critical issues in discourse analysis*. Blackwell.

Wild, K., Church, A., McCarthy, D., & Burgess, J. (2013). Quantifying lexical usage: Vocabulary pertaining to ecosystems and the environment. *Corpora, 8*(1), 53–79.

Wilkinson, M. (2019). "Bisexual oysters": A diachronic corpus-based critical discourse analysis of bisexual representation in The Times between 1957 and 2017. *Discourse & Communication, 13*(2), 249–67.

Wilson, A., & Rayson, P. (1993). Automatic content analysis of spoken discourse. In C. Souter & E. Atwell (Eds.), *Corpus-based computational linguistics* (pp. 215–26). Rodopi.

Wodak, R., & Meyer, M. (2009). Critical discourse analysis: History, agenda, theory and methodology. In R. Wodak & M. Meyer (Eds.), *Methods of critical discourse analysis* (pp. 1–33). Sage.

Wohlleben, P. (2015). *The hidden life of trees: What they feel, how they communicate—Discoveries from a secret world*. Greystone Books.

Wulf, A. (2015). *The invention of nature: Alexander von Humboldt's new world*. Vintage.

Yuan, M. (2010). Mapping text. In D. Bodenheimer, J. Corrigan, & T. Harris (Eds.), *The spatial humanities: GIS and the future of humanities scholarship*. Indiana University Press.

Zuo, X. (2019). An ecological analysis of Emily Dickinson's "The Grass." *Theory and practice in language studies, 9*(7), 849–53.

Index

Abdulkarim, Z. 120
Abram, D., *The Spell of the Sensuous* 87
academic disciplines 56, 162
Alexander, R. 42–3, 50
   Framing Discourse on the Environment: A Critical Discourse Approach 43
Almiron, N. 115
Ana, O. S. 20
Ancarno, C. 40, 162
Animal Crossing: New Leaf simulation game 158
animals 94–5. *See also* nonhuman animals/species
   animal-as-criminal framing 159
   animal escapes 25, 110, 118–19, 122–4, 126, 159
   animal farming industry and welfare 109–10, 115–16, 124, 128–9, 159
   killing of 114
annotation 13–14, 33, 106, 142, 152
AntConc 35, 163
Anthropocene/Anthropocentrism/anthropocentric 54, 61, 70, 113, 129, 131–2
anti-Jewish sentiment 58
anti-Semitism 58
applied linguistics 56, 65
a priori language model 14, 111
ArcGIS 133
Archer Corpus of Historical English Registers 55
Atkinson, D. 56
Attenborough, D. 131
Atwood, M., *Oryx and Crake* 89
Augusta Resources, Vancouver 145
Austen, J. 91
Australian Conservation Fund (ACF) 112

Bailey, E. T., *The Sound of a Wild Snail Eating* 87
Baker, P. 56–7, 160
   Corpora and Discourse Studies 163
   Using Corpora for Discourse Analysis 163
Basso, K., *Wisdom Sits in Places: Language and Landscape among the Western Apache* 49
Bayes Factor 100
Bednarek, M. 47
Bellamy, B. R. 89
Bevitori, C. 44–6, 60
Biber, D. 14, 19
biological diversity 150
Blue Diamond company 109–10
The Blue Marble image 4, 75, 131
Boaz, F. 5
Bogost, I. 158
Bonnefille, S. M. 44, 59
Bonnelli, E. 13
Bootcat web crawler 30
British National Corpus (BNC) 29, 38, 48, 162
British Petroleum (BP) 42–3
   Deepwater Horizon Oil Disaster case 43, 64
   Gulf of Mexico Restoration webpage 43
Brooks, M., *War Z: An Oral History of the Zombie War* 88–9
Brown Corpus 11, 55–6
Bruno, K. 42
Buenavista Mine of northwestern Mexico 145
Burgess, A., *A Clockwork Orange* 91
Burroughs, J. 88
Bush, G. W. 44, 59

Canadian Wildlife Federation (CWF) 112
Caple, H. 47
Carbaugh, D. 49, 132, 135–6, 145, 159–60
Carson, R., *Silent Spring* 7, 75, 84, 87
Carto GIS platform 133, 138, 141–2, 151
Castello, E. 50
   Laudato Si 36
Casy, J. 85

chemotaxis 56
Chesapeake Bay Foundation (CBF) 139–40, 143, 148–51
Clark, J. 91
classism 53, 88
CLAWS POS tag schema 13
CLAWS Tagger 96, 141, 152
CliC Dickens Project 92
climate change 21–2, 24, 29–36, 44, 50, 59–61, 80, 87, 89, 155, 161. *See also* global warming
climate crisis 3, 20–1, 27–8, 32–3, 35–7, 45, 60, 80–1, 83–4, 86, 89, 111, 119, 139, 155, 157, 160–1
    disasters 24, 27, 43, 47–8, 89, 145, 152
    discourse 27, 30–6, 38, 161
    place 49–50
cluster analysis technique 27, 35, 92
CoBuild Bank of English 120
Collins, L. 33
collocation 17, 20, 24, 32, 34–5, 41, 44, 117, 120, 123, 125–6, 128, 133–4, 145, 147, 149
    adjective 24, 53, 62–3, 65, 70–4, 77, 79, 123–5
    carbon 34–5
    collocational analysis technique 27, 35, 45, 47
    diachronic 155
    environment 44
    evaluation and analysis 62–7
    immigration 15, 17, 20–1, 63
    LGTBQ labelling words 57
    4L-4R 62–3, 68, 71–2, 147
    pristine 75–6
    semantic class 65–6
    taste 40
    wilderness 24, 53–4, 58, 62–3, 66–8, 80, 119, 151, 155–7
        boundless 78
        evolving evaluations of 69–79
        western 71
commodities/commodification 22, 47, 115, 159
communication 2, 4. *See also* language/language system
    corporate 15, 43–5
    environmental 25, 27–8, 31, 38, 50–1, 137–8, 150, 152–3, 162

computational word embedding technique 57
concordance 35, 39, 63, 76, 92, 105, 114, 123–6, 148
Conservation International 139
Constancia Mine of Peru 145
content analysis 31
contrastive analysis technique 34, 48
Cook, D., *The New Wilderness* 81
Cook, G. 39–40, 162
corpora 11–13, 25, 28–30, 37, 55, 58, 62, 96, 99–100, 111, 117, 119–20, 134, 138, 142–3, 147–8, 150–2, 160–3
    balanced 55
    diachronic corpus 17, 24, 29, 41–2, 44, 53, 59, 155
    general corpus 28–9, 162
    and Kendall's Tau correlation coefficient 67–8
    and semantic tagging 140–2
    specialized corpus 12, 25, 27–30, 37–8, 43, 45–6, 66, 111, 119, 137, 159, 162
corporate discourse 24, 42–5, 161
Corps of Civil Engineers 152
corpus-assisted discourse studies (CADS) 1, 12–20, 23–5, 27–8, 30–1, 45–7, 63–5, 68, 84, 90–1, 93, 111, 117, 120, 130, 133–5, 138, 142, 147, 151, 159–62
    D-CADS 55–9, 155–6
corpus-assisted ecolinguistics 23–5, 27–8, 36–8, 44, 48, 50–1, 53–4, 60–2, 83–5, 90, 93, 95, 106, 132, 134, 138, 151–3, 155, 157–61
    constructing corpus 95–7
    diachronic 24, 61, 62, 79–80, 155
    and GIS 138–42
corpus-assisted eco-stylistics 24, 119, 158, 160
corpus-assisted humor studies 119
corpus-based critical discourse approach 57
corpus linguistics (CL) 1, 10–15, 17, 19–20, 25, 30–3, 49, 55, 59, 62, 91–2, 96–7, 116–17, 134, 138, 147
Corpus of Contemporary American English (COCA) 28–30, 96, 103, 119–20, 122–6, 128, 149, 162, 165 n.1 (Ch 4)

Corpus of Historical American English
   (COHA) 24, 29, 37, 41, 57, 61,
   67–8, 71–2, 74–5, 77, 119, 165 n.1
   (Ch 3)
Corpus of Lake District Writing 135
corpus stylistics 25, 84, 90–3, 96, 157
criminal justice system 125–6
critical discourse analysis 3, 17, 19, 63,
   112, 120, 136
critical discourse studies (CDS) 1, 18–20,
   43, 45, 47, 90
   and ecolinguistics 20–3, 32
Cronon, W. 54, 70
   The Trouble with Wilderness 105–6
Culpeper, J. 91
culture 3–6, 9, 34, 46, 49, 61, 64, 70–1, 80,
   89, 95, 139
culturomics approach 61

Dahl, T. 34
Darwin, C. 4
   On the Origin of Species 5
data-driven approach 13, 17, 30, 57, 65,
   87, 163
diachronic corpus 17, 24, 29, 41–2, 44,
   53, 155
diachronic corpus-assisted discourse study
   (D-CADS) 55–9, 155–6
Dickens, C., *Bleak House* 92
Dickinson, E. 93
digital simulation game/digital gaming
   107, 158
discourse analytic method 2, 7–8, 18, 40,
   147, 159, 163
discursive patterns 17, 36, 80, 105–6
do Couto, H. H. 6, 10
Donaldson, C. 135

ecocriticism 95
eco-friendly 107, 158
eco-keywords 24, 44, 62, 80, 156
EcoLexicon English Corpus 162
ecolinguistics 1, 7, 53, 59, 65, 67, 84–5,
   90–1, 95, 110–12, 130–2, 138, 147,
   155–60, 162–3. *See also* linguistics
   analysis of literary texts 93–5, 107
   and CDS 20–3, 32
   corpus-assisted (*see* corpus-assisted
     ecolinguistics)
   defining 1–3
   diachronic studies in 59–62, 80, 156–7,
     161
   history of 3–10
   IEA's definition of 10
   studies of place in 135–8
ecological discourse analysis (EDA) 2,
   51
ecology 1–2, 4–5, 7–9, 44, 63, 85
   ecological awareness 85, 88, 90, 93,
     157, 163
   ecological consciousness 4, 50, 85, 87,
     90, 151
   ecological crisis 2, 9, 80, 83, 157–8
   ecological degradation 7, 23–4, 43, 64,
     79–80, 110, 145
   ecological thinking 4, 7, 10, 93
   eco-relevant terms 45–7 (*see also*
     specific terms)
   language 4–7, 49
economy/economic 35, 44, 47, 59, 64,
   148–9
   commodification (*see* commodities/
     commodification)
   economic growth 9, 44, 59, 118
   exploitation 47
ecosophy 9, 53, 64–5, 67, 90, 130, 163
ecosystem 5, 10, 21, 23, 70, 81, 146,
   157
Eggins, S. 16
El Estor Mine of Guatemala 145, 150
Emerson, R. W. 84
English-Corpora.org 12
English Language Newspaper Corpus 58
Environmental Protection Agency 37,
   152
environment/environmentalism 1–2, 7–8,
   24, 44, 47, 60, 80, 106–7, 137
   environmental catastrophe 43
   environmental communication 25,
     27–8, 31, 38, 50–1, 137–8, 150,
     152–3, 162
   environmental degradation 42–3
   environmental discourse 137–8, 151–2,
     162
   environmental issue 24, 32, 44, 47–8,
     156
   environmental organizations corpus
     140

environmental studies 162
environmental writing (genres) 83–90, 95, 106
   eco-horror 88
   fiction/non-fiction 84–91, 95
   New Nature writing 85–8, 90
   science fiction 88
   speculative fiction 85, 88–9, 95, 106, 157, 160
   organism-environment relations 5
   physical 2–3, 6, 10
   unsustainable 8
ergative verbs 48, 94, 157
ESRI GIS platform 133
euphemism 42, 113
Europe/European 5, 7, 31, 69–71
The Everglades Foundation 140

farming discourse 22, 109–10, 115–16, 124, 128–9, 159
Firth, J. R. 62
Fischer-Starke, B. 91
Fisher, M. 22–3
Fitzsimmons-Doolan, S. 58, 100
Flaco, M. 120
Flin Flon Mine of Manitoba 145
Fløttum, K. 34–5
Forbes, S., "The Lake as Microcosm" 5
Fortanet, I. 66
France 31–2
Frayne, C. 37, 41, 61, 156–7
Freeman, C. 22, 115
Freiberg-Lancaster-Oslo Bergen (FLOB) Corpora 55
Fries, C. F. 11
Fusari, S. 29, 41, 156–7

Gabrielatos, C. 97, 100
gender 13, 56
   equality 2–3
general corpus 28–30, 34, 162
genres 12, 14, 18, 29, 66–7, 85–90, 96, 106, 158, 162
geographical information systems (GIS) 49–50, 132, 138, 151–3, 159–60
   corpora and semantic tagging 140–2
   and corpus-assisted ecolinguistics 138–42

historical GIS 134
   mapping places 142–51
geographical text analysis (GTA) 133–5
Gerbig, A. 48
Germany 31–2
Gesualto, S. 50
Laudato Si 36
Gilbert, I. 22
Gilquin, G. 38, 112
GIS-CADS approach 134–5, 152, 160
Gjerstad, Ø 35
Gjesdal, A. M. 35
Glenn, C. B. 115
global warming 30–3. *See also* climate change
Gnann, A. 56
Goatly, A. 39, 93–4, 114, 117, 119–20
Goodall, J. 38
Google Books Corpus 24, 60–1, 67, 69–72, 77
Google Ngram Viewer corpus 37, 41, 46, 67, 69
grammar 4, 8, 93–4, 102, 113
   grammatical features/structure 13, 16–17, 28, 55–6, 59, 117
   grammatical metaphor 112
   lexicogrammatical features 18, 39, 91, 157
The Grand Canyon Trust (GCT) 139, 141, 143–4, 148, 150–1
Grant, W. J. 60–1, 80
Greeley, H. 71
green 27, 44–6
greenhouse effect 31–2
Greenpeace 137
greenwashing 42–5, 119
Greer, J. 42
Gregory, I. 49, 134–5, 138, 152
Gries, S. T. 55
Grieve, J. 132, 152
Grundmann, R. 31–2
Guo, D. 132, 152
Gupta, A. F. 38

Haeckel, E. 4, 7
Generelle Morphologie der Organismen (*General Morphology of Organisms*) 5
Hahn-Powell, G. 56
Haig, E. 152

Halliday, M. A. K. 2, 8, 16, 102-3, 112, 157
  "New Ways of Meaning: The Challenge to Applied Linguistics" 8, 111, 163
Hardie, A. 49, 100, 134, 138, 152
Hardt-Mautner, G. 19
Harmonious Discourse Analysis (HDA) 10
Haugen, E. 1, 6, 8
  The Ecology of Language 6-7, 111
Helsinki Diachronic Corpus of English Texts 55
Hewings, M. 65
Hilpert, M. 55
historical linguistics 55
Hoey, M. 117
Hoffman, S. 55
Holthaus, E., *The Future Earth* 163
homonymy/homophony 121, 123
Hudbay Mineral Resources, Toronto 145
Hueberger, R. 113
humans 2, 5-7, 10, 16, 21-3, 76, 80, 84, 95, 101-5, 110, 113, 118, 122, 126, 128, 131, 156-7
  and animals 109-10 (*see also* animals)
  and ecosystems 157
  humanities 25, 27, 49, 85, 88, 95, 131-3, 157, 160
  human-nature relationship 25, 54, 62, 71, 101
  killing of 114
  and nonhuman animals 2, 16, 22-3, 39, 41 (*see also* nonhuman animals/species)
humor/humorous 110-11, 117-21, 123
Hunston, S. 65
Hyland, K. 14
Hymes, D., "Studies in Southwestern Ethnolinguistics" 6
Hyon, S. 66

idioms 113, 122-3, 125
Information Deficit Model 83
International Ecolinguistics Association (IEA) 9-10
Itäranta, E., *Memory of Water* 89

Jacobs, G. M. 38, 112
Japanese Whaling Research Institute 137
Jaspal, R. 32

Jepson, J. 113
Johansson, C. 55
Johnson, M. 9

Kasakoff, A. 132, 152
Kendall's Tau correlation coefficient 24, 54, 57, 73-4, 76-7, 79, 155
  and corpora 67-8
Kennedy, J. F. 60, 71
keyness analysis technique 97-101, 106, 147, 161
  log likelihood statistic 97, 99-101
keyword analysis technique 27, 32-3, 36, 48
Khazaal, N. 115
Kidner, K. 136
  Athabasca Tar Sands/Athabasca Oil Sands study 136-7
King, M. L., Jr. 71
Klein, N., *On Fire: The Burning Case for a Green New Deal* 86-7
Kolbert, E., *The Sixth Extinction: An Unnatural Extinction* 86
Koteyko, N. 32-5
Krishnamurthy, R. 31

Lakoff, G. 9, 118
Lancaster Newsbooks Corpus 134
Lancaster-Oslo Bergen (LOB) Corpus 55
LancsBox 163
language/language system 1-3, 8-10, 13-14, 35, 46-7, 53, 63, 90, 93-4, 96, 102, 109, 114, 116-18, 132-3, 145, 155, 158-61. *See also* communication
  anthropocentric 113
  anthropomorphic 112-13
  authentic 11, 13, 15, 19, 111
  change 28-9, 55-6, 59, 61
  corpus-assisted analysis of 65, 67
  data 11, 111
  ecology 4-7, 49
  humorous 119
  patterns 3, 16, 18, 32, 102, 111, 119, 130, 133, 161
  practices 9, 22-3, 79-80, 110, 112-13, 130
  Sapir on 6
  second language writers 12

studies 5–6, 10, 14, 132
users 15–17, 22, 69–70, 75, 77, 103, 117
Law & Order, CSI:Miami, and *Hawaii Five-O* crime drama 122
Leech, G. 55
legitimate/legitimacy 16, 20, 22, 34, 40
Lei, L. 57
Leopold, A., *The Sand County Almanac* 84
lexical items 11, 13, 16–17, 28, 31, 33, 37, 41, 56, 58, 62–5, 75, 97, 100–2, 105, 112, 114–15, 117–18, 123–6, 128, 142
lexical priming and framing 111, 116–18, 130, 159–60
lexicography 11, 18
lexicon 46
LGTBQ labelling words 57
Li, C. 47
light detection and ranging (LIDAR) technology 75, 131–2
linguistics 1, 3, 5, 15–16, 25, 28, 39, 97. *See also* ecolinguistics
    choices 15–16, 91
    patterns 7, 17, 23, 36–7, 40, 48, 91, 117, 120, 133
    practices 3, 9, 42, 90, 115, 156
Lischinsky, A. 43–4
Liu, M. 47
Lopez, T. 120
Luzón, M. J. 66

MacFarlane, R. 86
Mad Cow disease 115
Mahlberg, M. 46, 92
Mair, C. 55
Mango Maps GIS platform 133
Mapping the Lakes project 135
Marchi, A. 58
    Corpus Approaches to Discourse 163
Marsh, G. P. 4
Martin, J. R. 110
    Grammaticalizing Ecology: The Politics of Baby Seals and Kangaroos 112
McCarthy, M., *The Moth Snowstorm: Joy and Nature* 87–8
McEnery, T. 20
    Corpora and Discourse Studies 163

McKibben, B.
    The End of Nature 86–7
    Falter: Has the Human Game Started to Play Itself Out 86
media and communication studies 28, 30–1, 155
metaphors 5, 7–9, 20, 27, 41, 43–4, 91, 112–13, 116
methodological synergy 19. *See also* synergy/synergies
metonymy 44, 116
Meyer, M. 20
Miller, Arthur, *The Crucible* 54
mining corporations 13, 29, 49–50, 137–8, 144–6, 148, 152
Mnuchin, S. 32
modal auxiliaries 14, 16, 34
modal verbs 55
Monbiot, G. 87
    Feral 88
monitor corpus 28–9
morality 58
Mount Polley Mine Disaster 145
Mühlhäusler, P. 53, 75
Muir, J. 4, 54

National Aeronautics and Space Administration (NASA) 36
national media 31–2
National Public Radio (NPR), article from 22–3
nature 2, 4–5, 36, 39, 47, 53–4, 87, 94–5, 102, 114
Nature Genetics journal 14
Nerlich, B. 32–3
News on the Web (NOW) Corpus 119, 122–3, 126
node corpus 29, 33, 97, 100, 110
nonhuman animals/species 16, 21–5, 27, 53, 61, 84, 86–7, 94, 101, 106, 109–10, 118, 125, 128, 155–6, 159. *See also* animals; humans
    companion animal 41
    corpus of nonhuman animal escape articles 121
    findings and discussion 121–8
        alternative discourse 128
        framing 125–8

puns 121–3
reference 123–5
and human 2, 16, 22–3, 39, 41 (see also humans)
killing of 114
method and corpus 118–21
representations of 36–42, 111–16
norming method 141
North America/North Americans 6–7, 17, 63, 84–5, 95, 132, 139
environmentalism in 84, 106
and wilderness 54, 76

Oakley, L., *Life* 29, 37–8
Obama, B. 60
oecology 5
onomatopoeia 122
ozone depletion 47–8

Painter v. Blue Diamond case 109–10
Partington, A. 15, 55–6, 58
Linguistics of Laughter 121
part of speech (POS) tags 13–14, 47, 96, 106, 152
Pearce, F., *The New Wild: How Invasive Species Will Be Nature's Salvation* 86
Pebble Mine 138–9, 143
Peltier, A. 120
People, Products, Pests, and Pets: The Discursive Representation of Animals project 161
Pet Responsibility Act of Argentina 114
phrase 13, 41, 46, 125–6
phrasal verb 123
Plappert, G. 14
political discourse 14, 42–5, 152
Poole, R. 13, 56, 66, 107, 158
Potts, A. 13, 47
Powers, R., *The Overstory* 24–5, 84, 95–7, 100, 105–6, 119, 157–8, 161
animation and agency of trees 101–5
character names 100–1
concordance lines of tree 105
keywords in 98–9, 101–5
verbal patterns with trees 104
prepositions 55, 114
Project Gutenberg 96
pronoun 27, 38, 112–13, 128, 147

racism 53, 88
reality 2–3, 8, 16, 23, 48, 53, 56, 62, 110, 112, 125, 129, 157, 160
cruel reality 115
reciprocal verbs 157
reference corpus 14, 29, 33, 48, 58, 96–7, 100, 119–20, 165 n.1 (Ch 4)
religion/religious faith 36, 58, 70–1
Rich, N., *Odds against Tomorrow* 89
Rosemont Mine 49, 137–9, 143, 146
Rosemont Mine Truth (RMT) 138, 140, 144–6, 148, 150–1
Rudnick, L. 49, 145

Salem Witch Trials 54
Sandberg, C. 3
Santa Rita Mountain 16, 49–50, 143
Sapir, E. 4–5
The Ecolinguistics Reader: Language, Ecology, and Environment 6, 8
on language 6
"Language and Environment" 5
Save Bristol Bay (SBB) 138–9, 141, 143
Save the Bay blog 140
Save the Santa Ritas Organization 140
The Scarlett Letter 54
Schmidt, A. 31
Schneider-Mayerson, M. 89
Scott, M. 32
Sealey, A., *Life* 29, 37–8
seed words 46
semantic domain analysis 45–6, 106
semantic frames 45, 50, 70, 91, 128, 147, 150
semantic prosodies 13, 35, 57, 124, 159
semantic tags/tagging 13–14, 150–1
and corpora 140–2
frequencies with place names 142
of money 147–8
semantic tag analysis technique 27, 33, 47
sentient beings 37, 103, 123, 128
sexism 53
sexual identity 57
Shakespeare, W., *Romeo and Juliet* 91
Shi, Y. 57
Shumacher, E. F., *Small Is Beautiful* 64
Shutz, N., Jr. 6
The Sierra Club group 139

Sinclair, J. 12
Singer, P. 22
Sjolander, A. E. 44
Skalicky, S. 117, 119–20
Smith-Harris, T. 113
Smith, N. 55
social cognition 17
social interaction 15
social media 111, 119, 140, 146, 152–3
social sciences 2, 14, 27, 132–3
social semiotic system 15
sociolinguistics 13, 55
Southern Reach Trilogy 88
Spangler, S. 107, 158
Spatial Humanities 25, 132, 160
specialized corpus 12, 25, 27–30, 37–8, 43, 45–6, 66, 111, 119, 137, 159, 162
speciesism 113, 115, 129
Stanford Tagset 152
State of the Union addresses (SOTUA) 59
Steinbeck, J., *The Grapes of Wrath* 85
Stibbe, A. 21–2, 50, 93, 95, 113, 115, 118, 129
  Animals Erased 116
  on ecolinguistics 9, 64
  Ecolinguistics: Language, Ecology, and the Stories We Live By 9, 157
Strathy Corpus of Canadian English 12, 29, 41
stylistics. *See* corpus stylistics
sub-corpus 33, 40, 58, 67–8, 96, 162
sustainability 3, 23–4, 27, 44–5, 53, 64, 80, 90, 107, 157, 161
  sustainable development 45–6, 118
synergy/synergies 11, 23, 134
  methodological 19
systemic functional grammar (SFG) 39
systemic functional linguistics (SFL) 15–16, 47

TagAnt software 13
Taylor, J. 135, 160
  Corpus Approaches to Discourse 163
Tesseract OCR engine 96
Theroux, M., *Far North* 89
Thompson, G. 65
Thoreau, H. D. 4, 54, 84
Thunberg, G. 22, 119
TIME Magazine Corpus 55

Toronto, Canada 145
transgression 42, 53–4, 117, 119–20, 159
TreeTagger POS tag schema 13
Trexler, A., *Anthropogenic Fictions: The Novel in Times of Climate Change* 85
Twitter 152
Tyson Foods 115

UCREL Semantic Tag Analysis System (USAS) 33, 96, 142, 152
United Kingdom 31–2, 39, 45, 86
United Nations Climate Summit (2019) 22
The United States 5, 7, 25, 31–2, 45, 49, 54, 57, 67, 69, 74, 80, 88, 132, 138, 161
  Arizona 138–9, 141, 150
  COVID-19 pandemic in 37
  Earth Day 7, 75
  Hurricane Katrina 13, 47, 89
  immigration in 58
  U.S. Wilderness Act of 1964 75

Vancouver, Canada 145
VanderMeer, J. (*Annihilation, Authority,* and *Acceptance* trilogy) 88–9
Van Dijk, T. 17
Vegan Life 120, 128–9
vegetarian/vegan/plant-based 45–6, 61, 109–10
Vincent, B. 91
Voegelin, C. 5–6
Voegelin, F. 5–6
von Humboldt, A. 3, 5
  Ein Naturgemälde der Anden 4
  Essays on the Geography of Plants 4
von Humboldt, W. 4

Walden 54
Wallace-Wells, D., *The Uninhabitable Earth* 87
Walsh, E. 60–1, 80
Washington, G. 71
Whorf, B. L. 4–5
  Whorfian Hypothesis 39
  Whorfianism 114
Wilkinson, M. 57

Wilson, E. O.
   The Anthropocene Epoch 86
   Half-Earth: Our Planet's Fight for Life 86
WMatrix platform 13, 96, 141–2, 163
Wodak, R. 20
wordplays 25, 117–18, 121–4, 129
Wordsmith keyword analysis 100
Wordsmith Tools 100, 163

Wordsworth, W. 94
   The Prelude 93–5
World Bank 21, 34
World Summit on Sustainable Development, Johannesburg 46
Wulf, A. 4

Yuan, M. 134

Plate 1 Adjective + wilderness in the Google Books Corpus 1800–2010

Plate 2 Place name mentions globally across all corpora
Legend: Purple: Save Bristol Bay; Green: Rosemont Mine Truth; Red: Grand Canyon Trust; Blue: Chesapeake Bay Foundation

Plate 3 Place name mentions in the United States
Legend: Purple: Save Bristol Bay; Green: Rosemont Mine Truth; Red: Grand Canyon Trust; Blue: Chesapeake Bay Foundation

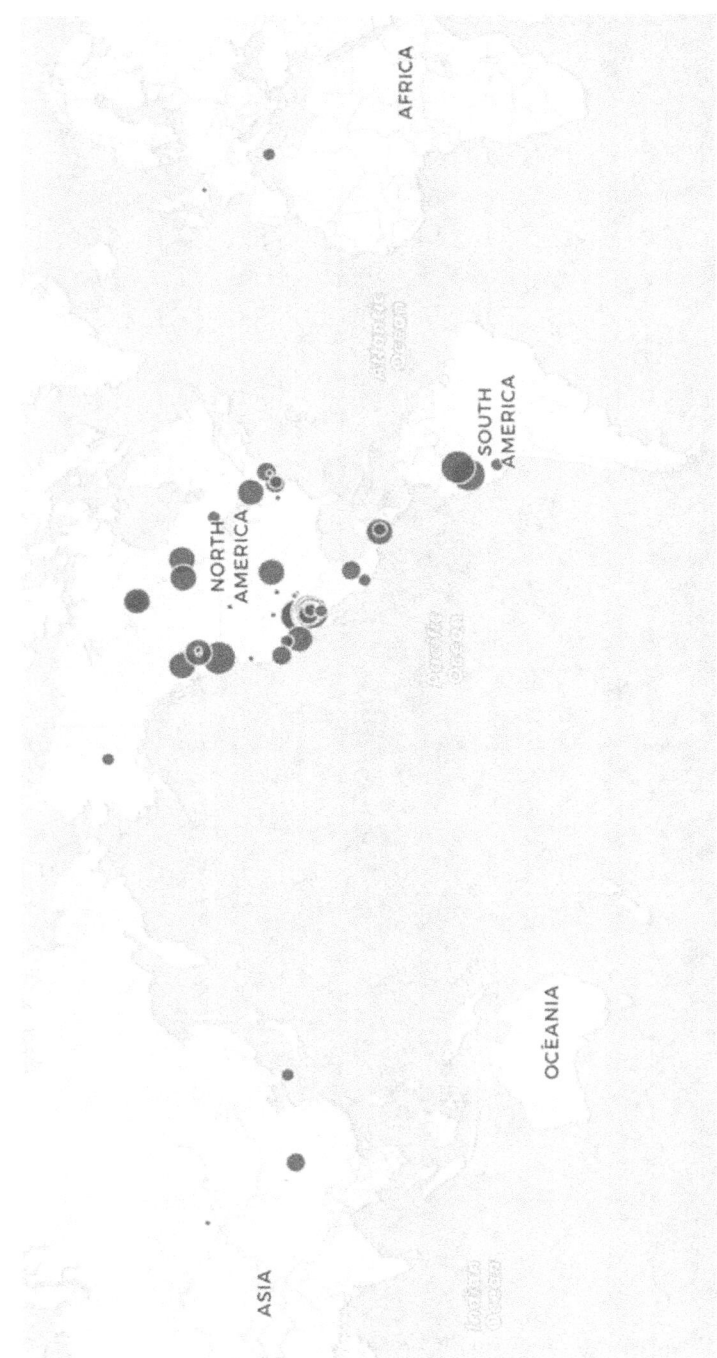

Plate 4 Place name mentions in the Rosemont Mine Truth Corpus

Plate 5 Rosemont Mine cartoon (author unknown)

Plate 6 Place and money

Legend: Purple: Save Bristol Bay; Green: Rosemont Mine Truth; Red: Grand Canyon Trust; Blue: Chesapeake Bay Foundation

Plate 7 Place and money (United States)
Legend: Purple: Save Bristol Bay; Green: Rosemont Mine Truth; Red: Grand Canyon Trust; Blue: Chesapeake Bay Foundation

Plate 8 Place and life
Legend: Purple: Save Bristol Bay; Green: Rosemont Mine Truth; Red: Grand Canyon Trust; Blue: Chesapeake Bay Foundation

www.ingramcontent.com/pod-product-compliance
Lightning Source LLC
Chambersburg PA
CBHW061827300426
44115CB00013B/2273